Mind Games

The Dual Facets of

Manipulation & Dark Psychology

David Alan Binder

Pharos Books

ISBN: 978-93-59839-15-8
eISBN: 978-93-59835-94-5

Publisher: Pharos Books (P) Ltd.
Plot No.-55, Main Mother Dairy Road
Pandav Nagar, East Delhi-110092
Phone: 011-40395855, +4049916623
WhatsApp: +91 8368220032
E-mail: sales@pharosbooks.in
Website: www.pharosbooks.in
First Edition: 2023

MIND GAMES
By David Alan Binder

In heartfelt dedication, this book is lovingly dedicated to Katherine Anne (Malone) Binder, celebrating the enduring love, prosperity, and shared journey between us.

We take great pride in and hold deep love for our family.

To Mahip Bhatia, Neeharika Lodhi and Pharos Books Private Limited for providing the Printing Services, Publishing Services, Cover Page Design

Thanks to all those who played a role in bringing this book to the light of day.

To all my readers and followers.

CONTENTS

FOREWORD

In the realm of human interaction, the subtle art of manipulation and the enigmatic allure of dark psychology have long been subjects of fascination and concern. As we delve into the captivating world of these mind games, we embark on a journey that traverses the delicate balance between good and evil.

In this exploration, we must recognize the undeniable truth that, as always, there are two sides to everything. The wielding of techniques such as manipulation and dark psychology can be employed as a means to an end, leaving indelible imprints on the course of history. On one end of the spectrum, we encounter the infamous figures who employed these tools to sow seeds of malevolence and chaos. Their actions bear testament to the grave consequences of harnessing these powers for sinister purposes.

However, let us not overlook the other side of this profound narrative. Among the annals of history, we find those who wielded control and manipulation for ostensibly altruistic motives. These famous individuals skillfully employed their influence to bring about positive change, to inspire the masses towards noble causes, and to lead with resilience and compassion.

It is essential to acknowledge that control and manipulation are universal traits. In varying degrees, they manifest in every facet of life, and they touch the lives of each one of us. The boundaries that define the morality of these actions are often blurred, and the interpretation of their intent lies within the minds of those on whom they are bestowed.

This book beckons us to contemplate the intricate interplay of human psychology and the manipulation of minds. Through riveting tales and insightful analyses, we aim to offer a glimpse into the dual nature of these techniques—the darkness that can consume hearts and minds, and the light that can illuminate the path to progress and change.

As we embark on this journey, we must tread carefully, for the very fabric of human society is woven from the threads of manipulation and control. May this exploration inspire us to ponder our own roles, our motivations, and the impact of our actions on those around us. In this quest for understanding, let us strive to discern the shades of gray and seek the path that leads us towards a more enlightened and compassionate existence.

Remember, dear reader, that within the realm of MIND GAMES, the lines between good and evil may blur, but it is within the realm of human consciousness that the ultimate judgment lies.

Manipulative tactics and control techniques can be employed by various types of individuals, and it's important to recognize these behaviors to protect ourselves from their negative influence. Here are some categories of people who may use manipulative tactics and control techniques:

Manipulative Partners: Individuals who use emotional manipulation, gaslighting, guilt-tripping, and other tactics to control their romantic partners.

Narcissists: People with narcissistic personality traits who seek to dominate and exploit others for their own gain and self-importance.

Sociopaths/Psychopaths: Individuals with antisocial personality traits who lack empathy and manipulate others to achieve their goals without remorse.

Toxic Bosses: Managers or supervisors who use intimidation, fear, or favoritism to control their employees and maintain power.

Abusive Parents: Parents or guardians who use emotional, physical, or psychological abuse to manipulate and control their children.

Cult Leaders: Individuals who establish and maintain cults by using mind control, indoctrination, and isolation techniques to exert complete control over their followers.

Cyberbullies/Trolls: Internet users who engage in online harassment and manipulation to torment and control others on social media platforms or online forums.

Politicians: Some politicians may use manipulative tactics, misinformation, and fear-mongering to sway public opinion and gain support for their agendas.

Salespeople: Certain salespeople may use high-pressure sales tactics, emotional manipulation, or misinformation to persuade customers to make purchases they may not necessarily want or need.

Religious Leaders: While the majority of religious leaders are genuine and compassionate, a few may use manipulation and fear-based tactics to control their followers. More about these are below and need special significance.

Stalkers: Individuals who engage in stalking behaviors may use manipulation, control, and intimidation to invade their victims' privacy and maintain power over them.

Online Scammers: People who use various deceitful tactics to defraud others and gain financial or personal information.

Work Colleagues: Some coworkers may use manipulation and control techniques to undermine their colleagues or gain an advantage in the workplace.

Insecure Friends: Individuals who manipulate and control their friends to feel superior or to ensure they are always the center of attention.

Caregivers: Unfortunately, some caregivers may use manipulation to exploit vulnerable individuals under their care.

Remember that not everyone in these categories will resort to manipulative tactics and control techniques, and it's essential to approach people with an open mind while being aware of the signs of manipulation and setting healthy boundaries if needed.

Certainly, religious leaders of all types can also fall into the category of individuals who may use manipulative tactics and control techniques. It's important to note that the vast majority of religious leaders are dedicated, compassionate individuals who genuinely seek to help and guide their followers. However, a few may exploit their position of authority for personal gain or to exert control over their followers. Here are some examples of religious leaders who may use manipulative tactics:

Authoritarian Leaders: Religious leaders who demand unquestioning loyalty, obedience, and submission to their authority, using fear and guilt to keep followers in line.

Prosperity Gospel Preachers: Some prosperity gospel preachers may use manipulative techniques to persuade their followers to give large donations or offerings in the belief that they will receive financial blessings in return.

Cult Leaders: As mentioned earlier, certain religious leaders may establish cult-like groups, using mind control, isolation, and manipulation to control and exploit their followers.

Doomsday Prophets: Leaders who use fear of the apocalypse or impending disaster to manipulate followers into taking extreme actions or giving up personal autonomy.

Religious Extremists: Extremist leaders who manipulate their followers' beliefs and emotions to justify violence or harmful actions in the name of their religion.

Guilt Manipulators: Some religious leaders may use guilt as a tool to control their followers, making them feel ashamed or sinful for not adhering to certain practices or beliefs.

Exclusivity Preachers: Leaders who promote a sense of elitism within their religious group, claiming that only their followers have access to divine truth, and using this exclusivity to control their community.

False Prophets: Individuals who claim to have special insights or direct communication with the divine, using these claims to manipulate and deceive their followers.

It's important to remember that these examples may represent a minority of religious leaders, and the majority of religious figures genuinely strive to promote peace, love, and understanding among their followers. Nonetheless, it is crucial for individuals to remain vigilant and critically assess any leader's teachings or behaviors that seem manipulative or controlling.

All religions, at their inception, were often regarded as cults by the broader society. This is due to several factors and historical patterns that have been observed across various religious movements.

When a new religious movement emerges, it typically starts with a small group of followers who believe in the teachings and doctrines of the founder or spiritual leader. During this early stage, the movement's beliefs and practices may be perceived as unconventional or even threatening to established religious norms and societal norms.

The reasons why newly formed religions are labeled as cults are multifaceted:

Unfamiliarity: When a religious group is new and unfamiliar to the majority of people, it can be seen as strange or eccentric. People tend to be cautious or apprehensive about what they don't understand, leading to labeling such groups as cults.

Counter-cultural Elements: Many new religious movements challenge existing social norms, traditions, or power structures. These countercultural elements can be seen as a threat to the status quo, leading to negative perceptions and labeling as a cult.

Secrecy and Closed Practices: Some new religious movements may adopt secretive practices or limit access to information about their beliefs and rituals. This secrecy can fuel suspicion and contribute to the cult label.

Strong Group Identity: Early followers of a new religious movement often display a strong sense of group identity and loyalty to their leader. This cohesion may be seen as exclusive or cult-like by outsiders.

Media Sensationalism: The media's portrayal of new religious movements can play a significant role in shaping public opinion. Sensationalist reporting or biased coverage may emphasize negative aspects, reinforcing the cult stereotype.

As time passes and a religious movement grows, it may undergo changes that can lead to its acceptance as a mainstream religion. Factors contributing to this evolution include:

Increased Membership: As a religious group attracts more followers and becomes more visible, it gains recognition and legitimacy.

Social Acceptance: If the religious teachings align with prevailing values and do not challenge societal norms, it becomes more accepted.

Institutionalization: Establishing formal structures, traditions, and institutions can help a religious movement gain respectability and be seen as an established religion.

Time and Tradition: Religions that have withstood the test of time and become ingrained in cultures tend to be seen as more legitimate and less like cults.

Influence and Power: Religions that amass political or economic power may gain social acceptance and be treated as legitimate institutions.

It's important to note that the label "cult" is often subjective and can carry negative connotations. As societies become more diverse and tolerant, it is crucial to evaluate religious groups based on their actions, values, and impact rather than solely relying on historical labels or stereotypes. Additionally, not all new religious movements evolve into mainstream religions, and some may indeed retain cult-like characteristics that raise valid concerns about their practices and effects on followers.

While it is essential not to single out religion as the sole source of culpability, it's essential to recognize that the potential for manipulative tactics and control techniques exists in various organizations, clubs, and memberships. This acknowledgement stems from the understanding that human behavior and group dynamics can lead to the emergence of unhealthy power structures and manipulative behaviors within any organized community.

In any organization, whether religious, social, or professional, certain conditions and factors can contribute to the manifestation of manipulative tendencies:

Authority and Hierarchy: Hierarchical structures, where power is concentrated at the top, can create opportunities for leaders or those in authority positions to abuse their power and manipulate others below them.

Groupthink: In cohesive groups, the desire for consensus and conformity may discourage dissenting opinions, allowing manipulative individuals to exploit the group's collective mindset.

Ideological Devotion: Strong adherence to a specific ideology or belief system can create a fertile ground for charismatic leaders to manipulate followers using emotional appeals and dogmatic reasoning.

Charismatic Leaders: Charisma, while not inherently negative, can be used by certain individuals to captivate and manipulate their followers' emotions and loyalty.

Isolation: Organizations that isolate their members from external influences may prevent critical thinking and create an echo chamber, making it easier for manipulators to control information and perspectives.

Fear and Guilt: Manipulators may use fear tactics or guilt-tripping to control and manipulate members, exploiting their vulnerabilities and emotions.

Emotional Exploitation: Manipulative individuals may use emotional manipulation to gain trust, loyalty, and submission from their followers.

Group Identity: Strong group identity and loyalty can create an "us vs. them" mentality, fostering an environment where questioning the leader or the group's practices is discouraged or seen as disloyalty.

Lack of Transparency: Organizations that lack transparency in their decision-making processes or finances may foster suspicion and allow for manipulative practices to go unchecked.

Dependency: Manipulative leaders may encourage dependency on the organization or themselves, making it difficult for members to break free from their control.

It is crucial to emphasize that not all organizations or religious groups exhibit manipulative behaviors. Many groups promote positive values, foster a sense of community, and genuinely aim to help their members. However, awareness of the potential for manipulative tactics should encourage individuals to be vigilant and critical thinkers. Healthy skepticism and a willingness to question authority can safeguard against falling victim to manipulation within any organizational setting.

Promoting openness, transparency, and fostering an environment that encourages constructive dialogue and diversity of thought can help mitigate the risk of manipulative behaviors and create a more inclusive and healthy community for all members.

The Infamous with Malevolence and Chaos

Throughout history, there have been several infamous individuals who used manipulation and dark psychology to achieve their goals or exert control over others. Here are some examples:

Adolf Hitler: The German dictator and leader of the Nazi Party, Adolf Hitler, is perhaps one of the most notorious figures in history. He used propaganda, fear, and hate speech to manipulate the masses and gain support for his genocidal policies, which led to the Holocaust and World War II.

Joseph Stalin: The Soviet leader Joseph Stalin was known for his ruthless tactics to maintain power. He used a combination of propaganda, purges, and fear to control the Soviet Union and eliminate perceived threats to his authority, resulting in the deaths of millions of his own people.

Vlad the Impaler: Vlad III, also known as Vlad the Impaler, was a 15th-century ruler of Wallachia (now part of Romania). He earned his infamous reputation through brutal methods, including impaling his enemies and political opponents. His use of fear and cruelty was intended to intimidate and control his subjects.

Elizabeth Bathory: Known as the "Blood Countess," Elizabeth Bathory was a Hungarian noblewoman in the 16th and 17th centuries. She allegedly tortured and killed numerous young women, believing that bathing in their blood would preserve her youth. Her actions exemplify sadistic and psychopathic behavior.

Jim Jones: The leader of the Peoples Temple, Jim Jones, orchestrated the mass suicide and murder of over 900 of his followers in Jonestown, Guyana, in 1978. Through manipulation and mind control, Jones convinced his followers to obey his every command, even to the point of their own deaths.

Charles Manson: Charles Manson was the leader of a cult known as the Manson Family. In the late 1960s, he manipulated his followers into committing a series of brutal murders, including the infamous Tate-LaBianca killings. Manson's charisma and control over his followers are considered classic examples of dark psychology.

Heinrich Himmler: As one of the key architects of the Holocaust, Heinrich Himmler was the head of the SS and the Gestapo in Nazi Germany. He used psychological manipulation and fear to maintain control over the Nazi regime's vast security apparatus and to orchestrate the genocide of millions.

Ivan the Terrible: Ivan IV of Russia, commonly known as Ivan the Terrible, was the first Tsar of Russia. He used terror, violence, and manipulation to consolidate his power and suppress opposition during his reign in the 16th century.

Gilles de Rais: A 15th-century French nobleman and military captain, Gilles de Rais is believed to have murdered hundreds of children in a series of heinous crimes. He manipulated and lured young victims, showcasing a horrifying example of dark psychology.

Aileen Wuornos: Aileen Wuornos was a serial killer in the United States who murdered seven men between 1989 and 1990. Her traumatic upbringing and troubled past contributed to her becoming a manipulative and violent individual.

These individuals are examples of historical figures who used manipulation and dark psychology to exert control, instigate violence, or achieve their sinister ambitions. Their actions serve as a grim reminder of the potential for human depravity and the importance of understanding and guarding against such manipulation in society.

The Famous with Altruistic Motives

While the concept of using manipulation and dark psychology for "good" is controversial and can be subject to interpretation, there are historical figures who exhibited strong leadership and employed persuasive tactics to achieve positive outcomes or advance noble causes. It is essential to recognize that their methods might still have been morally ambiguous or ethically questionable, and the perceived "good" achieved through manipulation may have come at a cost. Here are some examples:

Winston Churchill: During World War II, Winston Churchill, the British Prime Minister, used masterful rhetoric and psychological tactics to boost the morale of the British people and rally them against Nazi Germany. His speeches and radio broadcasts inspired hope and unity during some of the darkest moments of the war.

Franklin D. Roosevelt: As the President of the United States during the Great Depression and World War II, FDR employed various manipulative techniques, such as delivering fireside chats, to connect with the American public and garner support for his policies. His efforts helped restore confidence and facilitate recovery.

Mahatma Gandhi: The leader of India's independence movement, Mahatma Gandhi, effectively utilized non-violent resistance and civil disobedience to bring about social and political change. His ability to mobilize masses through moral influence and manipulation of public opinion played a significant role in India's struggle for independence.

Nelson Mandela: While imprisoned for 27 years, Nelson Mandela utilized strategic manipulation and diplomacy to negotiate with the South African government for an end to apartheid. His efforts contributed to the peaceful transition to a democratic nation.

Abraham Lincoln: As the 16th President of the United States during the Civil War, Abraham Lincoln skillfully managed public opinion, navigating the complexities of the war and garnering support for the abolition of slavery.

Martin Luther King Jr.: A prominent leader in the American Civil Rights Movement, Martin Luther King Jr. used persuasive and manipulative techniques in his speeches and protests to inspire change and challenge racial segregation and discrimination.

Elizabeth I of England: Queen Elizabeth I skillfully used manipulation and strategic alliances to navigate the challenges of her reign, solidify England's position as a world power, and bring stability to the country.

Joan of Arc: Joan of Arc, the French peasant girl who led French troops during the Hundred Years' War, used her deep faith and charisma to inspire and manipulate the troops, playing a pivotal role in securing several military victories for France.

Dalai Lama: The spiritual leader of Tibetan Buddhism, the Dalai Lama, uses his influence and wisdom to advocate for non-violence, compassion, and human rights on the global stage.

Florence Nightingale: Known as the founder of modern nursing, Florence Nightingale used her persuasive abilities and manipulation of societal norms to improve medical care and sanitation practices, significantly reducing mortality rates during the Crimean War.

It's crucial to remember that while these figures achieved positive outcomes, their methods might not always be deemed entirely "good" by everyone. The use of manipulation and psychology, even with seemingly positive intentions, can still be ethically complex and raise questions about the means justifying the end.

PART I: LAYING THE FOUNDATION

CHAPTER 1

INTRODUCTION TO DARK PSYCHOLOGY

Unveiling the Shadows: An Introduction to Dark Psychology

Introduction

The human mind is a complex and fascinating realm, capable of both extraordinary goodness and profound darkness. In this chapter, we embark on a journey to explore the enigmatic landscape of dark psychology, an intricate web of manipulation, deception, and hidden motives that exist within the human psyche. As we delve into this subject, we will unravel the mysteries surrounding dark psychology, understand its historical context, and contemplate the ethical implications that arise when confronting its darker aspects.

Defining Dark Psychology

Dark psychology is a multifaceted field that examines the subtle and often malicious ways individuals manipulate, influence, and control others for personal gain or to inflict harm. It encompasses a wide range of tactics and strategies aimed at exploiting vulnerabilities, playing on emotions, and distorting perceptions. Throughout this book, we will delve into the various aspects of dark psychology, shedding light on the techniques employed by individuals with malevolent intentions.

Historical Context and Notable Figures

Dark psychology is not a modern invention; its roots can be traced back to ancient times. Throughout history, there have been notable figures who exemplify the mastery of manipulative tactics, leaving a lasting impact on society. From Machiavelli's cunning political strategies to cult leaders who mesmerized their followers, we will examine how dark psychology has manifested through different eras and contexts.

Ethical Considerations

- As we navigate through the realms of dark psychology, ethical dilemmas inevitably emerge. It is crucial to confront these questions head-on to foster a responsible and informed approach to the subject matter. Throughout this book, we will grapple with the ethical implications of studying and discussing dark psychology, acknowledging the potential risks and responsibilities that come with exploring the darker aspects of the human mind.

- The Balance between Knowledge and Responsibility: Understanding the importance of acquiring knowledge about dark psychology while being mindful of the potential harm it may cause if misused or irresponsibly disseminated. In this chapter, we delve into the delicate equilibrium between gaining insight into the intricacies of dark psychological techniques and the ethical responsibility that accompanies this knowledge. We explore the significance of approaching this subject with caution, emphasizing the need for ethical guidelines and responsible dissemination of information to avoid unintended harm to individuals or society as a whole. By striking a balance between knowledge acquisition and ethical conduct, we aim to promote a well-informed understanding of dark psychology while prioritizing the well-being and safety of those affected.
- Ethical Use of Knowledge: Exploring how the understanding of dark psychological techniques can be used for ethical purposes, such as detecting manipulation and protecting oneself and others from harm. This chapter delves into the potential positive applications of knowledge about dark psychology. By examining the ethical use of this knowledge, we highlight how individuals can leverage their understanding to identify manipulative tactics and protect themselves and others from falling victim to such tactics. We emphasize the importance of using this knowledge responsibly and compassionately, aiming to empower individuals to recognize and respond effectively to manipulation while upholding ethical standards in their interactions.
- Considerations for Vulnerable Individuals: Recognizing the vulnerability of certain individuals to manipulative tactics and the need to safeguard their well-being. This chapter focuses on the understanding that certain individuals may be more susceptible to manipulation and its detrimental effects. We discuss the significance of recognizing vulnerability in various contexts, such as children, the elderly, or individuals facing mental health challenges. By addressing the unique needs of these vulnerable populations, we strive to promote awareness and empathy, encouraging readers to adopt protective measures and support systems to safeguard the well-being of those at risk.

- The Role of Intent and Impact: Analyzing the intentions behind studying dark psychology and assessing the potential impact of sharing this knowledge on a wider scale. In this chapter, we delve into the motives and intentions that drive individuals to explore the realm of dark psychology. We encourage readers to reflect on their personal reasons for seeking this knowledge and its potential consequences on themselves and others. Additionally, we discuss the impact of disseminating this information on a larger scale, highlighting the ethical implications and the responsibility to use such knowledge judiciously. By promoting mindfulness and awareness of intent and impact, we aim to foster a thoughtful and responsible approach to the study and dissemination of dark psychological concepts.

Conclusion

As we embark on this journey into the shadows of the human mind, it is essential to approach the study of dark psychology with curiosity, responsibility, and empathy. By understanding its complexities, historical context, and ethical considerations, we aim to shine a light on the darkness, empowering ourselves and others to navigate a world where manipulation lurks behind deceptive veils. Through knowledge, awareness, and empathy, we strive to foster a society that is more resilient and resistant to the machinations of those who seek to exploit our vulnerabilities.

CHAPTER 2

THE SHADOW SELF

Unraveling the Hidden Depths: Exploring the Concept of the Shadow Self

Introduction

Within each human being lies a psychological realm concealed from conscious awareness – the shadow self. In this chapter, we will embark on an introspective journey to understand the concept of the shadow and explore the unconscious aspects of the human psyche. By shedding light on our hidden depths, we can come to terms with our dark desires and suppressed emotions, fostering self-awareness and emotional growth.

Understanding the Concept of the Shadow

The shadow self, first introduced by Swiss psychiatrist Carl Gustav Jung, refers to the collection of repressed, denied, or unacknowledged aspects of an individual's personality. These aspects often contain qualities, desires, or emotions deemed socially unacceptable, leading individuals to hide or disown them from their conscious awareness. By acknowledging and integrating the shadow self, individuals can achieve a greater sense of wholeness and authenticity.

- The Nature of the Shadow: This embarks on a profound exploration of the shadow self, uncovering its multifaceted and enigmatic nature. We delve into the myriad elements that compose the shadow, ranging from primal instincts and innate desires to the influence of societal norms and repressed emotions. By delving into the depth and complexity of the shadow, readers gain a deep understanding of the hidden aspects of their psyche that often elude conscious awareness. This exploration serves as an invitation to engage in self-reflection and introspection, leading to a more profound understanding of the self and the potential for personal growth and integration. By embracing the shadow's presence, readers can begin to acknowledge and integrate the disowned aspects of themselves, leading to a more authentic and wholehearted way of living.

- Unconscious Projection: This fascinating phenomenon of unconscious projection, a psychological process in which individuals project their unacknowledged aspects onto others. Through a careful examination of projection dynamics, we explore how our own unresolved traits, fears, and insecurities can unconsciously be attributed to those around us. By shedding light on the mechanisms of projection, readers gain valuable insights into the intricacies of interpersonal relationships and potential conflicts that arise when projecting our shadow onto others. The aim is to promote self-awareness and empathy, encouraging readers to embrace their shadow self with compassion and authenticity. This newfound understanding can lead to healthier and more harmonious connections with others, as we become more mindful of our projections and work towards integrating the disowned parts of ourselves. Ultimately, this chapter empowers readers to foster empathy, both towards themselves and others, thus enriching their emotional intelligence and relational dynamics.

Unconscious Aspects of the Psyche

The unconscious mind holds a vast reservoir of thoughts, emotions, and memories that influence our behaviors and perceptions. Delving into the depths of the unconscious, we uncover the origins of the shadow self and its impact on our daily lives.

Freud's Contribution to the Unconscious: Reflecting on Sigmund Freud's foundational work on the unconscious mind and its relevance to the concept of the shadow.

The Collective Unconscious: Exploring Jung's concept of the collective unconscious and its role in shaping shared archetypes and symbols present in myths, dreams, and cultural narratives.

Dark Desires and Suppressed Emotions

The shadow self often encompasses our darkest desires, suppressed emotions, and untamed impulses. By confronting these aspects, we can gain insight into our own vulnerabilities and motivations.

- Repression and Denial: In this thorough exploration, we delve into the intricacies of the psychological processes of repression and denial. These mechanisms are influenced by societal norms and personal experiences, leading individuals to bury certain desires and emotions deep into their unconscious. Cultural expectations and perceived social norms play a significant role in shaping these repressive tendencies. Additionally, we examine how past traumas and painful experiences may result in denial as a protective mechanism to shield oneself from emotional distress. By understanding these complex processes, readers are encouraged to engage in introspection and self-exploration, fostering a deeper understanding of themselves. This knowledge empowers individuals to confront and embrace their suppressed emotions, allowing for a more authentic and integrated sense of self.

- The Duality of Human Nature: This topic delves into the profound concept of the duality inherent in all human beings. Within each individual, both positive and negative aspects coexist, forming the shadow self and the conscious self. Acknowledging and embracing this dual nature is essential, as suppressing the shadow aspects can lead to psychological imbalances and inner conflicts. By recognizing and accepting both the light and darkness within, individuals can cultivate a deeper level of self-awareness and inner harmony. This understanding allows individuals to navigate their emotions and behaviors with greater insight and compassion, fostering a healthier relationship with themselves and others.
- Unraveling Suppressed Emotions: In this chapter, we venture into the emotional terrain of the shadow self, where repressed emotions such as anger, fear, or grief may reside. These suppressed emotions often have a profound impact on an individual's well-being and relationships. Understanding the significance of acknowledging and processing these emotions is crucial for personal growth and healing. By unraveling and expressing these emotions in a healthy and constructive manner, individuals can experience emotional release and find greater authenticity in their emotional experiences. We explore various therapeutic approaches and practices that can facilitate this process, from psychotherapy to mindfulness techniques. The goal is to promote emotional well-being and foster a more profound and compassionate connection with oneself. By embracing and integrating these suppressed emotions, individuals can embark on a journey of self-discovery and emotional liberation.

Conclusion

The journey into the depths of the shadow self is not an easy one, as it necessitates facing aspects of ourselves we may have long avoided. However, by embracing the concept of the shadow, understanding the influence of the unconscious mind, and acknowledging our dark desires and suppressed emotions, we can embark on a path of self-discovery and self-acceptance. By integrating the shadow self with the conscious aspects of our personality, we can achieve a more authentic and balanced existence, fostering emotional resilience and fostering a deeper connection with ourselves and others.

CHAPTER 3

THE ART OF MANIPULATION

Strings of Deception: Mastering the Art of Manipulation

Introduction

Manipulation, an intricate dance of deception and influence, weaves its way into the fabric of human interactions. In this chapter, we will explore the art of manipulation, unraveling the techniques and strategies employed by manipulators to achieve their objectives. By understanding how cognitive biases are exploited and recognizing instances of psychological manipulation in everyday life, we can arm ourselves with the knowledge to protect against deceptive maneuvers.

Manipulation Techniques and Strategies

Manipulators are skilled in the art of subtle persuasion, using various techniques to influence the thoughts, emotions, and behaviors of others. In this section, we will examine some of the most common manipulation tactics employed by individuals with malicious intent.

- Gaslighting: Gaslighting refers to a sophisticated form of psychological manipulation wherein the perpetrator distorts reality and intentionally undermines the victim's perception of events, leading them to doubt their own memory, feelings, and sanity. By sowing seeds of confusion and making the victim question their reality, the gaslighter gains power and control over their target.
- Emotional Blackmail: This manipulative tactic involves leveraging emotions such as guilt, fear, and empathy to control and influence others' actions or decisions. Emotional blackmailers use emotional pressure to force compliance, making their victims feel responsible for the manipulator's emotions and actions.
- Charm and Flattery: Charm and flattery are powerful tools used by manipulators to win the trust and admiration of others. By showering their targets with compliments, affection, and attention, manipulators create a false sense of connection and intimacy, making it easier to exploit and control their victims.

- Isolation and Control: Manipulators often employ tactics of isolation to weaken their victims' support systems and increase their control. They might subtly or overtly isolate the victim from friends, family, or other sources of emotional support, leaving the victim more vulnerable to the manipulator's influence and control.

Exploiting Cognitive Biases

The human mind is susceptible to cognitive biases, and unconscious mental shortcuts that affect decision-making and judgments. Manipulators deftly exploit these biases to steer individuals towards their desired outcomes.

- Confirmation Bias: Manipulators capitalize on confirmation bias, a cognitive bias that leads individuals to favor information that supports their preexisting beliefs and opinions. By presenting information that aligns with the victim's views, the manipulator reinforces their existing convictions, creating an echo chamber that discourages critical thinking and hinders objective analysis.

- Authority Bias: This bias refers to the human tendency to defer to authority figures or experts, even when their statements may be questionable. Manipulators exploit this tendency by positioning themselves as authority figures, using their perceived expertise to gain compliance and loyalty from their targets.

- Availability Heuristic: Manipulators use the availability heuristic, a mental shortcut where people judge the likelihood of an event based on how easily they can recall relevant examples. By selectively presenting information or highlighting specific examples, manipulators shape their victims' opinions and perceptions, leading them to make judgments based on the information readily available to them.

Psychological Manipulation in Everyday Life

Psychological manipulation is not confined to extraordinary circumstances; it permeates everyday interactions, from personal relationships to public discourse. Recognizing instances of manipulation in our daily lives empowers us to protect ourselves and others from its insidious effects.

- Manipulation in Personal Relationships: This focuses on recognizing indications of manipulation within various personal relationships, including romantic partnerships, friendships, and family dynamics. By examining subtle and overt signs of manipulation, individuals can become more aware of potential harmful dynamics and take steps to protect themselves and foster healthier relationships.

- Manipulation in Social Media and Advertising: Delving into the world of social media and advertising, this section investigates the psychological techniques employed to influence user behavior and consumer choices. From targeted advertisements to persuasive content, understanding these manipulative tactics empowers individuals to be critical consumers and safeguard their mental well-being in the digital age.
- Manipulation in the Workplace: Within the context of professional environments, this chapter explores power dynamics and manipulative tactics that can arise in the workplace. By recognizing these behaviors and their potential impact on individuals and teams, employees can navigate such situations more effectively and contribute to fostering a healthier work culture.

Conclusion

The art of manipulation is a double-edged sword that can be used for both nefarious and benign purposes. By shining a light on the techniques and strategies employed by manipulators, as well as the cognitive biases that make us susceptible, we become better equipped to navigate the intricate dance of deception. Awareness of psychological manipulation in everyday life enables us to develop a discerning mind, fostering resilience against manipulation and promoting healthier, more authentic interactions. As we delve deeper into the labyrinth of manipulation, we must remain vigilant, arming ourselves with knowledge and empathy to protect ourselves and others from the puppeteer's strings of deception.

CHAPTER 4

THE POWER OF PERSUASION

The Art of Influence: Unleashing the Power of Persuasion

Introduction

Persuasion, an essential aspect of human communication, holds the key to inspiring action and shaping beliefs. In this chapter, we explore the captivating realm of persuasion, delving into its core principles and distinguishing it from manipulation. We will uncover the various tactics that persuasive communicators employ to sway opinions and nudge individuals towards certain choices, while also shedding light on the darker side of manipulative persuasion.

Principles of Persuasion

Persuasion is an art that draws upon psychological principles and communication techniques to change minds and encourage action. By understanding these foundational principles, we can become more conscious of the persuasive forces that influence our decisions.

- Reciprocity: This is the principle of reciprocity, wherein offering something of value to others can trigger a sense of indebtedness and, consequently, increased compliance. Understanding how this powerful psychological mechanism operates allows individuals to utilize it ethically in their interactions, fostering positive relationships and cooperation.

- Social Proof: This uses the influence of others' actions and opinions to shape our own choices and behaviors. By recognizing the impact of social proof, individuals can be more mindful of how they perceive information and make decisions, avoiding potential manipulation driven by the actions of others.

- Authority: Examining the sway of authority figures and expertise in persuading individuals to trust and follow, this section offers insights into recognizing genuine authority from deceptive manipulation. Equipping individuals with this understanding empowers them to make informed judgments and resist blindly obeying those who may exploit authority for personal gain.

- Consistency and Commitment: Investigating the tendency of people to stay true to their commitments and align with previous actions, this chapter sheds light on the importance of staying consistent and honoring commitments. By recognizing this principle, individuals can avoid falling prey to manipulative tactics that exploit their desire for consistency.
- Scarcity: Explored here is the allure of limited resources and opportunities, which can lead to increased desirability. By understanding the impact of scarcity on decision-making, individuals can guard against impulsive choices driven solely by the fear of missing out and maintain a more balanced perspective in their actions.

Persuasion versus Manipulation

Though persuasion and manipulation both aim to influence others, they differ fundamentally in their ethical approach and intent. In this section, we draw a clear distinction between the two, highlighting the importance of ethical persuasion.

- Voluntary versus Coerced: This provides a comprehensive exploration of the critical differentiation between persuasion and manipulation. It sheds light on how persuasion relies on seeking genuine consent from individuals, whereas manipulation may resort to coercive and deceitful tactics to achieve its goals. By grasping this fundamental distinction, individuals gain the ability to discern between authentic persuasion and manipulative strategies, enabling them to make well-informed decisions in their interactions.
- Empowerment versus Exploitation: This examines the stark contrast between ethical persuasion and manipulation. Ethical persuasion empowers individuals to exercise their autonomy and make choices aligned with their values, while manipulation seeks to exploit vulnerabilities and exert control over others. Understanding this juxtaposition equips individuals with valuable insights, enabling them to identify and resist manipulative influences effectively. This newfound knowledge fosters a sense of empowerment and self-determination, allowing individuals to navigate their lives with greater confidence.
- Transparency and Honesty: This underscores the paramount importance of transparency and honesty in the realm of ethical persuasion. Open and truthful communication serves as the foundation of genuine persuasion, fostering trust and mutual respect in relationships. Conversely, manipulation thrives on deception and hidden agendas, using these tactics

to sway others for personal gain. By recognizing the significance of transparency and honesty, individuals can establish and nurture authentic connections with others, while remaining vigilant against manipulative maneuvers that seek to deceive and mislead.

Manipulative Persuasion Tactics

Manipulative persuasion represents a darker shade of influence, where the line between persuasion and manipulation becomes blurred. In this section, we explore some of the most commonly used manipulative persuasion tactics, which can be subtle yet potent.

- False Scarcity: This manipulation technique capitalizes on the human tendency to act impulsively in response to perceived scarcity or urgency. Manipulators create a false sense of limited availability, time-sensitive offers, or exclusive opportunities to prompt individuals into making hasty decisions without thoroughly evaluating their choices. By exploiting the fear of missing out or losing out on a supposed opportunity, manipulators can lead people to act against their best interests, making impulsive decisions they might later regret.
- Bait-and-Switch: This strategy involves enticing individuals with an attractive proposition or offer initially, only to shift their attention to a less desirable alternative once they are engaged. Manipulators employ this technique to lure people in, generating excitement and interest in a particular product, service, or opportunity. However, once individuals are invested emotionally or mentally, the manipulator switches to a less appealing option, hoping that the initial attraction will influence the decision-making process. This tactic can lead to feelings of disappointment, frustration, and even a sense of being tricked or deceived.
- Emotional Appeals without Substance: In this manipulative tactic, individuals' emotions and vulnerabilities are targeted without providing credible information, logical reasoning, or concrete substance to support the emotional appeal. Manipulators might use fear, guilt, sympathy, or other strong emotions to influence decisions without offering any substantive evidence or valid reasons for their assertions. By bypassing rational thinking and appealing directly to emotions, manipulators can gain control over individuals' actions and choices, steering them in a direction that might not align with their best interests or values. This tactic can be particularly insidious, as it exploits people's emotional responses while withholding necessary information for informed decision-making.

- Exploiting Fear and Insecurity: Instilling fear or insecurity to gain compliance and control over others.

Conclusion

The power of persuasion can be a force for positive change, inspiring individuals to embrace new ideas, adopt beneficial habits, and build meaningful connections. By understanding the principles of persuasion and recognizing the boundary between persuasion and manipulation, we can harness the art of influence ethically and responsibly. As we navigate the intricate landscape of persuasive communication, we must remain vigilant against manipulative tactics that seek to exploit vulnerabilities and distort truths. Armed with the knowledge of ethical persuasion, we can become more discerning communicators, using the art of influence to promote mutual understanding, cooperation, and a more harmonious society.

CHAPTER 5

THE NARCISSISTIC MIND

Behind the Mirror: Unraveling the Narcissistic Personality

Introduction

The narcissistic mind, an enigmatic labyrinth of grandiosity and self-absorption, holds both fascination and trepidation. In this chapter, we delve into the complexities of narcissistic personality traits, exploring the manipulative tactics narcissists employ, such as gaslighting, to control and exploit others. Additionally, we will offer insights into coping mechanisms to protect ourselves from the effects of interacting with narcissistic individuals.

Narcissistic Personality Traits

Narcissistic individuals exhibit a distinctive set of personality traits characterized by an inflated sense of self-importance, a constant need for admiration, and a lack of empathy. By understanding these traits, we can gain insight into the mechanisms that drive narcissistic behavior.

- Grandiosity and Entitlement: This facet of narcissistic behavior involves an inflated sense of self-importance and an unwarranted belief in one's superiority over others. Narcissists tend to overvalue their abilities, accomplishments, and traits, leading them to seek admiration, recognition, and special treatment from others. This belief in their exceptionalism fuels a sense of entitlement, wherein they expect preferential treatment and unquestioning compliance from those around them. The grandiose nature of narcissists can manifest in various aspects of their lives, from personal relationships to professional settings, where they may demand constant validation and recognition of their supposed greatness.

- Fragile Self-Esteem: Despite their grandiose facade, narcissists often harbor deep-rooted insecurities and fragile self-esteem beneath the surface. Paradoxically, their need for constant validation and admiration stems from an underlying fear of rejection and inadequacy. They use their grandiosity as a defense mechanism to shield themselves from feelings of vulnerability and low self-worth. The tiniest criticism or perceived threat to their self-image can trigger intense emotional reactions, leading them to engage in defensive behaviors, such as projecting blame onto others or engaging in manipulative tactics to protect their fragile ego.

- Lack of Empathy: Empathy, the ability to understand and share the feelings of others, is notably absent in narcissistic individuals. They struggle to genuinely connect with the emotional experiences of those around them, often dismissing or trivializing others' emotions and needs. This lack of empathy allows them to prioritize their own desires and agenda without regard for how their actions impact others. Manipulation and exploitation of others' vulnerabilities become easier for narcissists due to their limited capacity to empathize, as they are less concerned with the consequences of their actions on others' well-being.
- Manipulative Charm: Narcissists often exhibit charming and charismatic behavior, which serves as a powerful tool to draw others into their web of influence. Their charm can be alluring, making them appear engaging, confident, and captivating. They may use flattery, compliments, and other forms of social charm to gain the trust and admiration of others. This charm, however, is often calculated and deployed strategically to serve their own self-centered motives. Behind the charismatic facade lies a desire to manipulate and exploit others for personal gain, reinforcing their sense of grandiosity and entitlement.

Narcissistic Manipulation and Gaslighting

Narcissists are skilled at manipulating others to fulfill their desires and maintain control over their relationships. Gaslighting, a common tactic employed by narcissists, involves distorting reality and undermining the victim's perception of truth to gain power.

- Gaslighting Tactics: In this comprehensive analysis the following intricate and manipulative techniques are employed by narcissists to gaslight their victims. Gaslighting is a form of psychological manipulation where the narcissist systematically undermines the victim's perceptions, memories, and beliefs, causing doubt and confusion. We delve into the various gaslighting tactics, such as trivializing the victim's emotions, distorting facts, and denying their experiences, all aimed at destabilizing the victim's sense of reality. By understanding these insidious tactics, readers gain valuable insights into the dynamics of gaslighting relationships and can recognize the warning signs of this emotional abuse.

- Psychological Impact of Gaslighting: This is the profound emotional and psychological toll gaslighting can inflict on its victims. Gaslighting erodes the victim's self-esteem, confidence, and mental well-being, leading to a state of emotional dependency on the gaslighter. We explore the long-term effects of gaslighting, such as anxiety, depression, self-doubt, and a distorted perception of reality. Understanding the devastating impact of gaslighting is crucial for victims and their loved ones to empathize with the victim's experience and provide the necessary support and validation.
- Breaking Free from Gaslighting: There are strategies and empowering insights for recognizing and countering gaslighting to regain clarity and self-confidence. Victims of gaslighting often struggle to trust their own perceptions and instincts, but through various coping mechanisms and self-care practices, they can reclaim their sense of self. We explore the importance of setting and enforcing boundaries, seeking support from trustworthy individuals, and engaging in self-reflective practices. Additionally, we delve into the role of therapy and professional guidance in assisting victims on their journey of healing and breaking free from the grasp of gaslighting. By empowering victims with tools to resist manipulation and rebuild their self-worth, we aim to foster resilience and liberation from gaslighting's toxic effects.

Coping with Narcissistic Individuals

Interacting with narcissists can be emotionally challenging and draining. This section offers insights and coping mechanisms for protecting one's well-being when dealing with narcissistic individuals.

- Setting Boundaries: This is the critical aspect of setting boundaries in relationships to safeguard oneself from manipulation and emotional harm. We explore the significance of establishing clear and firm boundaries that delineate acceptable behaviors and interactions. By doing so, individuals can protect their emotional well-being and assert their autonomy. Understanding the importance of boundaries empowers readers to communicate their needs and limits effectively, fostering healthier and more respectful relationships.
- Developing Emotional Resilience: A comprehensive journey of building emotional resilience as a crucial defense against manipulation. Emotional resilience refers to the ability to bounce back from adversity and maintain a sense of self-worth despite challenging circumstances. Throughout this

chapter, we explore various strategies and practices that aid in cultivating emotional resilience, such as mindfulness, self-compassion, and positive reframing. By enhancing emotional resilience, individuals become better equipped to withstand the manipulative tactics of narcissistic individuals and maintain their emotional equilibrium.

- Seeking Support: The value of seeking support from trusted friends, family, or professionals when navigating relationships with narcissistic individuals. We emphasize the importance of reaching out for help and validation, as dealing with manipulative behavior can be emotionally taxing and isolating. Readers are encouraged to lean on their support network to gain perspective, validation, and guidance in coping with challenging relationships. Seeking support from mental health professionals can also provide invaluable insights and tools to manage the emotional toll of dealing with narcissistic behavior.
- Self-Care and Empowerment: The integral role of self-care in promoting emotional well-being and empowerment is used when faced with narcissistic behavior. Self-care encompasses various practices, including mindfulness, healthy boundaries, and prioritizing one's emotional needs. By nurturing oneself through self-care, individuals strengthen their emotional resilience, maintain a sense of self-worth, and assert their rights in the face of manipulation. Emphasizing the importance of self-empowerment, this section aims to guide readers in reclaiming their power and taking charge of their emotional health in challenging relationships.

Conclusion

The narcissistic mind remains a captivating yet complex facet of human psychology. By understanding narcissistic personality traits and recognizing manipulative tactics like gaslighting, we can navigate interactions with narcissistic individuals more effectively. Armed with knowledge and coping strategies, we can protect our emotional well-being, maintain our sense of self, and foster healthier relationships. While the narcissistic mind may present challenges, it also provides an opportunity for personal growth and empowerment as we navigate the intricate web of narcissistic manipulation and strive to forge more authentic connections in our lives.

PART II: EXPLORING DARK PSYCHOLOGICAL TECHNIQUES

CHAPTER 6

EMOTIONAL MANIPULATION

Strings of Emotion: Unmasking the Tactics of Emotional Manipulation

Introduction

Emotional manipulation, a subtle dance of emotions and control, can be a potent force in human relationships. In this chapter, we uncover the art of emotional manipulation, exploring the tactics used to exploit emotions, such as emotional blackmail and guilt-tripping. By learning to identify emotional manipulation and implementing strategies to shield ourselves from its influence, we can reclaim our emotional autonomy and build healthier connections.

Identifying Emotional Manipulation

Emotional manipulation operates within the realm of emotions, making it challenging to recognize. In this section, we unravel the signs and signals that hint at emotional manipulation, empowering us to become more discerning and aware of its presence in our lives.

Subtle Signs of Emotional Manipulation: Identifying the seemingly innocent gestures and language that mask deeper manipulative intent.

- Exploiting Vulnerabilities: The intricate ways emotional manipulators identify and exploit vulnerabilities to gain control and influence over their targets are voluminous. Manipulators keenly observe their victims' emotional needs, insecurities, and fears, strategically using this knowledge to manipulate and manipulate their emotions. By understanding the tactics used to exploit vulnerabilities, readers gain insights into their own emotional triggers, empowering them to recognize and protect themselves from potential manipulation. Through this exploration, we aim to foster greater self-awareness and resilience, enabling individuals to build healthier and more authentic relationships.
- Trusting Your Intuition: The profound significance of trusting our instincts and feelings when detecting emotional manipulation. Intuition acts as an invaluable compass, providing subtle cues about the authenticity of

interactions and the intentions of others. By encouraging readers to tune into their intuition, we equip them with an internal guidance system to discern between genuine connections and manipulative behavior. This chapter also explores the factors that may cloud our intuition, such as self-doubt or gaslighting, and offers strategies to strengthen the connection with one's intuition. Emphasizing the power of intuition in protecting oneself from manipulation, we empower readers to listen to their inner voice and make informed choices in their relationships.

Emotional Blackmail and Guilt-Tripping

Two powerful tools wielded by emotional manipulators are emotional blackmail and guilt-tripping. In this section, we shed light on these tactics and explore their impact on emotional well-being.

- Emotional Blackmail: The intricate workings of emotional blackmail consist of wherein manipulators utilize threats, ultimatums, or emotional leverage to coerce compliance from their targets. These tactics are employed by emotional blackmailers, such as using fear, shame, or guilt, and readers gain a deeper understanding of the power dynamics at play in manipulative relationships. Recognizing the signs of emotional blackmail enables individuals to assert their boundaries and protect their emotional well-being from such toxic influences. Through this exploration, we aim to empower readers to recognize and confront emotional blackmailers, fostering a sense of self-empowerment and assertiveness in their interactions.
- Guilt-Tripping: The manipulative use of guilt as a tool to influence behavior, often leading individuals to act against their own desires or needs to avoid feeling guilty. We explore how guilt-tripping involves emotional coercion and plays on a person's sense of responsibility or loyalty, creating a sense of indebtedness that can be exploited. Understanding the mechanics of guilt-tripping helps readers discern between genuine expressions of concern and attempts to manipulate emotions for personal gain. By empowering readers to recognize and challenge guilt-tripping behavior, we aim to foster healthier relationships based on open communication and mutual respect.
- Emotional Toll: The profound emotional toll that emotional blackmail and guilt-tripping take on victims' self-esteem and self-worth is devastating. Emotional blackmailers and guilt-trippers erode their targets' confidence and sense of agency, creating a cycle of emotional turmoil and self-doubt.

Through examining the psychological impact of these manipulative tactics, readers gain insights into the importance of emotional healing and self-care. We explore strategies for building emotional resilience and self-compassion, allowing individuals to reclaim their emotional well-being and establish healthier boundaries in their relationships. By addressing the emotional toll of emotional blackmail and guilt-tripping, we hope to empower readers to break free from manipulative influences and foster more authentic and supportive connections with others.

Shielding Yourself from Emotional Manipulation

Protecting ourselves from emotional manipulation requires a combination of self-awareness and boundary-setting. This section offers strategies to shield ourselves from emotional manipulation and maintain emotional independence.

- Developing Emotional Resilience: The essential process of building emotional resilience, which empowers individuals to withstand emotional manipulation and maintain their personal autonomy is crucial. The components of emotional resilience, such as self-awareness, emotional regulation, and coping mechanisms, can equip individuals to navigate challenging emotional situations with greater strength and adaptability. Understanding the importance of emotional resilience enables readers to embrace setbacks as opportunities for growth and transform adversity into opportunities for personal development. The target needs to foster a sense of inner strength and self-confidence, allowing individuals to protect themselves from emotional manipulation and maintain a strong sense of self amidst challenging circumstances.
- Setting Boundaries: Define where the boundaries are plus using those to establish and communicate clear boundaries in our relationships and interactions. This is how setting boundaries is an act of self-care and self-preservation, enabling individuals to safeguard their emotional well-being and protect themselves from manipulation. By understanding the role of boundaries in healthy relationships, readers gain insights into the art of assertiveness and self-advocacy, empowering them to set limits and communicate their needs effectively. This skill is essential in recognizing and responding to emotional manipulation, as it helps individuals to assert their autonomy and protect their emotional space. Through exploring the concept of boundaries, we aim to promote healthier and more balanced relationships, where mutual respect and emotional safety are prioritized.

- Assertiveness and Communication: The power of cultivating assertiveness in expressing our needs and desires, while maintaining open and honest communication with others is also essential. Assertiveness is a key component of emotional intelligence and is crucial for navigating emotional manipulation effectively. By developing assertiveness skills, readers can articulate their boundaries, expectations, and emotions with clarity and confidence. This empowers them to resist manipulative tactics and communicate their feelings and boundaries assertively. Through exploring assertive communication techniques, we aim to equip individuals with the tools to protect themselves from emotional manipulation and promote healthier communication in all areas of their lives.
- Seeking Support: The value of seeking support from trusted friends, family, or professionals when dealing with emotional manipulation is also crucial. Recognizing that emotional manipulation can be emotionally taxing, seeking support is essential for processing emotions and gaining perspective on challenging situations. We explore the significance of vulnerability and reaching out for help as a strength rather than a weakness. By seeking support, individuals can gain validation, encouragement, and guidance in navigating emotional manipulation, allowing them to feel less isolated and more empowered to take action. Through exploring the role of support in emotional well-being, we aim to promote resilience and healing in the face of emotional manipulation and foster a sense of connectedness within a supportive network.

Conclusion

Emotional manipulation is an intricate web that entangles the hearts and minds of those caught within its grasp. By recognizing the signs of emotional manipulation and understanding the tactics employed, we can empower ourselves to break free from its chains. Armed with emotional resilience, self-awareness, and assertiveness, we can safeguard our emotional well-being and forge healthier connections based on trust and respect. As we navigate the complexities of emotional manipulation, we strive to create relationships that are grounded in genuine emotions, fostering a sense of emotional freedom and authenticity in our interactions with others.

CHAPTER 7

GASLIGHTING: THE MANIPULATION OF REALITY

Distorting Truth: Understanding Gaslighting and Its Effects

Introduction

Gaslighting, a form of psychological manipulation, distorts an individual's perception of reality, leaving them questioning their sanity and truth. In this chapter, we delve into the intricacies of gaslighting, exploring its definition, common examples, and the devastating impact it can have on victims. We also delve into strategies for detecting gaslighting behavior and healing from the emotional turmoil caused by this insidious form of manipulation.

Definition and Examples of Gaslighting

Gaslighting is a manipulative tactic aimed at making a person doubt their memory, perception, or sanity through persistent denial, misdirection, and contradiction. In this section, we define gaslighting and provide real-life examples to illustrate its various forms.

- Undermining Reality: These insidious tactics are used by gaslighters to undermine the victim's perception of reality. Gaslighters employ various techniques to deny or distort events, causing the victim to question their own recollections and experiences. By sowing seeds of doubt and confusion, gaslighters erode the victim's confidence in their memory and judgment, leaving them unsure of what is real and what is manipulated. Through a thorough exploration of these gaslighting tactics, readers gain a deeper understanding of the psychological impact of such manipulation. This awareness empowers individuals to recognize and resist gaslighting attempts, allowing them to maintain a stronger sense of self and reality.

- Blaming the Victim: The manipulative tactic of shifting blame onto the victim is a common strategy used by gaslighters to escape accountability for their actions. By making the victim feel responsible for the manipulation and any ensuing problems, gaslighters seek to disempower and control their targets further. The emotional toll of this blame-shifting, leads victims to internalize guilt and question their own worth. By exploring the dynamics of victim-blaming, readers gain insights into the ways gaslighters exploit vulnerability and manipulate emotions. Armed with this knowledge, individuals can better protect themselves from falling into the trap of self-blame and regain a sense of agency and self-worth.

- Minimizing Emotions: The emotionally invalidating tactics employed by gaslighters to minimize the victim's feelings and experiences can be devastating. Gaslighters may dismiss, trivialize, or outright deny the validity of the victim's emotions, leaving them feeling unheard and unimportant. By examining the impact of emotional invalidation, we highlight the harm done to the victim's emotional well-being, self-esteem, and mental health. Understanding the mechanisms used to diminish emotions empowers readers to recognize when their emotions are being manipulated and devalued. This awareness allows individuals to prioritize their emotional needs, cultivate self-compassion, and assert their right to have their feelings acknowledged and respected. Through this exploration, we aim to promote emotional validation and self-advocacy, enabling individuals to shield themselves from the harmful effects of emotional manipulation.

Detecting Gaslighting Behavior

Gaslighting can be challenging to recognize, as it often occurs gradually and subtly. This section equips readers with insights to identify gaslighting behavior and protect themselves from its harmful effects.

- Trusting Your Intuition: The profound importance of relying on our intuition when detecting gaslighting behavior is required. Intuition, often referred to as our "gut feeling," is a powerful internal compass that guides us in recognizing subtle cues and signals that something may be amiss in our interactions. The role of intuition helps us identify gaslighting attempts, then we gain a deeper understanding of the instinctive responses that signal manipulation. Emphasizing the significance of trusting one's gut feelings empowers individuals to validate their own experiences and perceptions, even in the face of doubt or denial from gaslighters. This newfound trust in intuition enables victims to reclaim their inner knowing, build self-confidence, and protect themselves from further manipulation.
- Documenting Evidence: The importance of maintaining a record of events and conversations as a means of validating one's experiences is necessary as well. Gaslighters often rely on the tactic of distorting or denying past

occurrences to sow seeds of confusion and doubt in the victim's mind. By keeping a detailed account of interactions, individuals have tangible evidence that supports their recollections, providing a powerful defense against gaslighting attempts. The various methods of documenting evidence, such as journaling, saving messages or emails, and recording conversations when appropriate. This practice not only serves as a validation tool for the victim but also facilitates communication with external sources, such as friends, family, or professionals, who can offer support and validation based on the documented evidence.

- Seeking External Perspectives: There is value in seeking support and feedback from trusted external sources to gain an objective perspective on gaslighting experiences. Victims of gaslighting may often find themselves isolated and doubting their reality, making it essential to seek validation and feedback from individuals who can provide an outside view of the situation. Friends, family members, or mental health professionals can offer invaluable insights and observations, helping to confirm the presence of gaslighting behavior and providing a supportive network for the victim. By recognizing the significance of external perspectives, individuals are encouraged to reach out for assistance, knowing they are not alone in their experiences. This collaborative effort fosters a sense of empowerment and collective understanding, ultimately aiding victims in breaking free from the clutches of gaslighting manipulation.

Healing from Gaslighting Experiences

Healing from gaslighting experiences is a journey towards reclaiming one's sense of reality and self-worth. In this section, we offer guidance and coping strategies for survivors of gaslighting.

- Validating Your Experience: The vital process of acknowledging the impact of gaslighting and validating the emotions and experiences of victims is also required. Gaslighting is a manipulative tactic that can leave individuals feeling confused, doubting their own perceptions, and questioning their reality. By delving into the emotional and psychological toll of gaslighting, readers gain a deeper understanding of the gaslighting dynamic and the feelings of vulnerability and self-doubt it may engender. The significance of validating the victim's experience is emphasized, as this validation fosters a sense of validation, affirmation, and recognition of their pain. By acknowledging the harm caused by gaslighting and offering validation, we aim to empower victims to reclaim their sense of reality, bolstering their emotional resilience and providing a foundation for healing and growth.

- Rebuilding Self-Trust: The essential process of nurturing self-trust and self-confidence after experiencing gaslighting is beneficial. Gaslighting can severely erode an individual's trust in their own judgments and perceptions, leaving them hesitant to trust their thoughts and feelings. Use strategies for rebuilding self-trust, such as engaging in self-reflection, embracing one's intuition, and celebrating personal strengths and achievements. By promoting self-compassion and self-acceptance, readers are encouraged to replace self-doubt with self-assurance, fostering a renewed sense of confidence in their abilities to discern truth from manipulation. Rebuilding self-trust is an integral step towards healing from gaslighting trauma, as it empowers individuals to rediscover their inner strength and agency.
- Setting Boundaries: The crucial importance of learning to establish and enforce (or reinforce) boundaries to protect oneself from present or future gaslighting attempts. Gaslighters often exploit weaknesses and cross personal boundaries to manipulate their victims. Understanding the significance of boundaries enables individuals to recognize their rights to safety, autonomy, and self-respect. We delve into strategies for setting and maintaining healthy boundaries in various relationships, whether romantic, familial, or professional. By effectively communicating boundaries and enforcing them, individuals can safeguard their emotional well-being and prevent future gaslighting attempts. This newfound sense of self-protection and empowerment strengthens resilience against manipulation and fosters healthier interpersonal dynamics.
- Seeking Support: The importance of seeking professional support and counseling to process the trauma of gaslighting and promote healing is crucial. Gaslighting experiences can have long-lasting effects on an individual's emotional and mental well-being, leading to feelings of anxiety, depression, and post-traumatic stress. Seeking support from mental health professionals who specialize in trauma and manipulation can provide victims with a safe space to explore their experiences, process their emotions, and develop coping strategies. We also highlight the value of seeking support from trusted friends and family, as having a supportive network can offer

additional validation and understanding. By encouraging readers to seek support, we aim to create a path towards healing and restoration, helping individuals reclaim their sense of self and navigate the aftermath of gaslighting with strength and resilience.

Conclusion

Gaslighting is a treacherous form of manipulation that shakes the foundations of an individual's reality and self-perception. By understanding gaslighting's insidious tactics, victims can reclaim their power and sense of self. Trusting one's intuition, seeking validation, and fostering emotional resilience are vital in breaking free from the clutches of gaslighting. Through support, healing, and self-compassion, survivors of gaslighting can emerge stronger, more self-aware, and equipped to navigate future interactions with resilience and authenticity. As we shed light on the dark corners of gaslighting, we empower individuals to recognize and resist this form of manipulation, creating a path towards emotional liberation and a strengthened sense of self.

CHAPTER 8

THE SEDUCTION GAME

Ensnaring Hearts: Unveiling the Dark Art of Seduction

Introduction

The seduction game, a tantalizing dance of attraction and influence, can be both alluring and perilous. In this chapter, we delve into the depths of seduction, exploring the manipulative tactics used to ensnare hearts in romantic relationships. By shedding light on the dark art of seduction, we equip readers with the knowledge to protect themselves from manipulative seduction and foster empowering connections built on authenticity and genuine affection.

The Dark Art of Seduction

Seduction, a skillful blend of charm and manipulation, is an age-old art employed to win affection and admiration. In this section, we delve into the darker aspects of seduction, revealing the tactics used to exploit vulnerabilities and create an illusion of genuine connection.

- Love Bombing: Love Bombing, is a manipulative tactic used to captivate and disarm targets. Love bombing involves overwhelming the target with an intense shower of affection, attention, and compliments, creating a euphoric emotional state. This is how manipulators exploit the target's vulnerabilities, insecurities, and desires for love and connection. The manipulator may use grand gestures, excessive flattery, and extravagant displays of affection to create an illusion of an idealized relationship. Understanding the mechanics of love bombing enables readers to recognize its seductive allure and become aware of potential manipulative attempts in their relationships.
- Mirroring and Validation: The manipulative tactic of mirroring and validation is employed by seducers to create a false sense of shared identity and validation. Mirroring involves mimicking the target's behaviors, interests, and values to establish a strong sense of connection and compatibility. By feigning shared interests and values, the manipulator aims to create the illusion of being the perfect match for the target, fostering

emotional intimacy and trust. Additionally, the manipulator validates the target's emotions, desires, and aspirations, making them feel heard and understood. We explore how mirroring and validation can be powerful tools in manipulating the target's emotions and perceptions, and how recognizing these tactics can empower individuals to maintain a critical and discerning mindset in their relationships.

- Emotional Manipulation: Emotional manipulation tactics are employed by love bombers to evoke intense feelings and emotional dependency in their targets. Emotional manipulation involves strategic maneuvers to control the target's emotions, making them more susceptible to the manipulator's influence. Common tactics include intermittent reinforcement, where the manipulator alternates between affection and withdrawal to create an addictive emotional rollercoaster, leaving the target yearning for more validation and attention. We also explore gaslighting and guilt-tripping techniques used to instill doubt in the target's perceptions and make them question their own emotions and experiences. By uncovering the emotional manipulation tactics, readers gain a deeper understanding of how love bombers exploit vulnerability to maintain control and domination in the relationship. Armed with this knowledge, individuals can develop emotional resilience and establish healthier boundaries to protect themselves from emotional manipulation.

Manipulative Tactics in Romantic Relationships

Romantic relationships can become battlegrounds for manipulative seduction. This section uncovers the subtle ways manipulators can use seduction to control and dominate their partners.

- Gaslighting in Love: The exploration of gaslighting in romantic relationships, sheds light on its insidious nature and its profound impact on the victim's perception of reality and emotions. Gaslighting involves manipulative tactics aimed at distorting the victim's sense of reality, making them doubt their own memory, perception, and judgment. Gaslighters employ subtle manipulations, such as questioning the victim's recollection of events, denying past conversations, and trivializing the victim's emotions, to create confusion and undermine their confidence. By understanding the mechanics of gaslighting, readers can recognize the warning signs early on in their relationships, empowering them to confront manipulation and maintain a healthy sense of self.

- Emotional Exploitation: Emotional exploitation tactics used by seducers in romantic relationships are used to exert control over their partners. Emotional exploitation involves leveraging the partner's emotional vulnerabilities, attachment needs, and desires for affection to manipulate and control their behavior. We explore how seducers may use love bombing, intense affection, and romantic gestures to evoke strong emotional responses and foster emotional dependency in their partners. By understanding the emotional manipulation tactics, readers gain insights into the power dynamics at play in their relationships and can identify whether their emotions are being genuinely reciprocated or emotionally exploited. Armed with this awareness, individuals can foster emotional resilience and set healthy boundaries to protect themselves from emotional exploitation.
- Isolation and Control: Seducers use isolation and control as tactics to create dependency and diminish the partner's support network. Isolation involves subtly or overtly cutting off the partner from their friends, family, and social circles, leaving them with limited external perspectives and emotional support. By fostering a sense of dependence on the seducer, the victim becomes more susceptible to manipulation and control. Additionally, we explore how control tactics, such as monitoring the partner's activities, controlling their finances, or imposing rigid rules, further reinforce the seducer's dominance in the relationship. Understanding these dynamics empowers readers to recognize signs of isolation and control early on, promoting a sense of autonomy and agency in their relationships. By establishing and maintaining healthy boundaries, individuals can foster relationships built on mutual respect and genuine connection rather than manipulation and dependency.

Empowering Yourself Against Seduction Manipulation

Empowerment lies in recognizing the signs of manipulative seduction and developing self-awareness to protect against its allure. In this section, we offer strategies to empower oneself in romantic relationships and cultivate genuine connections.

- Trusting Your Intuition: There is enormous significance in trusting one's instincts and being attuned to subtle red flags in romantic partners. Intuition serves as a valuable internal compass that can provide valuable insights into the authenticity of a relationship. By paying attention to gut feelings and subtle cues, individuals can identify signs of manipulation or deceit early on. We explore how gut instincts may manifest as feelings of discomfort, unease, or a sense of something being off in the relationship. Cultivating trust in one's intuition empowers individuals to make more informed decisions and avoid potentially harmful or manipulative relationships.

- Setting Healthy Boundaries: The importance of establishing and enforcing healthy boundaries to safeguard oneself from manipulative seduction is paramount. Healthy boundaries serve as protective barriers that delineate what is acceptable and unacceptable behavior in a relationship. By setting clear boundaries, individuals communicate their limits and expectations, promoting respect and mutual understanding. We delve into the process of identifying personal boundaries and assertively expressing them to potential partners. Understanding the role of boundaries in maintaining emotional well-being allows individuals to create relationships built on trust, respect, and genuine affection.
- Emotional Independence: This section highlights the significance of fostering emotional independence and resilience to resist emotional manipulation in romantic relationships. Emotional independence involves cultivating a strong sense of self-worth, self-awareness, and emotional regulation. By developing emotional independence, individuals are less susceptible to being emotionally dependent on others and more capable of making healthy relationship choices. We explore self-care practices and emotional coping strategies that promote emotional well-being, empowering individuals to navigate relationships from a place of strength and autonomy.
- Seeking Authentic Connections: In this chapter, we emphasize the value of pursuing relationships based on authenticity, mutual respect, and genuine affection. Genuine connections are built on honesty, vulnerability, and shared values. We discuss the importance of taking the time to get to know potential partners and assessing whether their intentions align with one's own relationship goals. Seeking authentic connections involves being open to forming meaningful bonds with individuals who value and respect one another. By prioritizing authenticity and genuine affection, individuals can build healthier, more fulfilling romantic relationships that are less vulnerable to manipulation and deceit.

Conclusion

The seduction game can be a captivating yet treacherous terrain, where genuine affection can be obscured by manipulative tactics. By understanding the dark art of seduction, we empower ourselves to detect and resist manipulation in romantic relationships. Trusting our intuition, setting healthy boundaries, and fostering emotional independence are crucial in navigating the complexities of romantic connections. As we unveil the seduction game's deceptive facade, we create opportunities for authentic, empowering, and nourishing relationships, where hearts are not ensnared by artful manipulation but are free to explore the depths of true emotional connection.

CHAPTER 9

MACHIAVELLIAN MINDSET

Navigating the Calculated Realm: Understanding the Machiavellian Personality

Introduction

The Machiavellian mindset, a calculated and strategic approach to interactions, has long intrigued scholars and observers. In this chapter, we delve into the characteristics of the Machiavellian personality type, exploring their strategic strategies and coping mechanisms for dealing with Machiavellian individuals. By understanding this intricate mindset, we equip ourselves with insights to navigate the realm of Machiavellianism and protect against potential manipulation.

The Machiavellian Personality Type

The Machiavellian personality type is characterized by a strategic, pragmatic, and manipulative approach to achieving goals. In this section, we examine the core traits that define the Machiavellian mindset.

- Strategic Calculations: The Machiavellian mindset emphasizes their innate inclination to make calculated decisions based on strategic benefits. Machiavellians are adept at analyzing every action and interaction with a focus on achieving their goals and enhancing their personal interests. Their approach is often marked by a keen awareness of power dynamics, potential alliances, and the consequences of their actions. We explore how this strategic mindset enables Machiavellians to navigate social situations with a calculated demeanor, carefully considering the outcomes of their choices. Understanding their strategic calculations empowers individuals to be cautious when interacting with Machiavellians and to recognize when their intentions may be driven more by self-interest than genuine concern.

- Manipulative Tendencies: The manipulative tendencies commonly exhibited by Machiavellians are as follows; manipulation is a tool they employ to gain advantages, maintain control, and achieve their objectives. Machiavellians are skilled at using deception, charm, and persuasive tactics to influence others' perceptions and actions. We examine various manipulative strategies used by Machiavellians, such as gaslighting, love bombing, and emotional exploitation. Recognizing their manipulative tendencies can help individuals be more cautious in their interactions, allowing them to protect themselves from potential manipulation and maintain autonomy in their decisions.

- Lack of Empathy: The Machiavellian's diminished capacity for empathy and concern for the well-being of others is obvious. Empathy, the ability to understand and share the feelings of others, is often lacking in Machiavellians. Their focus on self-preservation and pursuit of personal goals may lead them to disregard the feelings and needs of those around them. This lack of empathy can manifest in their callous behavior, indifference to others' suffering, and willingness to exploit people for their own gains. Recognizing their lack of empathy allows individuals to be cautious when engaging with Machiavellians, understanding that their actions may not be driven by genuine concern for others but rather by self-serving motives.

Strategies of the Machiavellian Mind

The Machiavellian mindset thrives on cunning strategies and calculated actions. This section explores the tactics employed by Machiavellian individuals to achieve their objectives.

- Exploiting Weaknesses: The Machiavellian's astute ability to identify and exploit weaknesses in others in order to gain the upper hand also is implemented. Their keen observation skills allow them to pinpoint vulnerabilities and use them strategically, whether to gain influence, control, or extract information from their targets. By understanding this aspect of Machiavellian behavior, individuals can become more aware of potential manipulative tactics and work towards fortifying their own boundaries and self-awareness.

- Feigning Trust and Loyalty: The Machiavellian's remarkable talent for feigning trust and loyalty as a means to achieve their objectives is astute. They can convincingly act as reliable confidants or allies, earning the trust of others, all while concealing their true intentions. By examining this deceptive behavior, individuals can become more cautious about whom they place their trust in and be mindful of any inconsistencies in people's actions and words.

- Building Alliances: The Machiavellian's skill in forming and manipulating alliances furthers their interests. They possess an acute understanding of group dynamics and use their charm and persuasion to rally support and gain influence within social circles. By understanding this aspect of Machiavellian behavior, individuals can be better prepared to assess the true motives behind seemingly charismatic individuals and maintain a healthy skepticism towards those who may seek to manipulate them for personal gain.

Coping with Machiavellian Individuals

Interacting with Machiavellian individuals can be challenging, requiring vigilance and self-awareness. In this section, we offer coping strategies to protect oneself from manipulation and navigate relationships with Machiavellian personalities.

- Setting Firm Boundaries: This facet delves into the significance of learning to establish and maintain strong boundaries as a means to protect oneself against Machiavellian influence. Machiavellians often seek to push boundaries and exploit weaknesses, but by developing firm and clearly defined limits, individuals can create a barrier that safeguards their autonomy and well-being. Understanding the importance of boundaries enables individuals to recognize when they are being pushed beyond their comfort zone and empowers them to assertively protect their personal space and values.
- Trusting But Verifying: Adopting a balanced approach when dealing with Machiavellian individuals is of the utmost importance. While it's essential to interact with others in a trusting manner, it's equally crucial to exercise a healthy skepticism and verify the information before placing complete trust in someone. Machiavellians are skilled at presenting themselves in a favorable light and may not always be forthcoming with their true intentions. By trusting but verifying, individuals can navigate relationships with greater awareness and discernment, preventing potential manipulation.
- Observing Patterns of Behavior: The significance of observing consistent patterns of behavior in individuals, especially those with Machiavellian tendencies is paramount. Actions often speak louder than words, and observing recurring behaviors can provide valuable insights into a person's true character and motives. By paying attention to patterns, individuals can identify potential manipulative tendencies and make informed decisions about the people they choose to engage with.

- Avoiding Emotional Manipulation: This facet focuses on the importance of developing emotional resilience to resist emotional manipulation and control from Machiavellian individuals. Emotional manipulation is a tactic often employed by Machiavellians to exploit vulnerabilities and gain control over others. By cultivating emotional awareness and resilience, individuals can become less susceptible to emotional manipulation, maintain a sense of personal agency, and protect their emotional well-being in challenging interactions.

Conclusion

The Machiavellian mindset operates within a realm of calculated strategy and manipulation, requiring careful navigation and self-awareness. By understanding the characteristics and strategies of Machiavellian individuals, we can protect ourselves from potential manipulation and make informed decisions in our interactions. Trusting our intuition, setting firm boundaries, and observing patterns of behavior are vital tools in dealing with Machiavellian personalities. As we explore the depths of the Machiavellian mindset, we empower ourselves to forge healthier, more authentic relationships while safeguarding against the artful manipulation of those who seek to advance their objectives at any cost.

CHAPTER 10

PERSUASIVE COMMUNICATION

The Power of Words: Unmasking Manipulation in Persuasive Communication

Introduction

Persuasive communication, a skillful craft of language and rhetoric, has the potential to sway opinions and shape beliefs. In this chapter, we delve into the intricacies of persuasive communication, examining how manipulators use language and speech patterns to exploit vulnerabilities and influence others. By becoming critical receivers of persuasive messages, we can navigate the sea of information with discernment and shield ourselves from the subtle currents of manipulation.

Language and Rhetoric in Manipulation

Language is a powerful tool that can be used to inspire, educate, and motivate. However, in the hands of manipulators, it can become a weapon to deceive and control. In this section, we explore how language and rhetoric are harnessed to manipulate perceptions and emotions.

- Emotional Appeals: The art of emotional manipulation is how manipulators skillfully use emotionally charged language to elicit specific reactions and override rational thought. Emotions can be powerful drivers of behavior, and manipulators capitalize on this by employing carefully crafted messages that evoke fear, sympathy, or excitement. By understanding the mechanics of emotional appeals, individuals can become more vigilant in recognizing when their emotions are being targeted and take a step back to critically evaluate the situation.
- Persuasive Techniques: Various persuasive techniques are employed by manipulators to sway opinions without providing substantial evidence. Some of these techniques include repetition, where messages are repeated to reinforce a particular belief, flattery, which fosters a sense of admiration and trust, and fear appeals, which exploit anxieties to influence decisions.

Recognizing these tactics enables individuals to become more discerning consumers of information and less susceptible to being swayed by superficial or manipulative persuasive efforts.

- Ambiguity and Vagueness: How manipulators use ambiguous language to create confusion and exploit interpretations and use these to their advantage. By employing vague statements or leaving crucial details unsaid, manipulators can control the narrative and avoid accountability for their actions. They take advantage of the human tendency to fill in gaps in information with assumptions, leading individuals to draw conclusions that may align with the manipulator's objectives. Understanding the use of ambiguity and vagueness allows individuals to question incomplete information and seek clarity before making important decisions.

Manipulative Speech Patterns

Speech patterns play a pivotal role in persuasive communication, shaping the impact of the message on the audience. In this section, we uncover the manipulative speech patterns used to influence beliefs and actions.

- Gaslighting through Language: The insidious use of gaslighting techniques in manipulators' speech is to instill doubt in their victims' perceptions and beliefs. Gaslighters employ subtle tactics like questioning the victim's memory, denying past events, or twisting the context to make the victim question their sanity and reality. By understanding these gaslighting methods, individuals can become more aware of manipulative language patterns and protect themselves from falling victim to psychological manipulation.
- Deflection and Distraction: Watch how manipulators use deflection and distraction to shift the focus away from the core issues at hand, thereby maintaining control of the conversation or situation. They may divert attention by changing the subject, attacking the messenger rather than addressing the message, or overwhelming others with irrelevant details. By recognizing these deflection tactics, individuals can stay focused on the key points of discussion and avoid being led astray by manipulative distractions.
- Intimidation and Belittling: The use of intimidation and belittling language by manipulators is used to undermine their targets' confidence and assert dominance over them. By using derogatory language, insults, or condescension, manipulators attempt to make their victims feel small, powerless, and unworthy. Understanding the impact of intimidation and

belittling allows individuals to recognize when they are being subjected to such tactics and empowers them to assert their boundaries and self-worth in the face of manipulation.

Becoming a Critical Receiver of Persuasive Messages

Becoming a critical receiver of persuasive messages empowers individuals to think critically, question assumptions, and assess the credibility of information. In this section, we offer strategies to develop discernment and protect oneself from manipulation.

- Fact-Checking and Research: This highlights the significance of fact-checking and conducting independent research when encountering persuasive messages. In a world filled with information, it becomes essential to verify the accuracy and reliability of claims and data presented to us. By engaging in fact-checking and research, individuals can ensure that they are making informed decisions based on credible and verified information, rather than being swayed by misleading or false claims.
- Analyzing Motives: Understanding the motives and intentions behind persuasive communication is crucial in evaluating its credibility. People often have underlying biases or hidden agendas that can influence the way they present information. By analyzing the motives of the communicator, listeners can gain insight into potential biases and assess the sincerity of the message. This allows individuals to approach persuasive communication with a critical mindset, avoiding being easily influenced by manipulative tactics.
- Identifying Logical Fallacies: Logical fallacies are common errors in reasoning that can mislead listeners and weaken the credibility of persuasive messages. Recognizing these fallacies is essential for discerning flawed arguments and avoiding being manipulated by deceptive rhetoric. By familiarizing themselves with logical fallacies, individuals can strengthen their critical thinking skills and become more adept at identifying weak or misleading arguments.
- Emotional Awareness: Cultivating emotional awareness is essential for making rational decisions and avoiding impulsive reactions to persuasive messages. Emotional appeals are powerful tactics used to influence individuals' feelings and elicit specific responses. By developing emotional awareness, people can recognize when their emotions are being manipulated

and consciously separate their emotional responses from logical judgments. This allows them to make more balanced and well-informed decisions, less susceptible to being swayed solely by emotional appeals.

Conclusion

Persuasive communication can be both enlightening and deceptive, depending on the communicator's intentions and methods. By understanding the language and rhetoric of manipulation, we can become critical receivers of persuasive messages, shielding ourselves from manipulation and making informed decisions. Trusting our instincts, conducting thorough research, and recognizing manipulative speech patterns are essential skills in navigating the sea of persuasive communication. As we hone our ability to discern truth from deception, we empower ourselves to stand firm in our beliefs, maintain our autonomy, and build relationships based on trust and authentic communication.

PART III: UNDERSTANDING THE DARK SIDE

CHAPTER 11

DARK TRIAD PERSONALITIES

Unveiling the Dark Triad: Exploring Narcissism, Machiavellianism, and Psychopathy

Introduction to the Dark Triad (Narcissism, Machiavellianism, Psychopathy)

The Dark Triad is a constellation of three malevolent personality traits – narcissism, Machiavellianism, and psychopathy – that have captivated researchers and psychologists for their shared penchant for manipulation, exploitation, and lack of empathy. In this chapter, we delve into the core characteristics of each trait, offering insights into the complex and often enigmatic realm of dark personalities.

Overlapping Traits and Characteristics

While each personality trait of the Dark Triad possesses unique characteristics, they share underlying traits that form the foundation of their malevolent nature. In this section, we explore the overlapping traits and behaviors that tie the Dark Triad personalities together.

- Manipulative Tactics: This aspect delves into the intricate web of manipulative strategies employed by individuals with dark personalities to achieve their objectives. These tactics often involve cunning and deceitful maneuvers aimed at controlling and influencing others for their own benefit. By understanding these manipulative tactics, individuals can become more aware of potential red flags and protect themselves from falling prey to manipulative individuals.

- Lack of Empathy: One of the defining traits of dark personalities is their shared deficit of empathy. This lack of empathy enables them to disregard the feelings, emotions, and well-being of others. They may exploit and manipulate others without feeling remorse or compassion for the harm they cause. Understanding this lack of empathy helps individuals recognize when they are dealing with someone who may not have their best interests at heart and encourages them to be cautious in their interactions.

- Exploitative Nature: Dark individuals often display a common tendency to exploit and use others for their personal gain. They may see relationships as opportunities to take advantage of others, viewing people as tools to achieve their goals. This exploitative nature can manifest in various aspects of their behavior, such as using charm and manipulation to gain trust and control over others. By analyzing this exploitative nature, individuals can better identify manipulative behaviors and protect themselves from being manipulated or harmed. Being aware of these exploitative tendencies empowers individuals to establish healthy boundaries and avoid being drawn into harmful relationships.

Impact on Personal Relationships and Society

The Dark Triad personalities can wreak havoc on personal relationships and have far-reaching consequences for society as a whole. In this section, we explore the detrimental effects these malevolent traits can have on individuals, families, and communities.

- Destructive Relationships: This aspect delves into the intricate and often devastating impact that dark personalities can have on personal relationships. It explores the emotional harm and psychological manipulation that may arise when individuals with Dark Triad traits, such as narcissism, Machiavellianism, and psychopathy, engage with others. Understanding the dynamics of destructive relationships is crucial for recognizing warning signs and protecting oneself from falling into harmful partnerships.

- Influence on Social Dynamics: Dark personalities can also have a broader impact on the social fabric of a community or society at large. This section examines how the presence of individuals with dark traits can affect trust, cooperation, and overall social well-being. Such individuals may exploit and manipulate others, eroding trust and undermining the collaborative nature of healthy social interactions. By comprehending the influence of dark personalities on social dynamics, society can take measures to counteract their negative effects and foster a more supportive and empathetic environment.

- Dark Leaders and the Corrosion of Institutions: This aspect analyzes the potential consequences of having dark personalities in positions of power and authority. When individuals with Dark Triad traits hold significant leadership roles, there can be serious implications for institutions and organizations. Their tendencies towards manipulation, corruption, and unethical decision-making can lead to the erosion of trust, transparency, and moral integrity within these institutions. Understanding this correlation between dark leaders and institutional corrosion is essential for promoting ethical leadership and ensuring that those in positions of power uphold the best interests of the collective, rather than serving their own agendas.

Conclusion

- The Dark Triad personalities, with their shared characteristics of manipulation, lack of empathy, and exploitation, form an intricate web of malevolence that can leave a trail of emotional devastation in their wake. By understanding the core traits of narcissism, Machiavellianism, and psychopathy and recognizing their overlapping tendencies, we gain insight into the complex nature of dark personalities. The impact of the Dark Triad on personal relationships and society at large underscores the importance of being vigilant and critical in our interactions, safeguarding ourselves and our communities from the corrosive influence of malevolent individuals. As we navigate the treacherous terrain of the Dark Triad, we strive for a society that values empathy, authenticity, and ethical behavior, fostering connections built on trust and mutual respect.

CHAPTER 12

THE PSYCHOLOGY OF CULTS

Beyond Belief: Understanding Cult Formation and Manipulation

Introduction

Cults, enigmatic and alluring, have long fascinated psychologists and researchers for their ability to captivate and manipulate followers. In this chapter, we explore the intricate psychology behind cult formation and the manipulative techniques used by cult leaders to gain control over their members. Additionally, we delve into the complexities of escaping the grip of cult manipulation and the path to recovery for those who have been ensnared by these compelling and often dangerous groups.

Cult Formation and Manipulation Techniques

Cults emerge through a combination of psychological, social, and emotional factors that create an environment conducive to manipulation. In this section, we examine the dynamics of cult formation and the techniques used by cult leaders to control their followers.

- Identity Erosion: This facet explores the insidious process through which cults dismantle individuals' pre-existing identities and replace them with the group's beliefs and values. Cult leaders often employ various psychological tactics to weaken personal identities, such as discouraging critical thinking and independent decision-making. By breaking down a person's sense of self and individuality, the cult can exert greater control over its members, making them more receptive to adopting the group's ideology and relinquishing their autonomy.

- Mind Control: The disturbing world of mind control techniques is used by cults to manipulate and dominate their followers. These techniques may include indoctrination, thought reform, and isolation from external influences. Cult leaders aim to create a closed system of beliefs and information that revolves solely around the group, fostering a sense of dependency and allegiance. The goal is to instill absolute loyalty to the cult leader and prevent any dissent or critical analysis of the group's teachings.

- Love-Bombing: Love-bombing is a manipulative tactic employed by cults to entrap new recruits and foster a deep emotional connection. During the initial stages of recruitment, new members are showered with overwhelming affection, attention, and acceptance. This excessive display of love and belongingness creates a powerful psychological bond with the group and its members. As a result, individuals may feel indebted to the cult and its leader, making it difficult to break free from the group's influence later on. Unraveling the mechanics of love-bombing helps individuals recognize this manipulative strategy and guard against being ensnared by its allure.

Cult Leaders and Their Tactics

Cult leaders often possess charismatic qualities that draw followers into their fold. This section delves into the traits and tactics used by cult leaders to establish and maintain control over their followers.

- Charismatic Leadership: This aspect delves into the art of charismatic leadership employed by cult leaders to wield influence and captivate their followers. Cult leaders often possess magnetic personalities, charm, and eloquence, which allow them to draw people in and create a sense of awe and admiration. Their persuasive communication and ability to inspire devotion make it easier for them to manipulate and control their followers. Understanding the dynamics of charismatic leadership helps shed light on how individuals can be swayed by a leader's allure, leading them to overlook red flags and critical evaluation.
- Authoritarian Control: The use of authoritarian tactics by cult leaders is used to establish dominance and control over their followers. Cults often operate under a hierarchical structure where the leader's authority is absolute, and any questioning or dissent is swiftly suppressed. Authoritarian leaders use fear, intimidation, and punishment to maintain their power and discourage independent thought. They create an atmosphere of obedience and blind loyalty, making it difficult for followers to break free from the group's grip.
- Exploitation and Abuse: This facet examines the dark underbelly of cult leadership, where leaders exploit their power to manipulate and abuse vulnerable members. Cult leaders may engage in psychological, emotional, and even physical abuse to keep their followers compliant and submissive. They might take advantage of their followers' trust and loyalty, manipulating them for financial gain or personal gratification. Recognizing the patterns of exploitation and abuse helps individuals identify the toxic dynamics of cults and protect themselves and others from falling prey to such harmful influences.

Escaping and Recovering from Cult Manipulation

Escaping the grip of cult manipulation is a challenging and emotionally taxing journey. In this section, we explore the process of breaking free from cult influence and the steps toward recovery and healing.

- Deconstructing Indoctrination: This aspect delves into the intricate process of undoing the deeply ingrained beliefs and thought patterns instilled by the cult. Indoctrination in a cult involves systematic manipulation and conditioning that can shape a person's entire worldview. Deconstructing this indoctrination requires critical self-reflection, questioning the beliefs, and identifying the techniques used by the cult to control minds. It may involve examining the logical fallacies, inconsistencies, and emotional manipulations employed by the cult. By understanding the mechanisms of indoctrination, individuals can gain clarity, break free from mental entrapment, and regain their intellectual autonomy.
- Rebuilding Self-Identity: After leaving a cult, individuals often face a profound crisis of identity, as their sense of self is heavily intertwined with the group's beliefs and values. Rebuilding self-identity involves embarking on a journey of self-discovery and rediscovery. It entails exploring one's authentic beliefs, interests, and values, free from the influence of the cult. This process may be challenging and require professional counseling or therapy to navigate feelings of confusion, loss, and reintegration into society. As individuals begin to redefine themselves outside of the cult's grasp, they can cultivate a stronger and more resilient sense of self.
- Seeking Support: Seeking support is an essential step in the recovery process for individuals who have left a cult. Leaving a cult can be emotionally and psychologically taxing, and having a support network is crucial for healing and adjustment. Friends, family, or support groups can provide empathy, understanding, and a safe space to share experiences and emotions. Professional help from therapists or counselors experienced in cult recovery can also offer valuable guidance and tools for coping with the aftermath of cult involvement. By seeking support, individuals can find reassurance and solidarity in their journey toward healing and reclaiming their lives.

Conclusion

The psychology of cults presents a perplexing tapestry of manipulation, charisma, and vulnerability that can lead individuals into a world of blind devotion and control. By understanding the dynamics of cult formation and manipulation techniques, we become more vigilant and cautious of the potential dangers cults pose to vulnerable individuals. The path to escape from cult manipulation is arduous, but it is possible with the right support and self-discovery. As we shine a light on the psychology of cults, we foster a society that encourages critical thinking, autonomy, and emotional resilience, empowering individuals to resist the allure of cult manipulation and to forge a path towards a more authentic and independent life.

CHAPTER 13

BRAINWASHING AND THOUGHT CONTROL

The Battle for Minds: Unmasking Brainwashing and Thought Control

Introduction

Brainwashing and thought control, mysterious and unsettling concepts, have long been associated with the manipulation of human cognition. In this chapter, we delve into the depths of these techniques, exploring the psychology behind brainwashing and the methods used to manipulate individuals' thoughts and beliefs. By understanding the intricacies of brainwashing and thought control, we equip ourselves with the knowledge to recognize and resist the insidious influence of these manipulative practices.

Understanding Brainwashing Techniques

Brainwashing techniques are designed to weaken an individual's sense of self and critical thinking, leaving them susceptible to adopting new beliefs and ideologies. In this section, we explore the psychological mechanisms behind brainwashing and the strategies used to manipulate minds.

- Isolation and Dependency: This aspect involves a comprehensive analysis of how manipulators employ isolation and dependency to achieve their aims. By isolating their targets from friends, family, and other support systems, manipulators create an environment where the victim becomes increasingly reliant on the manipulator for emotional and psychological needs. Isolation weakens the victim's access to alternate perspectives, making them more susceptible to the manipulator's influence. Dependency fosters a sense of indebtedness and loyalty to the manipulator, further reinforcing their control over the victim's thoughts and actions.

- Disruption of Reality: Manipulators engage in tactics that distort reality to control their victims' perceptions and beliefs. They may use gaslighting techniques to make the victim doubt their own memory, perceptions, and sanity. By sowing seeds of confusion and uncertainty, manipulators create an environment where the victim relies on the manipulator's version of reality. This distortion of reality enables the manipulator to establish and maintain power and control over the victim's thoughts and decisions.

- Repetition and Conditioning: Manipulators often employ repetitive messaging and conditioning to shape their victims' beliefs and behaviors. Through consistent repetition of certain ideas or beliefs, manipulators aim to normalize their narratives and suppress any dissenting opinions. Over time, the victim may internalize these messages and adopt the manipulator's worldview as their own. Conditioning techniques, such as rewards for compliance and punishment for resistance, further reinforce the manipulator's desired behaviors. As a result, the victim's autonomy and critical thinking abilities can become diminished, increasing the manipulator's control over their actions and decisions.
- Understanding the mechanisms of isolation and dependency, the disruption of reality, and the power of repetition and conditioning can help individuals recognize manipulative tactics and protect themselves from falling under the sway of manipulators. By fostering self-awareness, critical thinking, and emotional resilience, individuals can resist manipulation and maintain a sense of autonomy and agency in their lives.

Thought-Reform Programs and Indoctrination

Thought-reform programs and indoctrination aim to reshape individuals' thoughts and beliefs to align with a particular ideology or agenda. In this section, we explore the methods used in these programs and the impact they can have on individuals' cognition.

- Cult Indoctrination: This facet involves a comprehensive exploration of the intricate processes employed by cults to indoctrinate and control the minds of their followers. Cults use a combination of psychological techniques to create a closed, insular environment that fosters unquestioning loyalty and obedience. They often employ tactics such as love-bombing, where new recruits are showered with affection and attention to create a sense of indebtedness and loyalty. Cult leaders use charismatic charm and emotional manipulation to captivate and maintain the devotion of their followers. Additionally, cults often establish rigid belief systems and discourage critical thinking, making it challenging for followers to question or challenge the group's ideologies.
- Totalitarian Regimes and Thought Control: The diabolical methods are used by authoritarian regimes to manipulate public opinion and suppress dissent. Totalitarian regimes often utilize propaganda, censorship, and surveillance to control the flow of information and shape the narrative according to their

interests. By disseminating biased or false information, these regimes aim to sway public perception and maintain their grip on power. Thought control involves restricting access to alternative viewpoints, leading to a limited understanding of reality among the population. Fear and intimidation are also employed to silence dissent, creating an environment where individuals may self-censor to avoid punishment or persecution.

- Manipulative Advertising and Media: In this context, we explore how advertising and media can use thought-control techniques to influence consumer behavior and shape societal norms. Advertisers often employ psychological tactics, such as emotional appeals, to trigger specific reactions and override rational thought. They may create a sense of urgency or scarcity to drive impulsive decision-making. Additionally, media outlets may selectively present information or use sensationalism to grab attention and influence public opinion. The constant exposure to certain messages and imagery can lead to the normalization of certain behaviors and beliefs, shaping cultural norms and values.
- By understanding the intricacies of cult indoctrination, the methods used by totalitarian regimes for thought control, and the manipulative techniques employed by advertising and media, individuals can develop critical thinking skills and better navigate the influence of such tactics on their beliefs and behaviors. Building resilience against these influences allows individuals to make more informed decisions and maintain a sense of autonomy in a world where manipulation and control are pervasive.

Deconstructing Brainwashing Tactics

Recognizing brainwashing tactics is crucial in guarding against manipulation. In this section, we offer insights and strategies to deconstruct brainwashing techniques and maintain cognitive autonomy.

- Critical Thinking and Rational Analysis: This facet emphasizes the significance of cultivating critical thinking skills and employing rational analysis when confronted with information and claims put forth by manipulators. Critical thinking involves questioning the validity and reliability of the presented information, examining evidence, and evaluating arguments to reach well-informed conclusions. By engaging in critical thinking, individuals can better discern the accuracy and credibility of the messages they encounter, thus reducing the risk of falling prey to manipulative tactics.

- Seeking Diverse Perspectives: In this aspect, the focus is on the value of seeking diverse perspectives and information from a variety of sources. Echo chambers, where individuals are exposed only to like-minded viewpoints, can lead to biased and limited understandings of complex issues. By actively seeking out diverse viewpoints, individuals can gain a broader understanding of a topic and develop a more comprehensive perspective. This practice also helps in recognizing potential biases and manipulative narratives that may be prevalent in certain circles.
- Building Resilience to Manipulation: This dimension centers on nurturing emotional resilience and self-confidence to withstand attempts at thought control by manipulators. Emotional resilience involves the ability to cope with and recover from challenging emotional experiences. By building emotional resilience, individuals are less susceptible to emotional manipulation and can maintain their own beliefs, values, and sense of self even in the face of pressure. Additionally, fostering self-confidence helps individuals trust their own judgment and resist succumbing to manipulative tactics that aim to undermine their sense of self-worth and decision-making capabilities.
- By understanding and implementing critical thinking, seeking diverse perspectives, and building resilience to manipulation, individuals can fortify their mental and emotional defenses against manipulative influences. These skills empower individuals to navigate the complexities of the information age more effectively, make well-informed decisions, and maintain a sense of autonomy and personal agency in the face of manipulative attempts.

Conclusion

Brainwashing and thought control present a compelling and deeply troubling exploration of the human mind's vulnerability to manipulation. By understanding the techniques used in brainwashing, thought-reform programs, and indoctrination, we empower ourselves to recognize and resist attempts at mind control. The preservation of critical thinking, seeking diverse perspectives, and fostering emotional resilience are essential in protecting our cognitive autonomy and individuality. As we unmask the tactics of brainwashing and thought control, we pave the way for a society that values independent thought, promotes open dialogue, and safeguards against the insidious influence of manipulative forces.

CHAPTER 14

THE ROLE OF SOCIAL MEDIA IN MANIPULATION

The Digital Tangle: Unraveling Social Media's Role in Psychological Manipulation

Introduction

Social media, an integral part of modern life, has revolutionized communication and connectivity. However, it has also become a breeding ground for psychological manipulation and influence. In this chapter, we explore the complex interplay between social media and psychological manipulation, examining how algorithms and data are exploited to sway opinions and behavior. We also delve into strategies for safeguarding our mental well-being in the digital realm.

Social Media and Psychological Manipulation

Social media platforms offer unprecedented access to vast amounts of personal information, making them fertile grounds for psychological manipulation. In this section, we examine the ways social media is utilized for manipulation and influence.

- Targeted Advertising: This aspect delves into the world of personalized advertisements that utilize data and user information to tailor messages to specific individuals or groups. The goal of targeted advertising is to influence consumer behavior and increase the likelihood of converting leads into customers. By leveraging data such as browsing history, demographics, and online interactions, advertisers can create more relevant and personalized content, making their ads more appealing and persuasive to the target audience. Understanding targeted advertising sheds light on the intricate strategies used by businesses to effectively reach and engage potential consumers in an increasingly digital and data-driven world.
- Confirmation Bias and Echo Chambers: This dimension explores the psychological phenomenon of confirmation bias and its connection to the echo chamber effect observed in social media platforms. Confirmation bias refers to the human tendency to seek, interpret, and favor information that

confirms one's existing beliefs or opinions, while disregarding or dismissing contradictory evidence. Social media algorithms often prioritize content that aligns with users' preferences, creating echo chambers where individuals are exposed primarily to information that reinforces their preexisting viewpoints. This reinforcement can deepen ideological divisions and contribute to a polarized society. Recognizing the influence of confirmation bias and echo chambers helps individuals become more aware of their information consumption habits and encourages seeking diverse perspectives to foster a more well-rounded understanding of complex issues.

- Emotional Manipulation: This aspect delves into the use of emotional content and sensationalism in various forms of media to provoke strong emotional reactions and drive engagement. Emotional manipulation involves crafting messages with the intent of eliciting specific emotions, such as fear, anger, joy, or sadness, to captivate the audience and increase their response rate. In the context of media and advertising, emotionally charged content can lead to higher levels of sharing, commenting, and liking, effectively amplifying the reach and impact of the message. Analyzing emotional manipulation helps individuals recognize and critically assess the emotional triggers used in media content, allowing them to be more discerning consumers and make informed choices about the information they engage with.
- By understanding the mechanisms of targeted advertising, confirmation bias and echo chambers, and emotional manipulation, individuals can develop greater media literacy and critical thinking skills. These insights empower individuals to navigate the vast sea of information and media content more effectively, enabling them to make conscious choices about their information consumption, form well-rounded perspectives, and guard against being unduly influenced by manipulative tactics.

Exploiting Algorithms and Data

The pervasive collection of user data on social media provides manipulators with powerful tools to exploit individuals' preferences and vulnerabilities. In this section, we uncover the dark side of data exploitation.

- Data Mining and Profiling: This facet involves a comprehensive exploration of the process of data mining, where vast amounts of user data are collected from various sources, such as websites, social media, and online activities. The collected data is then analyzed to create detailed user profiles, which encompass preferences, behaviors, interests, demographics, and more. This level of profiling enables precision targeting of individuals with highly tailored content, products, or services. Data mining plays a crucial role in modern marketing and advertising strategies, allowing businesses to deliver personalized experiences and increase the effectiveness of their campaigns. However, it also raises concerns about data privacy, as users' personal information may be used without their explicit consent or knowledge.

- Polarization and Disinformation: This dimension explores the darker side of social media, where platforms can be weaponized to spread polarizing content and disinformation deliberately. By leveraging algorithms that prioritize engaging and emotionally charged content, malicious actors can manipulate public opinion and exacerbate ideological divisions. False or misleading information can be disseminated rapidly, reaching a wide audience before being fact-checked or debunked. The spread of disinformation can undermine trust in reliable sources and democratic institutions, leading to a polarized society with conflicting viewpoints. Recognizing the potential for polarization and disinformation on social media highlights the need for media literacy and critical thinking to discern reliable information from misinformation.
- Amplification of Extremism: This aspect delves into the unintended consequences of social media algorithms, which can inadvertently amplify extremist content. As platforms prioritize content that generates high engagement, controversial or extremist views may gain disproportionate visibility. The algorithm's aim is to keep users engaged and spending more time on the platform, leading to a "filter bubble" effect where individuals are exposed primarily to content that aligns with their existing beliefs. This reinforcement can contribute to radicalization, where individuals become increasingly isolated from diverse perspectives and exposed only to extremist ideologies. Understanding the role of algorithms in amplifying extremism calls for the development of algorithms that prioritize the promotion of credible and balanced content while still respecting users' individual preferences.
- By thoroughly understanding data mining and profiling, polarization and disinformation, and the amplification of extremism, individuals can better comprehend the dynamics of the digital landscape they navigate daily. This understanding equips them with the tools to critically assess the information they encounter, discern potential biases or manipulative tactics, and actively engage with a diverse range of perspectives. Through media literacy and responsible information consumption, individuals can counteract

the negative consequences of digital manipulation and promote a more informed, balanced, and harmonious digital society.

Protecting Your Mental Well-Being Online

The ubiquity of social media demands thoughtful strategies for maintaining mental well-being amidst the constant flow of information and manipulation attempts. In this section, we offer insights and practices to protect ourselves from the adverse effects of social media.

- Digital Detox and Time Management: This aspect explores the importance of practicing moderation in social media usage and adopting mindful time management strategies to prevent overexposure and negative effects on well-being. Social media platforms are designed to be engaging and addictive, often leading to excessive screen time and a constant need for validation through likes and comments. Engaging in a digital detox involves taking intentional breaks from social media and other digital devices to recharge, reconnect with the real world, and reduce feelings of being overwhelmed or anxiety caused by constant connectivity. Mindful time management entails setting boundaries and allocating specific periods for digital activities, allowing individuals to balance their online presence with other important aspects of life, such as work, family, and self-care.
- Fact-Checking and Critical Thinking: This dimension emphasizes the significance of fact-checking and employing critical thinking skills to verify the accuracy and reliability of information encountered online. The digital realm is inundated with vast amounts of information, some of which may be misleading or intentionally deceptive. Fact-checking involves conducting thorough research and seeking credible sources to corroborate claims before accepting them as truths. Critical thinking encourages individuals to question the validity of information, assess potential biases, and evaluate the credibility of the sources. By becoming adept at fact-checking and critical thinking, individuals can protect themselves from falling victim to misinformation and manipulation, contributing to a more informed and responsible digital society.
- Curating Your Digital Environment: This facet delves into the practice of consciously curating one's digital environment, particularly social media feeds, to prioritize positive and informative content. Social media algorithms are designed to show users content based on their previous interactions and preferences, creating an echo chamber effect where individuals are

exposed only to information that aligns with their existing beliefs. By intentionally curating the content they consume, individuals can diversify their perspectives, broaden their knowledge, and expose themselves to a wide range of viewpoints. This approach not only fosters a more balanced and informed digital experience but also mitigates the negative impact of echo chambers, where individuals may become increasingly polarized and isolated from diverse opinions.

- By thoroughly understanding digital detox and time management, fact-checking and critical thinking, and curating one's digital environment, individuals can cultivate a healthier and more mindful relationship with the digital world. Implementing these strategies empowers individuals to navigate the digital landscape responsibly, protect themselves from manipulation and misinformation, and maintain a balanced and positive online presence. In doing so, individuals contribute to creating a more constructive and harmonious digital space for themselves and others.

Conclusion

Social media's widespread use has opened new avenues for psychological manipulation and influence. By understanding the tactics of data exploitation and content manipulation, we can approach social media with greater discernment and critical thinking. Protecting our mental well-being in the digital realm requires conscious efforts to balance usage, verify information, and curate our digital environment. As we navigate the complexities of social media's impact on psychological manipulation, we empower ourselves to be more conscious and responsible digital citizens, fostering a digital landscape that promotes authentic connection, informed discourse, and safeguarded mental well-being.

CHAPTER 15

UNRAVELING THE PSYCHOPATH

Beyond the Mask: Understanding Psychopathic Traits and Protecting Against Their Influence

Introduction

Psychopathy, a personality disorder characterized by a lack of empathy, manipulative tendencies, and a superficial charm, remains one of the most enigmatic and dangerous traits in human psychology. In this chapter, we delve into the intricacies of psychopathy, exploring its defining traits and behaviors. We also discuss how to identify psychopathic individuals in various contexts and strategies to protect ourselves from their influence.

Psychopathic Traits and Behaviors

Psychopathy is marked by a distinctive set of traits and behaviors that set it apart from other personality disorders. In this section, we explore the core characteristics of psychopathy.

- Lack of Empathy: This facet delves into the profound psychological trait of psychopaths—their inability to experience empathy or genuine concern for others' emotions and suffering. Empathy is the capacity to understand and share the feelings of others, and it plays a crucial role in forming meaningful connections and caring for fellow human beings. However, psychopaths lack this essential emotional ability, which makes it easier for them to engage in manipulative and exploitative behaviors. They can deceive and harm others without remorse, as they do not experience the emotional impact of their actions on others. Understanding this lack of empathy is critical in recognizing and protecting oneself from potential harm in interactions with psychopaths.

- Superficial Charm: This dimension explores the captivating and charming facade that psychopaths often exhibit to manipulate and disarm their targets. Psychopaths are skilled at portraying a charming and engaging personality that draws people in and makes them feel special and valued. They may use this charm to create a false sense of intimacy and trust, making it easier to exploit and control others. Behind this facade, however, lies a lack of genuine emotional connection or concern for others. Understanding the nature of superficial charm enables individuals to distinguish between genuine warmth and manipulative behavior, allowing them to guard against falling victim to psychopathic manipulation.

- Impulsivity and Irresponsibility: This aspect delves into the psychopathic trait of impulsivity, where individuals act on their desires and impulses without considering the consequences or taking responsibility for their actions. Psychopaths often engage in risky and reckless behaviors, as they have a reduced ability to foresee potential negative outcomes. Their impulsivity can lead to impulsive aggression, deceit, and a disregard for social norms and rules. Additionally, psychopaths tend to avoid taking responsibility for their actions, blaming others or external circumstances for their misdeeds. Understanding this aspect of psychopathy helps individuals recognize the signs of impulsive and irresponsible behavior, which can serve as warning signals to protect themselves from potential harm.
- By thoroughly understanding the lack of empathy, superficial charm, and impulsivity and irresponsibility in psychopathy, individuals can become better equipped to recognize and protect themselves from manipulative and exploitative individuals. This knowledge empowers individuals to make informed decisions in their interactions, set appropriate boundaries, and maintain their emotional well-being. Additionally, awareness of these traits can aid in identifying potential red flags in personal and professional relationships, promoting a safer and more secure social environment for all.

Identifying Psychopathy in Various Contexts

Psychopathic individuals can be found in various settings, and identifying them is crucial in protecting ourselves from potential harm. In this section, we discuss how to recognize psychopathic traits in different contexts.\\

- Personal Relationships: This dimension involves a comprehensive exploration of psychopathy's red flags and warning signs in various personal relationships, including romantic partnerships, friendships, and familial connections. Psychopathic individuals may exhibit manipulative and exploitative behaviors that can harm their partners, friends, or family members emotionally and psychologically. By understanding these warning signs, individuals can become more aware of potential manipulative tendencies, allowing them to protect themselves and maintain healthier and more authentic relationships. Traits such as lack of empathy, superficial charm, and impulsivity might be evident in personal relationships, and recognizing these traits can help individuals make informed decisions about their involvement with psychopathic individuals.

- Professional Settings: This aspect focuses on how psychopathic individuals may display manipulative behaviors in the workplace or professional settings. In professional environments, psychopaths might exploit power dynamics to gain advantage or manipulate colleagues for personal gain. They may exhibit a lack of remorse or guilt for their actions and may engage in deceitful practices to advance their career or undermine others. Understanding the manifestation of psychopathic traits in professional contexts empowers individuals to be vigilant about potential manipulative colleagues or superiors and to protect their interests and well-being in the workplace.
- Social and Community Interactions: This facet involves recognizing psychopathic traits in social circles and community interactions. Psychopathic individuals may exploit social dynamics and use charm to win people's trust and loyalty, only to serve their personal interests later on. Being aware of psychopathic traits in social settings can help individuals avoid falling prey to manipulation and deceit. Moreover, understanding how psychopathic individuals may operate within communities can aid in identifying potential risks and protecting the collective well-being.
- By thoroughly examining psychopathic traits in personal relationships, professional settings, and social interactions, individuals can become better equipped to recognize warning signs and take appropriate measures to protect themselves and others. This knowledge fosters a safer and more informed social environment, enabling individuals to establish healthier connections and guard against potentially manipulative individuals.

Protecting Yourself from Psychopathic Influence

Protecting ourselves from psychopathic influence requires vigilance and self-awareness. In this section, we offer strategies to safeguard against the harmful effects of psychopathic individuals.

- Trusting Your Gut Instincts: This dimension highlights the significance of paying attention to one's intuition and inner feelings, particularly feelings of discomfort or unease. Gut instincts often serve as valuable early warning signs that something may be amiss in a relationship or interaction. By tuning into these intuitive signals, individuals can become more aware of potential manipulative behaviors or red flags, helping them make informed decisions and protect their well-being.
- Setting Boundaries: This aspect involves learning the importance of establishing and enforcing clear boundaries in various relationships and interactions. Boundaries act as essential protective mechanisms, shielding individuals from manipulation and exploitation. By setting boundaries, individuals communicate their limits and expectations, deterring potential manipulators from overstepping personal boundaries. This practice empowers individuals to maintain a sense of autonomy and self-respect, creating a healthier dynamic in their relationships.
- Seeking Objective Perspectives: Seeking support and feedback from trusted friends or professionals offers an objective and impartial viewpoint on relationships or interactions. Sometimes, when individuals are emotionally involved, they may struggle to recognize signs of manipulation or abusive behavior. Seeking objective perspectives can provide clarity and validation, allowing individuals to gain insight into potentially toxic dynamics and make informed decisions regarding the relationship.
- Developing Emotional Resilience: Building emotional resilience is vital in withstanding manipulation attempts and maintaining a strong sense of self-worth. Manipulators often target individuals' emotions, seeking to create self-doubt or dependence. By developing emotional resilience, individuals become better equipped to cope with emotional challenges and resist manipulation. This involves nurturing a positive self-image, fostering emotional independence, and cultivating coping mechanisms to handle stressful situations.
- Understanding and embracing these four dimensions—trusting one's gut instincts, setting boundaries, seeking objective perspectives, and developing emotional resilience—empower individuals to navigate relationships and interactions more effectively. By fostering self-awareness, emotional strength, and assertiveness, individuals can protect themselves from manipulation, maintain healthier connections, and cultivate a stronger sense of well-being.

Conclusion

Psychopathy remains a complex and formidable facet of human psychology, characterized by a lack of empathy and manipulative tendencies. By understanding the traits and behaviors associated with psychopathy, we become more adept at identifying potential psychopathic individuals in various contexts. Equipped with knowledge and self-awareness, we can protect ourselves from their harmful influence and create boundaries to ensure our emotional well-being. As we unravel the psychopath's facade and shield ourselves from their manipulation, we foster a society that values empathy, authenticity, and emotional resilience, promoting healthier and more authentic connections in our relationships and interactions.

CHAPTER 16

SELF-AWARENESS AND EMPOWERMENT

The Key to Liberation: Cultivating Self-Awareness and Strengthening Resilience

Introduction

In a world rife with psychological manipulation and influence, cultivating self-awareness and building emotional resilience become powerful tools for personal empowerment and protection. In this chapter, we explore the transformative potential of self-awareness and emotional intelligence, guiding readers on a journey to strengthen their inner defenses against manipulation and exploitation. As we embark on this path of self-discovery and empowerment, we equip ourselves with the knowledge and tools to break free from the shackles of manipulation and forge a path towards authenticity and emotional liberation.

Cultivating Self-Awareness

Self-awareness serves as a guiding light on our journey towards empowerment. In this section, we delve into the importance of self-awareness and offer practical strategies to deepen our understanding of ourselves.

- Recognizing Emotional Triggers: This dimension delves into the process of recognizing our emotional triggers and understanding their underlying roots. Emotional triggers are specific situations, words, or actions that evoke strong emotional reactions within us. By exploring these triggers, we gain valuable insights into our emotional responses and behaviors. Understanding the origin of these triggers, which can often be rooted in past experiences or traumas, allows us to develop more balanced and controlled reactions, reducing the potential for impulsive or harmful responses.
- Examining Core Beliefs: This aspect involves engaging in deep introspection to examine our core beliefs and question their origins. Core beliefs are the fundamental beliefs we hold about ourselves, others, and the world around us. Some of these beliefs may be limiting or negative, impacting our self-esteem, confidence, and relationships. Through self-reflection and

exploration, we can challenge and reframe these limiting beliefs, fostering personal growth and positive change. By recognizing and transforming our core beliefs, we empower ourselves to create a more constructive and empowering belief system.

- Mindfulness and Reflection: This dimension emphasizes the practice of mindfulness and regular self-reflection to cultivate greater self-awareness in our daily lives. Mindfulness involves being fully present and aware of our thoughts, feelings, and actions without judgment. By practicing mindfulness, we become attuned to our emotions and thought patterns, enabling us to respond to situations more consciously rather than reacting impulsively. Regular self-reflection complements mindfulness, allowing us to evaluate our experiences, behaviors, and emotions, fostering continuous personal growth and development.
- In summary, these three dimensions—recognizing emotional triggers, examining core beliefs, and practicing mindfulness and reflection—work together to deepen our self-awareness and emotional intelligence. By understanding the origins of our emotional reactions, challenging limiting beliefs, and cultivating mindfulness, we gain greater control over our responses to various situations. This enhanced self-awareness empowers us to make healthier choices, develop more meaningful relationships, and foster personal growth and well-being.

Strengthening Emotional Intelligence

Emotional intelligence is a powerful asset in navigating the complexities of human interactions. In this section, we explore the components of emotional intelligence and its role in protecting against manipulation.

- Understanding Emotions: This dimension revolves around developing a comprehensive understanding of emotions—both our own and those of others. Emotions play a crucial role in our lives, influencing our thoughts, behaviors, and relationships. By honing our emotional intelligence, we become adept at identifying and comprehending our own emotions, which leads to increased self-awareness and self-understanding. Additionally, recognizing emotions in others enables us to navigate social interactions with greater sensitivity and empathy, fostering deeper connections and more meaningful relationships.

- Empathy and Compassion: Cultivating empathy and compassion is vital for creating meaningful and authentic connections with others. Empathy involves putting ourselves in someone else's shoes, understanding their feelings, and validating their experiences. By actively practicing empathy, we acknowledge the struggles and joys of others, fostering a sense of camaraderie and understanding. Furthermore, compassion goes beyond understanding to actively expressing care and concern for others' well-being. When we demonstrate empathy and compassion, we build trust and emotional closeness with those around us, contributing to a more supportive and harmonious social environment.
- Emotional Regulation: Learning to regulate our emotions effectively is an essential skill for maintaining emotional balance and well-being. Emotions can be powerful and intense, and without proper regulation, they may lead to impulsive or irrational reactions that could harm ourselves or others. By developing emotional regulation, we become better equipped to respond to challenging situations with calmness and rationality. This enables us to make thoughtful decisions and communicate effectively, even in the face of adversity. Emotional regulation also helps in managing stress and preventing emotional overwhelm, fostering a healthier and more balanced emotional state.
- To recap, understanding emotions, cultivating empathy and compassion, and practicing emotional regulation are interconnected dimensions that contribute to emotional intelligence and personal growth. By enhancing our ability to identify and comprehend emotions, connecting empathetically with others, and effectively regulating our emotional responses, we foster healthier relationships, make sound decisions, and promote overall emotional well-being. These skills are essential for navigating life's complexities and building a supportive and compassionate social network.

Building Resilience Against Manipulation

Resilience acts as a shield against the manipulative tactics that seek to exploit vulnerabilities. In this section, we explore ways to build emotional resilience and protect ourselves from manipulation.

- Setting Boundaries: Setting and enforcing boundaries is a crucial aspect of maintaining emotional well-being and preserving personal autonomy. Boundaries serve as protective barriers that delineate what is acceptable and unacceptable in our interactions with others. By establishing clear boundaries, we communicate our needs and limits, ensuring that we are treated with respect and that our emotions are not disregarded or manipulated. Setting boundaries empowers us to prioritize self-care and prevent others from infringing upon our emotional space, ultimately fostering healthier and more balanced relationships.

- Developing Critical Thinking: Cultivating critical thinking skills equips us with the ability to evaluate information and ideas objectively and independently. In today's information age, we are bombarded with a constant stream of data, making it essential to discern truth from manipulation and misinformation. Critical thinking allows us to question the credibility and reliability of sources, assess the evidence supporting claims, and identify potential biases or hidden agendas. By engaging in critical thinking, we become less susceptible to fallacious arguments and deceptive tactics used to sway opinions and beliefs. This empowers us to make well-informed decisions and form opinions based on reason and evidence.
- Seeking Support and Community: Recognizing the value of seeking support from trusted individuals or professionals is essential for processing emotions and experiences effectively. Connecting with supportive friends, understanding family members, or skilled counselors provides an outlet for expressing our feelings and gaining perspective on challenging situations. Sharing our thoughts and emotions with others can lead to a deeper understanding of ourselves and our experiences, alleviating feelings of isolation or confusion. Moreover, being part of a supportive community fosters a sense of belonging and offers a safety net during difficult times, reinforcing the importance of seeking help and support when needed.
- To recap, setting boundaries, developing critical thinking, and seeking support and community are vital aspects of emotional well-being and personal growth. By establishing boundaries, we safeguard our emotional space and maintain autonomy in our relationships. Cultivating critical thinking enables us to navigate the influx of information and resist manipulation and deceit. Additionally, seeking support and community ensures that we have a support system to lean on during challenging times and fosters a sense of belonging. Combining these elements contributes to emotional resilience and enhances our capacity to lead fulfilling and authentic lives.

Conclusion

In a world where psychological manipulation can be pervasive, self-awareness and emotional resilience become essential tools for personal empowerment. By cultivating self-awareness, strengthening emotional intelligence, and building resilience against manipulation, we foster a sense of inner strength and authenticity. Armed with these transformative qualities, we navigate relationships and interactions with greater discernment and confidence, protecting ourselves from the allure of manipulation and forging a path towards emotional liberation and genuine connections. As we empower ourselves and others with self-awareness and emotional resilience, we foster a collective consciousness that values authenticity, empathy, and emotional autonomy, creating a society less susceptible to the influence of manipulative forces and more committed to fostering authentic human connections.

CHAPTER 17

BREAKING THE CHAINS OF MANIPULATION

Liberating the Self: Recognizing, Asserting, and Breaking Free from Manipulative Bonds

Introduction

The chains of manipulation can bind us in suffocating relationships, leaving us vulnerable and emotionally confined. In this chapter, we embark on a journey of self-liberation, focusing on recognizing manipulation in relationships, embracing assertiveness, and setting firm boundaries. By breaking free from manipulative bonds, we reclaim our emotional autonomy and rediscover the power to forge authentic and nurturing connections.

Recognizing Manipulation in Relationships

Manipulation can often be subtle, making it challenging to recognize until its impact becomes overwhelming. In this section, we explore the telltale signs of manipulation in relationships.

- Gaslighting and Distorted Reality: Gaslighting is a manipulative tactic employed by partners to undermine our sense of reality and doubt our perceptions. This can involve denying or twisting events, causing us to question our memory and judgment. The manipulator may invalidate our emotions, making us feel overly sensitive or irrational. Gradually, this erodes our self-confidence and makes us increasingly reliant on their version of reality. Understanding gaslighting is crucial because it helps us recognize the signs of manipulation and regain clarity in our own perceptions and experiences. By maintaining awareness of this tactic, we can protect our mental and emotional well-being, assert our own reality, and resist being manipulated.
- Emotional Blackmail: Emotional blackmail is a form of manipulation that involves using emotions like guilt, fear, or shame to control and coerce compliance from others. The manipulator may threaten to withhold love, affection, or support unless their demands are met. This tactic places us in a vulnerable position, making it challenging to assert our boundaries and

needs. Identifying emotional blackmail helps us become more aware of the power dynamics in our relationships and empowers us to resist giving in to unfair demands. By recognizing these manipulative techniques, we can set healthy boundaries and cultivate assertiveness, allowing us to protect our emotional well-being and prevent ourselves from being taken advantage of.

- Isolation and Dependency: Manipulative partners may employ tactics to isolate us from our support systems, such as friends and family while encouraging dependency on them for emotional and practical needs. This isolation weakens our sense of autonomy and makes us more reliant on the manipulator for validation and emotional sustenance. Recognizing the attempts at isolation and dependency allows us to break free from this cycle of control. By nurturing our existing relationships and seeking new connections, we can regain our support network, which offers objective perspectives and emotional support. Moreover, fostering emotional independence helps us develop the resilience to resist manipulation and maintain a healthier sense of self and interpersonal relationships.

Assertiveness and Setting Boundaries

Assertiveness becomes a beacon of self-empowerment, illuminating our path towards breaking free from manipulation. In this section, we delve into the power of assertiveness and the importance of setting clear boundaries.

- Speaking Your Truth: Speaking our truth involves the courage to express ourselves authentically, communicating our needs, emotions, and opinions openly and honestly. It requires self-awareness and the willingness to be vulnerable with others. By speaking our truth, we foster genuine and meaningful connections, as people can understand and relate to our authentic selves. Moreover, this practice promotes emotional well-being and self-esteem, as we are not suppressing our thoughts and emotions, but rather expressing them constructively.

- Saying No Without Guilt: Embracing the right to say no is crucial for maintaining personal boundaries and self-care. Many people struggle with saying no due to feelings of guilt or the fear of disappointing others. However, saying no when necessary is essential for protecting our well-being and maintaining a healthy balance in our lives. It empowers us to prioritize our needs and values, setting limits on our time and energy. By overcoming the guilt associated with saying no, we can build stronger self-advocacy skills and cultivate greater respect for our own boundaries.

- Firmly Enforcing Boundaries: Understanding and enforcing boundaries is vital in maintaining healthy relationships and protecting ourselves from manipulation and exploitation. Boundaries define what is acceptable and unacceptable behavior towards us, ensuring that our emotional and physical well-being is safeguarded. By firmly enforcing our boundaries, we show others that we value and respect ourselves, which encourages them to do the same. This can lead to more fulfilling and balanced relationships based on mutual respect and understanding. Moreover, setting and enforcing boundaries also helps us avoid burnout and maintain a sense of control in our lives, fostering a greater sense of agency and empowerment.

Steps to Break Free from Manipulative Bonds

Liberation from manipulation requires courage and determination. In this section, we outline the essential steps to break free from manipulative bonds and reclaim our emotional freedom.

- Self-Empowerment Through Knowledge: Self empowerment through knowledge entails actively educating ourselves about manipulation and its effects on our lives and relationships. By gaining insight into the tactics used by manipulators, we can develop a deeper understanding of how and why they work. This knowledge allows us to recognize manipulation when it occurs, which can prevent us from falling victim to it in the future. Moreover, understanding manipulation empowers us to protect ourselves and make informed decisions, fostering a sense of clarity and control in our interactions with others.
- Seeking Support: Seeking support is a crucial step in the journey of healing and empowerment after experiencing manipulation. Reaching out to trusted friends, family, or professionals allows us to share our experiences and emotions with others who can offer empathy, validation, and guidance. The act of seeking support helps us to feel less alone and isolated in our struggles, as well as provides an external perspective on our experiences. Supportive individuals can also provide insights and strategies for coping with the aftermath of manipulation, which can aid in the process of healing and regaining a sense of emotional well-being.
- Detaching Emotionally: Detaching emotionally from manipulative partners is a challenging but essential aspect of self-empowerment. Manipulators often thrive on eliciting emotional responses and reactions from their targets, which can cloud our judgment and keep us trapped in

unhealthy dynamics. By learning to detach emotionally, we can create space for reflection and gain a more objective perspective on the situation. This emotional distance allows us to assess the relationship or situation more rationally, recognize patterns of manipulation, and make decisions that prioritize our well-being and happiness.

- Embracing Healing and Growth: Engaging in healing practices and personal growth is an empowering way to recover from the effects of manipulation and build resilience. Self-care activities, such as mindfulness practices, exercise, or creative outlets, can help soothe emotional wounds and foster emotional well-being. Seeking therapy or counseling can be especially beneficial, as it provides a safe space to process emotions, explore underlying issues, and develop healthy coping mechanisms. Embracing personal growth involves setting and achieving meaningful goals, focusing on self-improvement, and rebuilding a strong sense of self. By embracing healing and growth, we reclaim our power, break free from the grasp of manipulation, and move forward with greater self-awareness and strength.

Conclusion

Breaking the chains of manipulation demands resilience, self-empowerment, and courage. By recognizing manipulation in relationships, embracing assertiveness, and setting firm boundaries, we embark on a transformative journey of self-liberation. With knowledge as our guide and support as our ally, we navigate the path towards breaking free from manipulative bonds and embracing emotional autonomy. As we liberate ourselves from the grip of manipulation, we inspire others to do the same, fostering a community of empowered individuals who prioritize authentic connections, emotional well-being, and the freedom to create meaningful and nurturing relationships.

CHAPTER 18

HEALING FROM PSYCHOLOGICAL MANIPULATION

From Wounds to Wisdom: Nurturing Emotional Well-Being and Growth After Manipulation

Introduction

The aftermath of psychological manipulation can leave deep emotional wounds, challenging our sense of self and trust in others. In this chapter, we embark on a journey of healing and growth, focusing on coping with the aftermath of manipulation, seeking professional help and support, and nurturing our emotional well-being. As we navigate the path from woundedness to wisdom, we empower ourselves to reclaim our emotional strength and forge a path towards healing and personal growth.

Coping with the Aftermath of Manipulation

The aftermath of psychological manipulation can leave us feeling emotionally bruised and vulnerable. In this section, we explore coping strategies to navigate the complex emotions that arise.

- Validating Our Feelings: Validating our feelings involves recognizing that the emotions we experience in response to manipulation are genuine and valid. Often, when we have been manipulated, we may doubt or dismiss our feelings, believing they are irrational or unwarranted. However, by acknowledging and accepting our emotions, we give ourselves permission to feel and validate the impact of the manipulation. This process is crucial for our emotional well-being, as it allows us to address and process the emotions we may have suppressed during the manipulative experience.
- Embracing Self-Compassion: Cultivating self-compassion is an essential aspect of self-healing and empowerment after experiencing manipulation. It involves treating ourselves with the same kindness, understanding, and support that we would offer to a friend going through a difficult time. Self-compassion allows us to be gentle with ourselves, acknowledging that we are not perfect and that it is okay to have vulnerabilities and

weaknesses. By embracing self-compassion, we counteract the self-blame and self-criticism that manipulators often instill in their targets. This practice creates a safe and nurturing space for us to process our emotions, promoting emotional healing and resilience.

- Processing the Experience: Processing the manipulation experience means allowing ourselves to fully acknowledge its impact on our emotions, thoughts, and perceptions. This can be a challenging and complex process, as manipulation often involves the distortion of reality and the erosion of trust in ourselves and others. To process the experience, we may need to confront difficult emotions, such as anger, sadness, or betrayal, and explore the beliefs and patterns that the manipulation has triggered. By engaging in this process, we gain clarity and understanding about the dynamics at play, helping us to identify the manipulative tactics used and recognize any vulnerabilities that were exploited. Processing the experience empowers us to reclaim our sense of self and build emotional resilience, preparing us for healthier and more authentic relationships in the future.

Seeking Professional Help and Support

Healing from manipulation often requires professional assistance and a supportive network. In this section, we explore the benefits of seeking professional help and support.

- Therapy and Counseling: Seeking therapy or counseling is a vital step in the healing process after experiencing challenges like manipulation. Professional therapy provides a safe and confidential environment where individuals can explore their emotions, thoughts, and experiences with the guidance of a trained mental health professional. Therapists and counselors offer valuable insights, tools, and coping strategies to help individuals process their emotions, rebuild their sense of self, and develop healthier relationship patterns. Through therapy, individuals can gain a deeper understanding of the impact of manipulation on their lives, identify any underlying issues that may have made them vulnerable to manipulation, and work towards healing and personal growth.

- Supportive Friends and Family: Having a support system of trusted friends and family members is essential in the healing journey. These individuals can offer emotional support, a listening ear, and a non-judgmental space where individuals can share their experiences and feelings openly.

Supportive friends and family can validate the survivor's emotions, which is especially important in cases of manipulation where the victim's feelings may have been invalidated or gaslighted. Their presence and understanding can help individuals feel less isolated and provide a sense of belonging and acceptance.

- Support Groups: Joining support groups that focus on healing from manipulation can be incredibly beneficial. These groups offer a unique opportunity to connect with others who have experienced similar challenges, providing a sense of community and shared understanding. In a support group, individuals can share their experiences, learn from others, and receive encouragement and empathy. Being part of a support group can reduce feelings of isolation and provide validation for survivors who may have struggled to be heard or believed by others. Additionally, support groups can serve as a platform for individuals to gain insights and coping strategies from others who have overcome similar experiences, fostering hope and resilience.

Nurturing Emotional Well-Being and Growth

Healing from manipulation goes beyond surviving; it involves nurturing our emotional well-being and fostering personal growth. In this section, we explore practices to support our emotional well-being and promote growth.

- Self-Care and Mindfulness: Prioritizing self-care and mindfulness is crucial for individuals who have experienced challenging situations, such as manipulation. Self-care involves actively taking care of one's physical, emotional, and mental well-being. Engaging in activities that promote relaxation, stress reduction, and emotional healing can contribute to inner peace and emotional resilience. Mindfulness, on the other hand, involves being fully present in the moment and observing one's thoughts and feelings without judgment. Practicing mindfulness can help individuals become more aware of their emotions and responses, allowing them to better cope with difficult emotions and reduce reactivity to triggers related to the manipulation experience.
- Rediscovering Identity and Values: After experiencing manipulation, individuals may feel disconnected from their authentic selves. Rediscovering one's identity involves exploring who they are beyond the influence of the manipulator. This process may involve reflecting on their values, beliefs,

passions, and interests. Reaffirming core values provides a strong foundation for self-discovery and growth. By aligning actions and choices with these values, individuals can restore a sense of integrity and authenticity, empowering them to make decisions that align with their true selves.

- Embracing Growth Opportunities: Facing and embracing challenges as opportunities for growth and learning is a powerful mindset for healing from manipulation. Rather than seeing difficult experiences as purely negative, individuals can view them as opportunities to learn about themselves, develop resilience, and expand their emotional intelligence. This growth-oriented perspective helps individuals see setbacks as temporary and offers hope for a brighter future. Embracing growth opportunities can lead to personal development and a stronger sense of self, enabling individuals to navigate future challenges with greater strength and confidence.

Conclusion

Healing from psychological manipulation is a transformative journey that requires compassion, support, and courage. By coping with the aftermath of manipulation, seeking professional help, and nurturing our emotional well-being, we embark on a path of healing and personal growth. As we traverse this path from woundedness to wisdom, we not only rediscover our emotional strength but also inspire others to embark on their journey of healing. Together, we foster a community of empowered individuals who support each other, prioritize emotional well-being, and embrace growth as a transformative force. As we heal from the effects of manipulation, we emerge wiser and more resilient, equipped to create meaningful and authentic connections, and dedicated to fostering a world where emotional well-being and personal growth are valued and nurtured.

CHAPTER 19

ETHICAL PERSUASION AND INFLUENCE

The Power of Integrity: Promoting Ethical Communication and Building Trust

Introduction

Persuasion and influence are natural aspects of human communication, but their ethical use is crucial for fostering healthy and genuine connections. In this chapter, we explore the principles of ethical persuasion and influence, emphasizing the importance of integrity, honesty, and empathy in our interactions. By promoting ethical communication and using persuasive techniques responsibly, we create a foundation for building relationships based on trust and authenticity.

Promoting Ethical Communication

Ethical communication serves as a moral compass in our interactions, guiding us towards honesty and transparency. In this section, we explore the principles of ethical communication.

- Truth and Honesty: Truthfulness and honesty are foundational values in effective communication. When we prioritize truth in our interactions, we commit to conveying accurate information and representing our thoughts and feelings authentically. Being honest builds trust and credibility with others, fostering genuine and meaningful connections. It is essential to avoid deception, half-truths, or manipulative tactics to maintain ethical and respectful communication.
- Empathy and Respect: Cultivating empathy involves actively seeking to understand others' emotions, perspectives, and experiences. When we approach conversations with empathy, we demonstrate genuine concern for the well-being of others and acknowledge their feelings and concerns without judgment. This empathetic approach enhances understanding and fosters a sense of connection and validation for the individuals involved. Respect goes hand in hand with empathy, as it involves valuing others' opinions and treating them with consideration and courtesy.

- Integrity and Consistency: Demonstrating integrity means aligning our words with our actions and upholding our values even in challenging situations. People who exhibit integrity are trustworthy and reliable, as they consistently follow through on their commitments and promises. By maintaining consistency in our communication, we build a sense of reliability and dependability with others. It is crucial to avoid contradictory statements or behaviors that can erode trust and create confusion.
- Incorporating truth and honesty, empathy and respect, and integrity and consistency into our communication style fosters an environment of open and transparent communication. Such an approach encourages positive and constructive interactions with others, enhances relationships, and promotes mutual understanding and growth. By focusing on these values, we contribute to a more compassionate, honest, and cohesive community.

Positive Use of Persuasive Techniques

Persuasive techniques can be employed responsibly to influence others in a positive and ethical manner. In this section, we explore the positive use of persuasion.

- Education and Information: Persuasion can be a powerful tool to educate and inform others. When used ethically, it empowers individuals to make informed decisions by providing them with accurate and relevant information. Educative persuasion aims to increase awareness, expand knowledge, and foster critical thinking. It encourages individuals to explore different perspectives and consider various options before reaching conclusions. By presenting information in a compelling and accessible manner, educative persuasion equips people with the tools they need to navigate complex issues and make well-informed choices.
- Encouragement and Inspiration: Motivational persuasion focuses on inspiring positive change and personal growth in others. Through encouragement and inspiration, persuaders tap into people's aspirations, values, and goals. This form of persuasion seeks to ignite enthusiasm and drive by highlighting the potential for improvement and achievement. By connecting with individuals' emotions and aspirations, motivational persuasion can boost self-confidence, resilience, and determination. It fosters a sense of empowerment, as individuals become motivated to take action and overcome challenges to reach their full potential.

- Empowering Choice: Persuasion that emphasizes empowering choice respects individuals' autonomy and agency in decision-making. It recognizes that people are more likely to embrace ideas or make decisions when they feel in control of the process. Empowering persuasion offers options, allowing individuals to select the path that aligns with their values, preferences, and needs. This approach encourages a sense of ownership and responsibility for the decisions made. By providing choices and respecting autonomy, empowering persuasion fosters trust and collaboration between the persuader and the audience.
- When employing education and information, encouragement and inspiration, and empowering choice in persuasion, it is crucial to be transparent and honest. Ethical persuasion aims to empower individuals rather than manipulate or exploit them. By using these approaches, persuaders can positively influence attitudes and behaviors while nurturing respect for others' autonomy and self-determination. Overall, ethical persuasion is a means to encourage personal and collective growth, foster meaningful connections, and promote positive change in society.

Creating Healthy Relationships Based on Trust

Trust forms the cornerstone of healthy and meaningful relationships. In this section, we explore how ethical communication and positive influence contribute to building trust.

- Transparency and Vulnerability: Building trust in any relationship starts with transparency and vulnerability. When we are open and honest about our intentions, feelings, and motivations, it creates a safe space for others to reciprocate. Transparency means sharing information without hidden agendas or deceit, fostering an environment of trust and authenticity. Additionally, being vulnerable and willing to show our imperfections and emotions allows others to relate to us on a deeper level. It signals that we are genuine and approachable, inviting others to do the same.
- Accountability and Reliability: Trust is further strengthened through accountability and reliability. When we take responsibility for our actions, admit our mistakes, and make amends when needed, it demonstrates integrity and shows that we can be counted on. Being reliable means following through on our commitments and promises consistently. People can trust us when they know they can rely on our words and actions, and that we will not let them down when they need us.

- Active Listening and Validation: Trust is nurtured when we actively listen to others and validate their feelings and experiences. Active listening involves being fully present and attentive to what the other person is saying without interrupting or judging. It shows that we value their thoughts and opinions, fostering a sense of respect and understanding. Validating someone's feelings means acknowledging and accepting their emotions without dismissing or invalidating them. It helps people feel heard, valued, and supported, leading to a deeper sense of trust in the relationship.
- In summary, transparency and vulnerability create an environment of openness and authenticity, while accountability and reliability demonstrate integrity and consistency. Active listening and validation foster understanding and respect. By embodying these qualities, we not only build trust in our relationships but also foster deeper connections and create a foundation for meaningful and supportive interactions. Trust is a fundamental element in any relationship, and nurturing it through these practices can lead to stronger bonds and more fulfilling connections with others.

Conclusion

Ethical persuasion and influence lie at the heart of meaningful and authentic connections. By promoting ethical communication, using persuasive techniques responsibly, and fostering trust in our relationships, we create a world where integrity and empathy guide our interactions. As we embrace ethical persuasion, we empower ourselves and others to make informed choices and forge connections based on mutual respect and trust. Together, we build a community of individuals committed to fostering ethical communication and positive influence, contributing to a society rooted in authenticity, compassion, and trust.

CHAPTER 20

THE LIGHT WITHIN: EMBRACING THE SHADOW

Embracing Wholeness: Integrating the Shadow Self for Personal Growth and Authenticity

Introduction

The concept of the "shadow" self, introduced by Swiss psychiatrist Carl Jung, represents the hidden and often denied aspects of our psyche. In this chapter, we embark on a journey of self-discovery, exploring the importance of embracing the dark side within and integrating our shadow self constructively. By doing so, we foster personal growth, achieve a sense of wholeness, and embrace authenticity in our lives.

Embracing the Dark Side Within

The shadow self encompasses aspects of ourselves that we often fear or suppress. In this section, we explore the significance of acknowledging and embracing the dark side within.

- Recognizing the Shadow: The concept of the shadow self, originally proposed by Swiss psychiatrist Carl Jung, refers to the unconscious part of our psyche that contains suppressed or disowned aspects of ourselves. These aspects can include traits, emotions, or desires that we deem unacceptable or undesirable. By acknowledging the presence of the shadow, we gain insight into the hidden parts of our psyche, allowing for a more holistic understanding of ourselves. This awareness enables us to recognize when the shadow influences our thoughts, behaviors, and relationships, ultimately leading to greater self-awareness and personal growth.
- Embracing Imperfections: Embracing our imperfections involves accepting and embracing the less favorable aspects of ourselves with compassion and kindness. Instead of denying or repressing these parts, we recognize that imperfections are a natural part of being human. Embracing imperfections does not mean that we condone harmful behaviors or negative traits, but rather that we acknowledge that they are a part of our

whole being. By embracing our imperfections, we free ourselves from the burden of striving for unattainable perfection and cultivate a deeper sense of self-acceptance and self-love.

- Letting Go of Judgment: Letting go of judgment involves releasing the harsh self-criticism and shame associated with our shadow aspects. Often, we are conditioned by societal norms and expectations to judge certain traits or emotions as undesirable. However, passing judgment on ourselves for having these aspects only perpetuates a cycle of inner conflict and suppression. By letting go of judgment, we create a safe and non-judgmental space within ourselves to explore and accept our shadow self. This process of self-compassion allows for healing and growth, as we learn to embrace our whole selves, including the aspects we once feared or rejected.
- In summary, recognizing the shadow self is about understanding the unconscious parts of ourselves that influence our lives. Embracing imperfections involves accepting all aspects of ourselves with kindness and understanding. Letting go of judgment liberates us from the burden of self-criticism and shame, allowing us to foster a more authentic and compassionate relationship with ourselves. By engaging in these practices, we embark on a journey of self-discovery and transformation, leading to greater self-awareness, acceptance, and personal growth.

Integrating the Shadow Self Constructively

Integration of the shadow self requires conscious effort and self-compassion. In this section, we explore ways to integrate the shadow self constructively.

- Self-Reflection and Self-Acceptance: Engaging in self-reflection involves taking the time to introspect and examine our thoughts, emotions, and behaviors without judgment. It's about cultivating a sense of curiosity and openness to understand the different facets of ourselves, including the shadow aspects. Through self-reflection, we can identify patterns, triggers, and unresolved issues that may be linked to our shadow. This process enables us to gain insights into the root causes of certain behaviors and emotions, empowering us to make conscious choices and grow as individuals. Additionally, self-acceptance plays a crucial role in this journey. It means embracing all parts of ourselves, including the shadow aspects, with compassion and understanding. Rather than rejecting or suppressing these elements, self-acceptance allows us to integrate them into our sense of self, fostering a more authentic and balanced inner landscape.

- Healing Past Wounds: Our past experiences, especially traumatic ones, can deeply impact our psychological well-being and contribute to the formation of the shadow. By addressing past wounds and traumas, we can facilitate the integration process of our shadow self. This healing journey involves seeking support from therapists, counselors, or other healing modalities to process and release emotional pain and negative beliefs that might have led to the creation of the shadow. Through healing, we gain the strength and resilience to confront the aspects of ourselves that we may have disowned due to past painful experiences. This process allows us to reclaim lost parts of ourselves, leading to greater wholeness and self-awareness.
- Creative Expression: Engaging in creative outlets, such as art, writing, dance, or music, provides a safe and expressive space to explore our shadow aspects constructively. Creativity allows us to tap into the depths of our subconscious, giving a voice to emotions, desires, and experiences that may have been buried in the shadow. Through creative expression, we can externalize and process these feelings, gaining valuable insights into ourselves. It offers an opportunity to explore our hidden parts in a non-threatening way, fostering self-discovery and personal growth. The creative expression also serves as a form of catharsis, helping us release emotional tension and find a sense of release and relief. As we engage in creative exploration, we may uncover hidden talents and strengths that were overshadowed by our fears and insecurities, leading to a deeper connection with our authentic selves.
- In summary, the process of self-reflecting and accepting all aspects of ourselves, including the shadow, is essential for personal growth and self-awareness. Healing past wounds enables us to integrate fragmented parts of ourselves, fostering a more balanced and integrated sense of self. Creative expression provides a valuable outlet to explore and understand our hidden aspects constructively. Embracing these practices invites us on a transformative journey of self-discovery, leading to greater authenticity, self-compassion, and empowerment.

Cultivating Personal Growth and Authenticity

Embracing the shadow self becomes a catalyst for personal growth and authenticity. In this section, we explore the transformative effects of shadow integration.

- Heightened Self-Awareness: Cultivating heightened self-awareness involves actively exploring and understanding the various aspects of ourselves, including our thoughts, emotions, beliefs, and behaviors. It requires a willingness to engage in introspection and self-reflection to gain insights into our motivations, desires, and fears. By developing this awareness, we become more attuned to our patterns and reactions, enabling us to make conscious choices and respond to situations with greater clarity and intention. Self-awareness also helps us recognize when our shadow aspects may be influencing our actions, allowing us to address them and work towards integration. This ongoing process of self-discovery empowers us to embrace our strengths and challenges, leading to a deeper sense of authenticity and fulfillment.
- Empathy and Compassion: Extending empathy and compassion to ourselves and others is a vital aspect of personal growth and meaningful relationships. Empathy involves the ability to put ourselves in someone else's shoes, understanding their feelings and experiences without judgment. When we practice empathy towards ourselves, we acknowledge and validate our own emotions, even if they are uncomfortable or difficult. This self-compassion creates a supportive and caring inner environment, fostering emotional resilience and self-acceptance.
- Similarly, extending empathy and compassion to others enhances our connections and fosters a sense of shared humanity. It allows us to connect on a deeper level, promoting understanding and cooperation in our relationships. By recognizing and acknowledging the struggles and vulnerabilities of others, we create a safe and nurturing space for mutual support and growth. Empathy and compassion also play a vital role in conflict resolution, as they promote open communication and encourage us to find common ground.
- Authenticity in Relationships: Embracing authenticity in our relationships involves showing up as our genuine selves, without masks or pretenses. It means expressing our thoughts, emotions, and desires honestly, even if they may not always align with societal expectations. By being authentic, we create an atmosphere of trust and vulnerability in our relationships, encouraging others to do the same. Authenticity allows us to connect on a deeper level, as we share our true selves with others, fostering genuine and meaningful connections.

- Furthermore, embracing authenticity enables us to attract and maintain relationships that align with our values and aspirations. When we are true to ourselves, we are more likely to attract like-minded individuals who appreciate and respect us for who we are. This authenticity also acts as a filter, helping us recognize and avoid relationships that may be based on manipulation or superficiality.
- In summary, cultivating heightened self-awareness empowers us to understand ourselves on a deeper level and make conscious choices. Extending empathy and compassion towards ourselves and others enhances our emotional well-being and fosters meaningful connections. Embracing authenticity in our relationships nurtures trust, vulnerability, and deeper connections with others. Together, these three elements form a powerful foundation for personal growth, self-fulfillment, and more fulfilling relationships.

Conclusion

Embracing the shadow self is an integral part of our journey towards personal growth and authenticity. By acknowledging and integrating our dark side, we uncover hidden potentials and become more whole and authentic individuals. As we embrace the light within and integrate the shadow self constructively, we cultivate a deeper sense of self-awareness, compassion, and empathy. Together, we embark on a path of growth, connection, and authenticity, fostering a community of individuals who celebrate their uniqueness and embrace their shadows with grace. As we embrace the light and darkness within us, we become beacons of authenticity, illuminating the path for others to embrace their shadows and journey towards wholeness and self-discovery.

PART IV: TOWARDS A BALANCED EXISTENCE

CHAPTER 21

MINDFUL LIVING AND RESILIENCE

Thriving Amidst Turbulence: Nurturing Mindful Living and Emotional Resilience

Introduction

In the pursuit of a balanced existence, mindfulness and emotional resilience become invaluable tools to navigate life's challenges with grace and strength. In this final part, we delve into the transformative power of mindful living and resilience, empowering ourselves to become impervious to manipulation and thrive amidst life's turbulence. As we embrace mindfulness, self-reflection, and resilience, we unlock the potential for profound personal growth and inner peace.

Practicing Mindfulness and Self-Reflection

Mindful living offers us the opportunity to be fully present and aware of our thoughts, feelings, and experiences. In this section, we explore the practice of mindfulness and self-reflection.

- Present Moment Awareness: Cultivating present moment awareness involves intentionally focusing our attention on the here and now, immersing ourselves in the present experience without dwelling on the past or worrying about the future. It requires letting go of distractions, preoccupations, and anxieties that may pull our minds away from the present moment. By fully engaging with what is happening right now, we become more attuned to our thoughts, feelings, and surroundings, enabling us to experience life with greater clarity and mindfulness. This practice of being present can help reduce stress, increase our ability to cope with challenges and enhance our overall well-being.
- Non-Judgmental Observation: Adopting a non-judgmental attitude towards our thoughts and emotions involves becoming an impartial observer of our inner experiences. Instead of reacting to our thoughts with criticism or attachment, we allow them to arise and pass without judgment. This does not mean suppressing or denying our feelings; rather, it entails acknowledging

and accepting them without adding further layers of evaluation or condemnation. By practicing non-judgmental observation, we develop a deeper understanding of ourselves and our patterns of thinking and feeling. This self-awareness can lead to greater emotional intelligence, improved decision-making, and increased self-compassion.

- Cultivating Gratitude: Fostering a sense of gratitude involves consciously recognizing and appreciating the simple joys and blessings in our lives. It goes beyond just saying "thank you" for what we have; it is about truly feeling and embodying gratitude in our daily lives. By focusing on the positive aspects of our experiences, even during challenging times, we shift our perspective from what is lacking to what is abundant. Gratitude has numerous benefits for our well-being, including increased happiness, improved relationships, and enhanced overall life satisfaction. It can also act as a buffer against stress and negative emotions, helping us navigate life's ups and downs with greater resilience.
- Incorporating these practices into our daily lives can significantly enhance our overall well-being and quality of life. Present moment awareness allows us to fully experience life as it unfolds, savoring each moment and finding joy in the simple pleasures. Non-judgmental observation helps us develop a deeper understanding of ourselves and our emotions, fostering greater self-acceptance and self-compassion. Cultivating gratitude shifts our focus from what we lack to what we have, cultivating a positive and appreciative mindset.
- By integrating present-moment awareness, non-judgmental observation, and gratitude into our lives, we can foster a greater sense of peace, fulfillment, and contentment. These practices serve as powerful tools to navigate the challenges of life with grace and resilience, enabling us to embrace the fullness of our experiences and find beauty in even the smallest moments.

Building Emotional Resilience

Emotional resilience equips us to weather life's storms with inner strength and bounce back from adversity. In this section, we explore strategies to build emotional resilience.

- Embracing Adversity as a Teacher: When we view challenges as opportunities for growth and learning, we shift our perspective on adversity. Instead of seeing setbacks as roadblocks, we see them as valuable experiences that can teach us important lessons. By reframing our approach to difficulties, we can transform setbacks into stepping stones towards success. Each challenge becomes an opportunity to build resilience, gain new insights, and develop valuable skills. This mindset not only empowers us to navigate adversity with a positive outlook but also fosters a sense of personal growth and accomplishment.

- Nurturing Supportive Relationships: During difficult times, having supportive relationships can make a significant difference in our ability to cope and thrive. Cultivating meaningful connections with others who provide emotional support creates a sense of belonging and reassurance. Supportive relationships offer a safe space where we can express our feelings, share our struggles, and receive understanding and encouragement. These connections remind us that we are not alone in our journey and that there are people who genuinely care about our well-being. The presence of a supportive network can increase our emotional resilience and help us face challenges with greater confidence and strength.
- Self-Compassion in the Face of Failure: When we encounter failure or make mistakes, it is essential to offer ourselves self-compassion and understanding. Recognizing that mistakes are an inherent part of the human experience allows us to embrace our imperfections without judgment. Instead of being overly critical or self-critical, we practice kindness and self-acceptance. Self-compassion acknowledges that we are not perfect and that everyone experiences failures and setbacks at some point. By treating ourselves with the same compassion we would offer a friend in a similar situation, we create a supportive and nurturing inner environment. This self-compassion can help us bounce back from failures, learn from our experiences, and continue to grow and evolve.
- Incorporating these practices into our lives can profoundly impact our well-being and resilience. Embracing adversity as a teacher empowers us to reframe challenges as opportunities for personal development and growth. Nurturing supportive relationships provides us with a sense of belonging and a strong support system during difficult times. Practicing self-compassion enables us to face failures and setbacks with greater self-acceptance and resilience.
- Together, these practices form a powerful foundation for navigating life's ups and downs with grace and strength. By embracing the lessons adversity offers, fostering meaningful connections with others, and extending compassion towards ourselves, we develop the inner resources to overcome challenges and thrive in the face of difficulties. Through this

journey of growth and self-discovery, we not only build resilience but also cultivate a deeper understanding of ourselves and our capacity for resilience and strength.

Becoming Impervious to Manipulation

The integration of mindfulness and resilience makes us more impervious to manipulation, safeguarding our emotional well-being and authenticity. In this section, we explore how mindfulness and resilience empower us to resist manipulation.

- Strengthening Self-Worth: Building a strong sense of self-worth and identity is a crucial step in protecting ourselves from manipulative tactics that target our insecurities. When we have a healthy and positive view of ourselves, we are less likely to fall prey to the attempts of manipulators who seek to exploit our vulnerabilities. A strong sense of self-worth allows us to recognize and appreciate our own value, making it harder for manipulators to undermine our confidence or self-esteem. By acknowledging our strengths and accepting our imperfections, we create a solid foundation of self-assurance that acts as a shield against emotional manipulation.
- Trusting Intuition: Our intuition, often referred to as our "gut feeling," can serve as a powerful guide in identifying manipulative behaviors and protecting ourselves from harm. It is an innate sense that helps us navigate situations, even when we may not have concrete evidence or reasons to explain our feelings. By learning to trust our intuition, we tap into a valuable source of inner wisdom that alerts us when something feels off or when we sense manipulation. Cultivating this trust in our intuition enables us to act decisively and protect our well-being when we encounter potentially harmful individuals or situations.
- Setting Boundaries with Confidence: Establishing and enforcing clear boundaries is a critical aspect of safeguarding ourselves from manipulation. When we assert our boundaries with confidence, we send a strong message to potential manipulators that we are not easily swayed or controlled. Having firm boundaries prevents others from encroaching on our emotional space, manipulating our decisions, or taking advantage of our vulnerabilities. It allows us to define our limits and communicate our needs effectively. By setting and maintaining these boundaries, we create a protective barrier that enhances our emotional well-being and safeguards our autonomy.

- By combining these practices, we equip ourselves with the tools to navigate the world more effectively, especially in the face of manipulative individuals. Strengthening self-worth empowers us to recognize and resist attempts at emotional manipulation, as we know our own value and refuse to be undermined by deceptive tactics. Trusting our intuition serves as an internal radar that warns us of potential dangers or toxic influences, guiding us away from harmful situations. Setting boundaries with confidence communicates our self-respect and ensures that manipulators understand their tactics will not be tolerated.
- In essence, these practices cultivate a sense of self-awareness, emotional resilience, and personal empowerment. As we build a stronger connection with ourselves and embrace our intuition, we become more adept at recognizing manipulative behaviors and safeguarding our emotional well-being. Setting boundaries enables us to take charge of our interactions and relationships, creating a healthier dynamic with others. Through this process of growth and self-protection, we develop a greater sense of control over our lives, fostering greater personal fulfillment and maintaining healthier, more authentic connections with others.

Conclusion

In the pursuit of a balanced existence, mindfulness and resilience stand as pillars of strength and self-awareness. By practicing mindfulness, self-reflection, and emotional resilience, we deepen our connection with the present moment, cultivate inner strength, and foster the imperviousness to manipulation. As we embrace mindful living and resilience, we become equipped to navigate life's challenges with grace, build authentic connections with others, and maintain our emotional well-being amidst turbulence. Together, we foster a community of individuals committed to nurturing mindful living and resilience, promoting a world where emotional balance, authenticity, and inner peace are celebrated and prioritized. As we step into a balanced existence, we inspire others to embark on their own journey of mindful living and emotional resilience, contributing to a collective consciousness that values compassion, self-awareness, and the pursuit of inner harmony.

CHAPTER 22

EMPATHY AND COMPASSION

Hearts Wide Open: Unleashing the Transformative Power of Empathy and Compassion

Introduction

Empathy and compassion are the threads that weave a tapestry of genuine connection and understanding in the fabric of human interactions. In this chapter, we embark on a journey of exploring the profound significance of empathy and compassion. By understanding the power of empathy, differentiating it from sympathy, and nurturing compassion for ourselves and others, we cultivate a world where empathy becomes a bridge that unites hearts and compassion becomes a force that heals and nurtures.

Understanding the Power of Empathy

Empathy stands as a profound capacity to feel and understand the emotions and experiences of others. In this section, we explore the transformative power of empathy.

- Emotional Resonance: Emotional resonance refers to the profound connection that can be established between individuals through the power of empathy. When we empathize with others, we are not merely sympathizing or feeling sorry for them; instead, we deeply connect with their emotions and experiences, stepping into their shoes and understanding their feelings on a visceral level. This resonance creates a sense of shared emotions, even if we have not personally experienced the same situation. By tapping into this emotional resonance, we can foster a genuine and meaningful connection with others, strengthening our relationships and building a sense of compassion and camaraderie.
- Fostering Understanding: Empathy serves as a gateway to understanding others' perspectives and experiences without judgment. When we engage in empathetic listening, we actively seek to comprehend the thoughts, emotions, and motivations behind someone's actions or words. This openness to

understanding allows us to move beyond preconceived notions or biases and approach interactions with an open mind. By embracing empathy as a tool for understanding, we create space for more profound and meaningful connections with others. It helps us recognize the complexity of human experiences, promoting acceptance and tolerance in our interactions.

- Building Empathic Bridges: Empathy plays a pivotal role in bridging gaps between individuals from diverse backgrounds and cultures. It enables us to connect with others on a human level, transcending differences and finding common ground. By empathizing with those who have different life experiences, values, or beliefs, we can build inclusive and supportive communities. Empathy fosters a sense of unity and solidarity, allowing us to appreciate and celebrate the diversity that enriches our society. Through building empathic bridges, we promote compassion, understanding, and cooperation, ultimately contributing to a more harmonious and empathetic world.
- In conclusion, the power of empathy lies in its ability to create emotional resonance, forging deep connections between individuals. By fostering empathy, we unlock the potential for a greater understanding of others' perspectives and experiences, leading to more meaningful and compassionate relationships. Empathy becomes a crucial tool in building bridges between diverse individuals, and promoting inclusivity and unity. As we cultivate empathy in our interactions and communities, we contribute to a more empathetic and compassionate world, where understanding and connection transcend boundaries and foster mutual respect and support.

Differentiating Empathy from Sympathy

Empathy and sympathy are often confused, but they differ in their emotional responses and impacts. In this section, we differentiate empathy from sympathy.

- Emotional Connection vs. Pity: Empathy goes beyond mere sympathy, as it involves emotionally connecting with others' experiences. When we empathize, we put ourselves in their shoes, trying to understand and feel what they are going through. This emotional resonance allows us to establish a deeper and more genuine connection with others. On the other hand, sympathy may lead to feelings of pity, where we may feel sorry for someone's situation without truly connecting with their emotions. Pity tends to create a sense of separation and distance, while empathy bridges the gap and fosters a sense of camaraderie.

- Validation vs. Fixing: Empathy offers validation to others' feelings by acknowledging their emotions as valid and important. By actively listening and showing understanding, we let them know that their feelings matter. On the other hand, sympathy may lead to the desire to fix others' problems or offer immediate solutions. While well-intentioned, this approach can sometimes undermine the individual's autonomy and sense of agency. Empathy allows individuals to feel heard and understood, creating a safe space for them to express their emotions without judgment or pressure to find immediate solutions.
- Empowerment vs. Dependency: When we empathize with someone, we empower them by recognizing and acknowledging their emotions. We convey that their feelings are legitimate and that it is okay to experience vulnerability. This sense of empowerment encourages individuals to navigate their emotions and challenges with self-confidence and resilience. On the contrary, sympathy may inadvertently foster dependency, as it can create a dynamic where one person assumes the role of providing solutions and support, while the other becomes reliant on external validation or assistance.
- In summary, empathy involves emotionally connecting with others' experiences, building a deeper and more genuine connection. It offers validation to their feelings, creating a safe space for emotional expression. Empathy empowers individuals by recognizing the legitimacy of their emotions and encouraging self-confidence. On the other hand, sympathy may lead to feelings of pity, create a desire to fix problems, and inadvertently foster dependency. By understanding the distinctions between empathy and sympathy, we can develop more meaningful and supportive relationships, offering genuine care and understanding to those around us.

Fostering Compassion for Self and Others

Compassion, a tender force of care and understanding, serves as a healing balm for the soul. In this section, we explore the significance of nurturing compassion for ourselves and others.

- Self-Compassion: Cultivating self-compassion involves treating ourselves with the same kindness, understanding, and care that we would offer to a dear friend in times of need. It means acknowledging our own struggles, mistakes, and imperfections without judgment or self-criticism. Self-compassion recognizes that being human means experiencing challenges and setbacks, and it allows us to respond to ourselves with empathy and love.

- Acts of Kindness: Practicing acts of kindness and compassion in our daily lives has a profound impact on both ourselves and those around us. Small gestures of kindness, such as a friendly smile, a listening ear, or a helping hand, can create ripples of positivity and influence. These acts not only bring joy and comfort to others but also boost our own sense of well-being and fulfillment.
- Healing through Compassion: Compassion acts as a healing force, not only for others but also for ourselves. When we offer compassion to others, we create a nurturing and supportive environment that fosters emotional healing and growth. This compassionate presence enables individuals to feel seen, heard, and understood, which can be deeply transformative.
- Similarly, embracing compassion for ourselves helps in healing emotional wounds and promoting resilience. Instead of ignoring or suppressing difficult emotions, self-compassion encourages us to embrace and process these feelings with gentleness and understanding. It helps us to be patient with ourselves during challenging times and encourages self-care as an essential aspect of well-being.
- Practicing self-compassion and extending it to others nurtures a cycle of emotional healing and empowerment. As we cultivate compassion within ourselves and express it in our interactions, we create a more compassionate and supportive world for everyone to thrive in. Compassion is a powerful force that can lead to personal growth, emotional well-being, and stronger connections with others. It enables us to build a more empathetic and caring society, where each person's struggles are met with understanding and where kindness is valued as a cornerstone of our relationships.

Conclusion

Empathy and compassion form the cornerstone of authentic connections and nurturing relationships. By understanding the power of empathy, differentiating it from sympathy, and nurturing compassion for ourselves and others, we become agents of positive change and healing in the world. Together, we foster a community that values empathy and compassion, creating a ripple effect of kindness and understanding. As we embrace empathy with open hearts and cultivate compassion for ourselves and others, we contribute to a world where empathy is a guiding light that bridges differences, and compassion becomes a source of healing and nurturing. As we unleash the transformative power of empathy and compassion, we inspire others to do the same, creating a collective consciousness that values empathy, compassion, and the celebration of our shared humanity.

CHAPTER 23

ETHICAL DECISION-MAKING

Guided by Integrity: Navigating Ethical Dilemmas with Moral Clarity

Introduction

Ethical decision-making is the compass that guides our personal choices, directing us towards a path aligned with moral integrity and values. In this chapter, we embark on a journey of exploring the vital role of ethics in our lives. By analyzing ethical dilemmas with discernment and strengthening our moral integrity, we empower ourselves to make choices that reflect the best of our values and contribute to a more ethical and principled world.

The Role of Ethics in Personal Choices

Ethics serve as a moral framework that shapes our behavior and influences our personal choices. In this section, we explore the significance of ethics in guiding our decisions.

- Defining Personal Values: Identifying and clarifying our personal values is the first step in ethical decision-making. Our values are the guiding beliefs and principles that shape our attitudes, behaviors, and choices. They are the compass that helps us navigate the complexities of life and make decisions aligned with our authentic selves. When we have a clear understanding of our values, we can better discern right from wrong and act in accordance with our moral compass.
- Aligning with Principles: Ethical decisions are rooted in principles that reflect our deeply held beliefs and values. These principles serve as the moral framework for our actions and guide us in upholding what we consider to be right and just. By aligning our decisions with these principles, we ensure that our choices are consistent with our core beliefs and maintain integrity in our actions.
- Impact on Others: Ethical decision-making extends beyond our own interests and considers the impact on others and the broader community. It involves empathizing with the perspectives and experiences of others and

considering the potential consequences of our actions on their well-being. By recognizing the interconnectedness of all individuals, we cultivate a sense of responsibility and promote compassion in our choices.

In-depth explanation of each:

- Defining Personal Values: Personal values are the beliefs and principles that guide our behavior and represent what is most important to us. They can encompass a wide range of aspects, such as honesty, compassion, fairness, respect for others, environmental sustainability, or social justice. When we take the time to define and clarify our personal values, we gain insight into what drives us and what we stand for. This self-awareness enables us to make decisions that are congruent with our deepest convictions and contribute to a sense of purpose and fulfillment.
- Aligning with Principles: Principles are fundamental truths or guidelines that govern ethical behavior. They serve as the ethical framework within which we make decisions and conduct ourselves. These principles may be derived from philosophical, religious, or cultural beliefs. For instance, the principle of "do unto others as you would have them do unto you" embodies the concept of treating others with kindness and respect, reflecting the value of empathy and consideration. When our decisions align with these guiding principles, we act in ways that are consistent with our values, promoting integrity and authenticity in our actions.
- Impact on Others: Ethical decision-making requires us to consider the effects of our choices on others and the broader community. It involves putting ourselves in the shoes of others and empathizing with their perspectives and emotions. By recognizing the interconnectedness of all individuals, we develop a sense of responsibility for the consequences of our actions. Ethical decisions prioritize the well-being and dignity of others, promoting a harmonious and compassionate society. This consideration for the impact on others fosters empathy and nurtures a culture of cooperation and mutual support. Ultimately, ethical decision-making encourages us to act with greater mindfulness and consideration for the collective welfare of humanity and the planet.

Analyzing Ethical Dilemmas

Ethical dilemmas challenge us to navigate complex situations that involve conflicting values and principles. In this section, we explore the process of analyzing ethical dilemmas with discernment.

- Identifying Conflicting Values: In ethical dilemmas, individuals may encounter conflicting values and principles that make decision-making challenging. Conflicting values are situations where two or more moral principles or beliefs come into opposition, making it difficult to determine the most ethical course of action. For instance, a person may value honesty, but they also value loyalty to a friend who has asked them to keep a secret that may harm others. Identifying these conflicting values is crucial as it allows individuals to delve deeper into the complexity of the situation and explore the underlying reasons behind their beliefs. By recognizing the presence of conflicting values, individuals can engage in a more introspective process to reconcile these opposing principles and make a well-informed ethical choice.
- Seeking Diverse Perspectives: Ethical decision-making involves considering a broad range of perspectives and viewpoints to gain a comprehensive understanding of the situation at hand. Different individuals may have unique cultural, social, or personal backgrounds that shape their moral judgments. By seeking diverse perspectives, we open ourselves up to a wider range of insights, which can help challenge our preconceived notions and biases. This process of considering diverse viewpoints fosters empathy and cultivates a deeper appreciation for the complexities of ethical dilemmas. Moreover, it enhances our ability to arrive at more well-rounded and fair decisions that account for the diverse needs and values of all stakeholders involved.
- Weighing Consequences: Ethical decision-making involves evaluating the potential consequences of each course of action on individuals and the broader community. Consequences can be both short-term and long-term and may affect various aspects of human life, such as physical well-being, emotional health, economic stability, or environmental sustainability. Weighing consequences requires careful consideration of the potential benefits and harms of each option. This includes anticipating potential unintended consequences that may arise from the chosen course of action. By thoroughly examining the implications of our decisions, we can strive to make choices that uphold the greatest overall good and minimize harm to others. This process of weighing consequences is vital in ensuring that ethical decisions prioritize the well-being and welfare of all those involved and promote a just and equitable society.

Strengthening Moral Integrity

Moral integrity stands as the cornerstone of ethical decision-making, requiring courage and commitment to act in alignment with our values. In this section, we explore ways to strengthen our moral integrity.

- Inner Reflection and Self-Awareness: Engaging in inner reflection and self-awareness is a fundamental step in ethical development. It involves taking the time to introspect and examine our beliefs, values, and motivations. Through self-reflection, we gain a deeper understanding of the guiding principles that shape our ethical compass. This process helps us identify our strengths and weaknesses, enabling us to make more conscious and informed decisions aligned with our core values. By understanding ourselves better, we become more mindful of how our actions impact others and the world around us, fostering a greater sense of responsibility and ethical awareness.
- Courage in the Face of Adversity: Cultivating courage is essential in upholding our values, especially when faced with challenging circumstances or ethical dilemmas. Ethical decision-making may require standing up for what we believe in, even if it means facing opposition or adversity. It takes courage to resist peer pressure, social norms, or personal interests that may conflict with our ethical principles. Embracing courage empowers us to take ethical action despite potential risks, promoting integrity and resilience in the face of moral challenges. By practicing courage, we demonstrate a commitment to ethical behavior, inspiring others to do the same and creating a culture of ethics and integrity.
- Practicing Ethical Leadership: Ethical leadership goes beyond personal ethical conduct; it involves being an example for others and inspiring ethical behavior in our communities. As ethical leaders, we demonstrate fairness, honesty, and accountability in our interactions with others. We lead by example, showing consistency between our words and actions. Ethical leaders prioritize the well-being and interests of others, foster inclusivity and diversity, and promote a culture of trust and respect. By embodying ethical leadership, we create a positive and ethical influence on those around us, encouraging others to adopt ethical principles in their decision-making and behavior. This ripple effect of ethical leadership can lead to more ethical and compassionate communities, contributing to a better and more just society as a whole.

Conclusion

Ethical decision-making is the compass that steers us towards a life guided by integrity and moral clarity. By recognizing the role of ethics in our personal choices, analyzing ethical dilemmas with discernment, and strengthening our moral integrity, we embrace a path that reflects the best of our values and principles. Together, we foster a community of individuals committed to making ethical decisions that positively impact others and contribute to a more principled world. As we navigate ethical dilemmas with moral clarity, we inspire others to do the same, creating a collective consciousness that values integrity, empathy, and ethical decision-making. Guided by ethics, we shape a world where our actions are driven by compassion, understanding, and the unwavering commitment to make choices that honor our values and elevate humanity.

CHAPTER 24

PROMOTING PSYCHOLOGICAL WELL-BEING

Thriving in Mind and Spirit: Nurturing Psychological Well-being for a Flourishing Society

Introduction

Psychological well-being is the foundation of a fulfilling and flourishing life. In this chapter, we explore the importance of psychological well-being and its profound impact on our overall quality of life. By embracing self-care practices for mental health and encouraging positive psychology in society, we foster a culture that prioritizes emotional well-being, compassion, and resilience, creating a society where individuals thrive in mind and spirit.

Psychological Well-being and Its Importance

Psychological well-being encompasses emotional, mental, and social aspects of our lives. In this section, we delve into the significance of psychological well-being and its role in our overall well-being.

- Emotional Resilience: Emotional resilience refers to the ability to adapt and cope with adversity, stress, and challenges in a healthy and constructive manner. It involves maintaining a stable and balanced emotional state even in difficult situations. Psychological well-being plays a crucial role in fostering emotional resilience. When individuals have good psychological well-being, which includes factors such as self-awareness, self-regulation, and a positive outlook, they are better equipped to face life's ups and downs with a sense of inner strength and composure. Emotional resilience enables individuals to bounce back from setbacks, learn from experiences, and grow stronger in the face of adversity.

- Positive Relationships: Our psychological well-being significantly influences our ability to form and maintain positive relationships with others. When we have good emotional health, we are more likely to engage in healthier interpersonal interactions. Positive relationships are built on empathy, understanding, and effective communication, which are nurtured by psychological well-being.

When we are emotionally resilient, we can manage our emotions effectively and respond to others' feelings with empathy and compassion. This fosters a sense of trust and connection in our relationships, making them more fulfilling and supportive. Additionally, individuals with strong psychological well-being are better equipped to handle conflicts and challenges in relationships, leading to more harmonious connections with others.

- Quality of Life: Psychological well-being is a key determinant of overall quality of life and life satisfaction. When we are emotionally resilient and have good psychological health, we experience a higher sense of well-being and contentment. It positively impacts our overall physical health, mental health, and social functioning. Psychological well-being contributes to greater self-esteem, a positive self-image, and a sense of purpose and meaning in life. Individuals with good emotional resilience are more likely to engage in healthy coping strategies, maintain a positive outlook, and experience reduced stress levels. As a result, they are more likely to enjoy a higher quality of life, experience greater life satisfaction, and find fulfillment in their personal and professional pursuits.

In summary, psychological well-being plays a vital role in fostering emotional resilience, building positive relationships, and enhancing overall quality of life. Cultivating and prioritizing psychological health can lead to increased emotional strength, healthier interpersonal connections, and a greater sense of fulfillment and satisfaction in life.

Self-Care Practices for Mental Health

Self-care practices form the pillars of maintaining and nurturing psychological well-being. In this section, we explore self-care practices for mental health.

- Mindfulness and Meditation: Mindfulness and meditation are practices that involve being fully present in the moment and cultivating a non-judgmental awareness of our thoughts, emotions, and sensations. By embracing mindfulness and meditation, we can develop a deeper connection with ourselves and the world around us, leading to increased inner peace and emotional balance. These practices encourage us to observe our thoughts without getting caught up in them, allowing us to respond to situations with greater clarity and composure. By regularly engaging in mindfulness and meditation, we can reduce stress and anxiety, improve our ability to manage difficult emotions and enhance our overall well-being.

- Healthy Boundaries: Healthy boundaries refer to the limits we set in our relationships and interactions with others to protect our mental and emotional well-being. Learning to establish and maintain healthy boundaries is essential for our self-care and personal growth. When we have healthy boundaries, we can assert our needs, express our emotions, and make decisions that align with our values without compromising our well-being. Healthy boundaries also prevent us from becoming overly responsible for other people's feelings and actions, promoting a healthier and more balanced dynamic in our relationships. By honoring our boundaries, we cultivate self-respect and build trust in ourselves, which contributes to greater emotional resilience and a stronger sense of self.
- Engaging in Meaningful Activities: Engaging in meaningful activities involves pursuing endeavors that bring joy, purpose, and fulfillment to our lives. When we participate in activities that align with our passions and values, we experience a deeper sense of satisfaction and happiness. These activities can be hobbies, volunteer work, creative pursuits, or any endeavors that give our lives meaning and purpose. By engaging in meaningful activities, we develop a greater sense of self-awareness and connection to our inner values and desires. This, in turn, fosters a sense of fulfillment and contentment in our lives. Meaningful activities can also serve as a form of self-care, providing a much-needed respite from the stresses of daily life and promoting overall well-being.

In summary, mindfulness and meditation can help us cultivate inner peace and emotional balance by increasing our present-moment awareness and non-judgmental observation of our thoughts and emotions. Healthy boundaries are essential for protecting our mental and emotional well-being in relationships and interactions with others, promoting self-respect and emotional resilience. Engaging in meaningful activities enhances our sense of fulfillment and happiness by connecting us with our passions and values, providing a meaningful sense of purpose in our lives. Together, these practices contribute to greater emotional well-being and a more fulfilling and balanced life.

Encouraging Positive Psychology in Society

Positive psychology seeks to enhance well-being and flourishing rather than merely treating mental illness. In this section, we explore ways to encourage positive psychology in society.

- Emphasizing Strengths and Resilience: By emphasizing strengths and resilience, individuals are encouraged to shift their focus from dwelling on weaknesses and limitations to recognizing and building upon their unique qualities and abilities. This approach empowers individuals to embrace their potential for growth and development, even in the face of challenges. When people are aware of their strengths and recognize their capacity to overcome obstacles, they become more self-confident and motivated to pursue their goals. Moreover, fostering a strengths-based mindset in communities and organizations can lead to a more supportive and encouraging environment, where individuals are celebrated for their accomplishments and encouraged to reach their full potential.
- Promoting Compassion and Empathy: Promoting compassion and empathy involves cultivating a culture of understanding, kindness, and support. When people are empathetic, they can connect with others on a deeper level and validate their feelings and experiences without judgment. This creates an atmosphere of trust and openness, allowing individuals to feel heard and supported. Compassion and empathy also facilitate positive relationships and cooperation within communities, leading to enhanced social bonds and collective well-being. When individuals feel understood and cared for, they are more likely to experience improved mental health and a sense of belonging.
- Nurturing Emotional Intelligence: Nurturing emotional intelligence involves prioritizing education and practices that enhance self-awareness, emotional regulation, and interpersonal skills. Emotional intelligence enables individuals to recognize and understand their emotions and reactions, allowing them to respond to situations more thoughtfully and effectively. By being aware of their emotional triggers and patterns, individuals can make conscious choices about how they express themselves and handle challenging situations. Developing emotional intelligence also includes the ability to empathize with others, fostering better communication and conflict resolution. Cultivating emotional intelligence in individuals and communities can lead to improved emotional well-being, reduced conflicts, and healthier relationships.

In summary, emphasizing strengths and resilience empowers individuals to recognize and build upon their unique qualities, fostering self-confidence and motivation. Promoting compassion and empathy cultivates a culture of understanding and support, creating an environment where individuals feel valued and cared for. Nurturing emotional intelligence involves developing self-awareness and interpersonal skills, enabling individuals to respond to emotions and social situations more effectively. Together, these practices contribute to a more supportive and empathetic society, where individuals can thrive and experience greater emotional well-being.

Conclusion

Promoting psychological well-being creates a society where individuals flourish in mind and spirit. By recognizing the importance of psychological well-being, embracing self-care practices for mental health, and encouraging positive psychology in society, we foster a culture that values emotional well-being, resilience, and empathy. Together, we create a community that nurtures psychological well-being and supports individuals in their pursuit of a fulfilling and meaningful life. As we prioritize psychological well-being in society, we inspire others to do the same, cultivating a collective consciousness that values emotional health, mental resilience, and compassion. Guided by the principles of psychological well-being, we shape a society where individuals thrive, and the spirit of positivity and growth uplifts the human experience.

CHAPTER 25

PROMOTING PSYCHOLOGICAL WELL-BEING

Nurturing the Mind: Embracing Psychological Well-being for a Flourishing Life

Introduction

Psychological well-being lies at the heart of a fulfilling and balanced life. In this chapter, we embark on a journey of exploring the significance of psychological well-being and its profound impact on our overall well-being. By embracing self-care practices for mental health and encouraging positive psychology in society, we pave the way for a culture that prioritizes emotional well-being, resilience, and collective growth, fostering a society where individuals thrive and flourish.

Psychological Well-being and Its Importance

Psychological well-being encompasses the emotional, mental, and social dimensions of our lives. In this section, we delve into the importance of psychological well-being and its role in shaping our overall quality of life.

- Emotional Resilience: Emotional resilience refers to the ability to bounce back and adapt in the face of adversity and life's challenges. When we have a strong sense of psychological well-being, which includes good mental health, emotional stability, and positive self-esteem, it acts as a buffer against stress and helps us cope with difficult situations more effectively. Psychological well-being provides us with the inner strength and emotional stability to navigate challenging circumstances with grace, allowing us to maintain a sense of balance and perspective even during tough times. It enables us to acknowledge our emotions, process them in a healthy way, and respond to situations in a constructive manner.
- Mental Clarity: Psychological well-being significantly influences our mental clarity and cognitive functioning. When our mental health is in a good state, we experience improved focus, concentration, and decision-making abilities. A positive and stable emotional state allows our minds to be more

receptive to new information, problem-solving, and critical thinking. On the other hand, when we are overwhelmed with stress or negative emotions, it can cloud our judgment, impair our cognitive abilities, and hinder our ability to make sound decisions. Therefore, nurturing our psychological well-being through self-care, stress management, and seeking support when needed can enhance our mental clarity and overall cognitive performance.

- Social Connections: Psychological well-being plays a vital role in enriching our social connections and fostering healthier relationships. When we feel emotionally stable and content within ourselves, it positively impacts our interactions with others. It allows us to be more empathetic, understanding, and supportive towards our friends, family, and acquaintances. Additionally, when we have a strong sense of well-being, we are better equipped to set healthy boundaries in our relationships, ensuring that they are mutually beneficial and respectful. Positive social connections, in turn, contribute to our overall well-being, as social support is a crucial factor in coping with stress and finding joy and fulfillment in life.

In summary, psychological well-being is a cornerstone of emotional resilience, empowering us to navigate life's challenges with grace and adaptability. It enhances our mental clarity, allowing us to make better decisions and process information effectively. Furthermore, it enriches our social connections, fostering healthier and more meaningful relationships with others. Prioritizing our psychological well-being through self-awareness, self-care, and seeking support can have a profound impact on our overall emotional health and quality of life.

Self-Care Practices for Mental Health

Self-care practices serve as a cornerstone of maintaining and nurturing psychological well-being. In this section, we explore self-care practices for mental health.

- Mindfulness and Meditation: Mindfulness and meditation are practices that involve being fully present in the moment, and paying attention to our thoughts, feelings and sensations without judgment. Embracing mindfulness and meditation allows us to cultivate inner peace and emotional balance. By becoming more aware of our thoughts and emotions, we can develop a deeper understanding of ourselves and our reactions to various situations. This increased self-awareness enables us to respond to life's challenges with greater clarity and composure.

- Mindfulness involves being fully attentive to the present moment, and acknowledging our thoughts and emotions without getting carried away by them. By practicing mindfulness, we can reduce stress and anxiety, as it encourages us to let go of worries about the past or future. Instead, we focus on what is happening right now, fostering a sense of calm and inner tranquility.
- Meditation is a deliberate practice of training the mind to achieve a state of mental clarity and emotional equilibrium. It often involves focusing on a specific object, such as the breath or a mantra, to anchor our attention and cultivate concentration. Through regular meditation, we can develop a greater capacity to remain centered, even in the midst of life's ups and downs. It helps us become more resilient to the challenges that come our way, enabling us to bounce back from adversity with greater ease.
- Healthy Boundaries: Healthy boundaries refer to the limits we set in our relationships and interactions with others to protect our mental and emotional well-being. Learning to set and maintain healthy boundaries is crucial for our emotional health and maintaining fulfilling relationships. Boundaries help us define what is acceptable to us in terms of how others treat us and what behaviors we are willing to tolerate.
- Setting healthy boundaries involves communicating our needs, feelings, and limits clearly and assertively. It allows us to prioritize self-care and ensures that we are not compromising our emotional well-being for the sake of others. By having clear boundaries, we can reduce the risk of being taken advantage of or feeling overwhelmed by the demands of others. This, in turn, contributes to greater emotional stability and a more balanced life.
- Engaging in Meaningful Activities: Engaging in meaningful activities involves pursuing hobbies, interests, and passions that bring us joy and a sense of purpose. When we invest our time and energy in activities that align with our values and interests, we enhance our sense of fulfillment and life satisfaction. Meaningful activities provide us with a sense of purpose and accomplishment, contributing to our overall well-being.
- Meaningful activities can range from creative pursuits like art or music, to volunteering for a cause we care about, to spending quality time with loved ones. When we are engaged in activities that are personally significant, we experience a greater sense of connection and purpose in life. It can also act as a form of self-care, as it allows us to recharge and find joy in the present moment.

In summary, mindfulness and meditation promote inner peace and emotional balance by enhancing our self-awareness and resilience. Healthy boundaries protect our mental and emotional well-being, ensuring that we prioritize self-care and maintain fulfilling relationships. Engaging in meaningful activities contributes to our overall well-being by providing us with a sense of purpose and joy in life. By incorporating these practices into our daily lives, we can cultivate greater emotional well-being and lead more fulfilling and balanced lives.

Encouraging Positive Psychology in Society

Positive psychology seeks to enhance well-being and flourishing, aiming beyond the mere absence of mental illness. In this section, we explore ways to encourage positive psychology in society.

- Fostering a Culture of Positivity: Cultivating a culture of positivity involves creating an environment where individuals are encouraged to focus on the positive aspects of situations, practice resilience, and embrace a growth mindset. In such a culture, people are supported in their efforts to learn from challenges, setbacks, and failures, rather than being discouraged by them. By valuing positivity, individuals are more likely to approach difficulties with optimism and determination, which can lead to increased motivation and productivity.
- Promoting Emotional Intelligence: Emotional intelligence refers to the ability to understand and manage one's emotions and effectively relate to the emotions of others. Prioritizing emotional intelligence education is essential for enhancing self-awareness, empathy, and interpersonal relationships. When individuals are emotionally intelligent, they can recognize their own emotions and the emotions of others, which enables them to respond to situations with greater sensitivity and understanding. This fosters healthier communication and collaboration, leading to more harmonious and productive interactions in personal and professional settings.
- Creating Supportive Environments: Designing supportive environments means establishing spaces, both physically and psychologically, where individuals feel safe, valued, and respected. In supportive environments, people are encouraged to express themselves freely without fear of judgment or criticism. This fosters a sense of belonging and psychological safety, enabling individuals to be more authentic and open in their interactions. Supportive environments are crucial for promoting well-being and mental health, as they provide the necessary support and resources for individuals to thrive and grow.

In summary, fostering a culture of positivity emphasizes embracing resilience and a growth mindset, encouraging individuals to learn and grow from challenges. Promoting emotional intelligence enhances self-awareness and empathy, leading to more meaningful and harmonious relationships. Creating supportive environments provides the necessary safety and support for individuals to express themselves authentically and promotes overall well-being. By incorporating these principles, organizations and communities can cultivate a healthier and more thriving environment for individuals to flourish and reach their full potential.

Conclusion

Promoting psychological well-being creates a society where individuals thrive and flourish. By recognizing the significance of psychological well-being, embracing self-care practices for mental health, and encouraging positive psychology in society, we pave the way for a culture that values emotional well-being, resilience, and collective growth. Together, we create a community that prioritizes psychological well-being and supports individuals in their pursuit of a fulfilling and balanced life. As we nurture psychological well-being in society, we inspire others to do the same, cultivating a collective consciousness that values emotional health, mental resilience, and empathy. Guided by the principles of psychological well-being, we shape a society where individuals not only survive but thrive, and where the spirit of positivity and growth elevates the human experience to new heights.

PART V: UNMASKING MANIPULATIVE TACTICS

CHAPTER 26

BEYOND THE SHADOWS: A BRIGHTER FUTURE

Illuminating the Path: Embracing Empathy, Resilience, and Personal Growth

Introduction

The journey through dark psychology has been transformative, shining a light on the intricacies of human behavior and the shadows that exist within us all. In this final chapter, we reflect on this profound journey and the lessons learned. By encouraging a more empathetic and resilient society and embracing the light within ourselves, we transcend darkness, paving the way for a brighter and more compassionate future.

Reflection on the Journey through Dark Psychology

The exploration of dark psychology has deepened our understanding of the human psyche, revealing the darker aspects that can influence behavior and relationships. In this section, we reflect on the lessons learned from this journey.

- Awareness of Manipulation: Recognizing the prevalence of manipulation in various aspects of life involves acknowledging that manipulative tactics can be found in personal relationships, professional settings, and even within larger societal structures. Being aware of manipulation allows us to be more vigilant and discerning in our interactions, helping us to identify potential red flags and protect ourselves from falling victim to manipulative schemes.
- Empowerment Through Knowledge: Embracing the empowerment that comes from understanding the mechanisms of dark psychology is crucial. When we educate ourselves about manipulative tactics and the psychology behind them, we gain the tools to protect ourselves and others from being exploited. Knowledge empowers us to recognize manipulative patterns, establish healthy boundaries, and make informed decisions, enabling us to navigate relationships and situations with greater confidence and assertiveness.

- Compassion for Victims and Manipulators: Cultivating empathy for both the victims of manipulation and those who engage in manipulative behaviors is an essential aspect of emotional intelligence and understanding human complexities. While manipulation can cause immense harm to its victims, it's important to recognize that manipulators may themselves be struggling with their own emotional issues, past traumas, or insecurities. Compassion does not excuse manipulative behavior, but it allows us to approach the situation with a deeper understanding of the underlying factors at play.
- By acknowledging the prevalence of manipulation, we empower ourselves to be more vigilant and proactive in protecting our well-being. Embracing knowledge about dark psychology equips us with the tools to recognize and respond to manipulation effectively. Additionally, cultivating compassion for both victims and manipulators fosters a more empathetic and understanding perspective on human behavior, which can contribute to more harmonious and supportive interactions in our personal and social lives.

Encouraging a More Empathetic and Resilient Society

Transcending the shadows requires a collective effort to build a more empathetic and resilient society. In this section, we explore ways to encourage such a society.

- Embracing Diversity and Inclusion: Celebrating the richness of diversity involves recognizing and appreciating the unique experiences, backgrounds, and perspectives that each individual brings to the table. In an inclusive society, people from all walks of life feel welcomed, respected, and valued for who they are. Embracing diversity not only fosters a sense of belonging but also promotes creativity, innovation, and a broader understanding of the world. It allows us to break down barriers, challenge stereotypes, and build bridges of understanding between different groups, fostering a more harmonious and cohesive society.
- Promoting Emotional Intelligence: Emotional intelligence is the capacity to understand and manage our emotions and the emotions of others effectively. By prioritizing emotional intelligence education, individuals gain valuable skills to navigate the complexities of their own emotions, fostering self-awareness and emotional regulation. Furthermore, emotional intelligence enables us to empathize with others, fostering deeper connections and more meaningful relationships. It helps us communicate more effectively, resolve conflicts peacefully, and promote a supportive and compassionate environment.

- Supporting Mental Health Initiatives: Mental health is a crucial aspect of overall well-being, and advocating for mental health support and resources is essential to address the psychological challenges faced by individuals and communities. By supporting mental health initiatives, we aim to break the stigma surrounding mental health issues, encourage open conversations about mental well-being, and ensure that people have access to professional help when needed. Investing in mental health services not only helps individuals cope with mental health conditions but also promotes resilience and psychological well-being for the entire community.
- In summary, embracing diversity and inclusion enriches our society by celebrating individual differences and promoting understanding among diverse groups. Prioritizing emotional intelligence equips us with the tools to navigate emotions and build stronger connections with others. Supporting mental health initiatives is vital to address psychological challenges and promote overall well-being for individuals and communities alike. By embracing these principles, we create a more compassionate, empathetic, and resilient society that values the well-being of every individual.

Embracing the Light Within and Transcending Darkness

The journey through dark psychology has also revealed the potential for personal growth and transformation. In this section, we explore ways to embrace the light within ourselves and transcend darkness.

- Cultivating Self-Compassion: Self-compassion involves treating ourselves with the same kindness and understanding we would offer to a friend. It's about acknowledging our humanity and accepting that we, like everyone else, are imperfect and make mistakes. Instead of being overly critical or judgmental towards ourselves, self-compassion encourages a gentle and supportive attitude. When we cultivate self-compassion, we become more understanding of our struggles and challenges, allowing us to respond to ourselves with care and empathy.
- Building Resilience: Resilience is the ability to bounce back from adversity, challenges, and setbacks. It involves developing inner strength and adaptability to cope with life's ups and downs. By building resilience, we learn to see difficulties as opportunities for growth and learning, rather than insurmountable obstacles. Resilient individuals are better equipped to handle stress and pressure, and they possess the capacity to persevere in

the face of challenges. Resilience allows us to maintain a sense of balance and stability even during difficult times, helping us to navigate life's uncertainties with greater confidence.

- Nurturing Empathy and Compassion: Empathy is the ability to understand and share the feelings of others, while compassion involves the desire to alleviate their suffering. Nurturing empathy and compassion allows us to connect with others on a deeper level, fostering genuine and meaningful relationships. When we practice empathy, we strive to listen actively and understand others' perspectives without judgment. Compassion leads us to offer support and care to those in need, creating a sense of interconnectedness and collective healing. By extending empathy and compassion to ourselves and others, we build a more compassionate and understanding world.
- In summary, cultivating self-compassion involves treating ourselves with kindness and acceptance, recognizing our shared humanity and embracing our imperfections. Building resilience empowers us to navigate life's challenges and setbacks with strength and adaptability, using difficult experiences as opportunities for growth. Nurturing empathy and compassion creates meaningful connections with others and promotes collective healing and understanding. By embracing these principles, we foster a positive and supportive inner world and contribute to creating a more compassionate and empathetic society.

Conclusion

The journey through dark psychology has taken us through the depths of human behavior, but it has also illuminated the path to a brighter future. By encouraging a more empathetic and resilient society and embracing the light within ourselves, we transcend darkness and create a world where empathy, compassion, and personal growth are valued and prioritized. Together, we foster a community that celebrates diversity, supports mental well-being, and encourages emotional intelligence. As we transcend the shadows and embrace the light, we inspire others to do the same, contributing to a collective consciousness that strives for a brighter, more compassionate future. Guided by our newfound awareness, empathy, and resilience, we shape a world where darkness is met with understanding and compassion, and where the light within us all shines brightly, illuminating the path towards a future of hope, growth, and healing.

CHAPTER 27

COVERT MANIPULATION TECHNIQUES

Unveiling the Veil: Exposing Subtle Covert Manipulation Strategies

Introduction

The realm of covert manipulation is where hidden agendas and subtle tactics are employed to exert control over others. Covert manipulation techniques are significant to humanity and these techniques provide insight into identifying these tactics and protecting ourselves from those who seek to manipulate us.

Subtle and Covert Manipulation Strategies

Covert manipulators are skilled at concealing their true intentions behind a facade of charm and charisma. In this section, we explore some of the subtle and covert manipulation strategies they employ.

- Gaslighting: Gaslighting is a form of psychological manipulation in which a person intentionally distorts and undermines someone else's perceptions, memories, and sense of reality. The term "gaslighting" originates from the 1938 play and later film "Gas Light," where a husband manipulates his wife into doubting her sanity by gradually dimming the gas lights in their home and then denying any change occurred when she questions it. In modern contexts, gaslighting involves similar tactics of subtly and persistently making the victim question their own judgment and memory.
- Gaslighting can be a powerful tool for emotional control, as it leads the victim to doubt their own thoughts, feelings, and experiences, making them highly vulnerable to the manipulator's influence. Over time, victims may lose confidence in their own perceptions and become increasingly dependent on the manipulator's version of reality. The gaslighter may use tactics such as denial, lying, twisting the truth, and even gaslighting others to further discredit the victim's version of events.
- Love Bombing: Love bombing is a manipulative tactic used by individuals, especially in romantic relationships or cult-like situations, to quickly gain control and emotional dependence over another person. During love

bombing, the manipulator showers their target with excessive affection, attention, compliments, and gifts. They create an intense emotional bond and make the target feel valued and cherished, often in a short period.

- The purpose of love bombing is to create an emotional attachment and sense of indebtedness in the target, making them more likely to comply with the manipulator's desires and demands. The manipulator may idealize the target and fulfill their desires initially to gain their trust and devotion. However, once the manipulator feels secure in their control, they may start exerting more power and begin to manipulate and exploit the target's feelings and emotions.
- Triangulation: Triangulation is a manipulative tactic used to create division and weaken relationships between individuals. The manipulator may involve a third person or create a rivalry between two people to foster conflict and insecurity. This manipulation tactic can be used in various contexts, including personal relationships, workplaces, and group settings.
- By creating a triangle of conflict, the manipulator diverts attention away from themselves and gains more control over the situation. They may spread rumors or lies about one person to the other, creating distrust and animosity. The ultimate goal is to isolate the targets, making them feel alienated and distrustful of each other, while the manipulator remains in a position of power and control. Triangulation is a highly effective tool for manipulators to manipulate the emotions and perceptions of others, often without their targets realizing they are being played against each other.

In summary, gaslighting involves deliberate manipulation to make someone doubt their reality and judgment. Love bombing is a tactic of overwhelming someone with excessive affection to create emotional dependence. Triangulation creates conflict and division among individuals, weakening their relationships and increasing the manipulator's control. Being aware of these manipulative tactics can empower individuals to recognize and protect themselves from emotional manipulation and control.

Identifying Hidden Agendas and Ulterior Motives

Covert manipulators often mask their true intentions, making it challenging to discern their ulterior motives. In this section, we explore ways to identify hidden agendas.

- Trusting Your Gut: Trusting our gut refers to relying on our intuition and instincts when something doesn't feel right or seems too good to be true.

Our gut feelings are often based on subtle cues, past experiences, and subconscious processing that we may not consciously recognize. These feelings can serve as valuable warning signals, helping us navigate situations that might involve manipulation or deceit.

- When we encounter a situation or an individual that triggers our gut feeling, it's essential to pay attention to these internal signals. We may feel uneasy, anxious, or skeptical without concrete evidence to justify these emotions. However, these feelings shouldn't be dismissed lightly, as they can be our subconscious mind alerting us to potential dangers or red flags. Trusting our gut means honoring and validating these feelings and being cautious about proceeding further until we gain a better understanding of the situation.
- Analyzing Patterns of Behavior: Manipulative individuals often employ consistent patterns of behavior to achieve their objectives. These patterns may involve charm, deceit, guilt-tripping, or other tactics designed to influence and control others. By analyzing patterns of behavior, we can recognize manipulative tactics and discern their intentions more clearly.
- It's essential to observe behavior over time rather than basing judgments on isolated incidents. People may exhibit various behaviors in different situations, but consistent patterns are more telling. By paying attention to repeated actions and responses, we can identify red flags and become more aware of any attempts at manipulation. Analyzing behavior patterns helps us make informed decisions about how we choose to interact with others and protect ourselves from potential manipulation.
- Seeking Objective Perspectives: When faced with a complex situation or interacting with someone who exhibits manipulative behavior, seeking objective perspectives from trusted friends, family, or professionals can offer valuable insights. Our personal emotions and biases may cloud our judgment, making it challenging to see a situation objectively.
- External perspectives from people we trust can provide a fresh viewpoint and offer feedback based on their observations. They can help us identify potential manipulation or validate our concerns. However, it's crucial to choose advisors who are genuinely objective and supportive, as seeking advice from individuals who might also be influenced or manipulated could lead to further confusion.

In summary, trusting our gut means acknowledging and respecting our intuition and instincts when something feels off or too good to be true. Analyzing patterns of behavior allows us to identify manipulative tactics and make informed decisions. Seeking objective perspectives helps us gain valuable insights from trusted individuals, providing a clearer understanding of complex situations and protecting us from potential manipulation. Together, these strategies can empower us to navigate relationships and interactions with greater awareness and discernment.

Protecting Yourself from Covert Manipulators

Protecting ourselves from covert manipulation requires awareness and assertiveness. In this section, we explore ways to safeguard against covert manipulators.

- Setting Boundaries: Setting boundaries involves establishing clear limits for ourselves and others in various aspects of life, such as our emotions, time, and personal space. Healthy boundaries act as protective barriers, safeguarding our well-being and preventing others from encroaching on our emotional or physical space without our consent. By defining what is acceptable and unacceptable behavior, we empower ourselves to maintain a sense of control over our lives and relationships.
- When we encounter situations or individuals who challenge our boundaries, it's essential to assert them firmly. This may involve saying no to requests that go against our values or expressing discomfort when someone violates our boundaries. By consistently enforcing these boundaries, we establish our self-worth and communicate our needs effectively. This, in turn, helps create healthier and more balanced relationships built on mutual respect and understanding.
- Limiting Personal Information: Being cautious about sharing sensitive personal information is a crucial step in protecting ourselves from potential manipulation and harm. In today's digital age, information is easily accessible, and disclosing too much personal data to individuals we don't fully trust can make us vulnerable to various forms of manipulation, such as identity theft or emotional exploitation.
- By being discerning about whom we share personal information with, we can reduce the risk of falling prey to manipulative tactics that target our vulnerabilities. It's essential to evaluate the trustworthiness and intentions

of the people we interact with before divulging sensitive details about our lives. Limiting personal information allows us to maintain a level of privacy and control over how others perceive and interact with us.

- Prioritizing Self-Care: Self-care is the intentional practice of taking care of our physical, emotional, and mental well-being. It involves activities that nourish and rejuvenate us, promoting a healthy sense of self and emotional resilience. Prioritizing self-care helps us build the inner strength needed to withstand manipulative influences and maintain a balanced perspective.
- Engaging in self-care activities, such as regular exercise, spending time with loved ones, or practicing mindfulness, can reduce stress and improve emotional regulation. When we prioritize self-care, we become more attuned to our emotional needs and can better recognize when external influences attempt to manipulate our emotions or actions.

In summary, setting boundaries is crucial for maintaining healthy relationships and safeguarding our emotional well-being. It allows us to communicate our needs and protect ourselves from manipulative influences. Limiting personal information helps us maintain a sense of privacy and protect against potential harm or exploitation. Prioritizing self-care fosters emotional resilience, empowering us to resist manipulation and maintain a sense of balance in our lives. Together, these strategies contribute to building a foundation of strength and self-awareness, enabling us to navigate life with greater clarity and confidence.

Conclusion

Unmasking covert manipulation techniques empowers us to protect ourselves and others from the harmful effects of manipulative behavior. By understanding the subtleties of these tactics, identifying hidden agendas, and prioritizing our emotional well-being, we become impervious to covert manipulation. Together, we create a community that values transparency, trust, and genuine connections, fostering a society where individuals are equipped to recognize and resist manipulation. As we unmask the veiled intentions and protect ourselves from covert manipulation, we contribute to a world where emotional integrity and authentic interactions prevail, paving the way for healthier relationships and a more compassionate society.

CHAPTER 28

EMOTIONAL INTELLIGENCE IN DEFENSE

The Armor Within: Harnessing Emotional Intelligence to Resist Manipulation

Introduction

Exploring the role of emotional intelligence as a powerful defense against manipulation, individuals can equip themselves with the necessary tools to navigate manipulative situations with clarity and assertiveness. The significance of emotional self-regulation, empathy, and embracing vulnerability without falling prey to exploitation is delved into in this chapter.

Strengthening Emotional Intelligence to Resist Manipulation

Emotional intelligence acts as a shield against manipulation, empowering us to recognize and respond to manipulative tactics effectively. In this section, we delve into how emotional intelligence aids in our defense.

- Self-Awareness: Cultivating self-awareness involves developing a deep understanding of ourselves, including our emotions, thoughts, beliefs, and behaviors. It is the process of becoming conscious of our own inner world and how it influences our interactions with others and the world around us. By being self-aware, we become more attuned to our emotions, triggers, and vulnerabilities, which are key aspects that manipulators may exploit. When we are aware of these aspects, we are better equipped to recognize potential manipulation attempts and safeguard ourselves from falling victim to them. Additionally, self-awareness allows us to be more mindful of our own behaviors and responses, enabling us to maintain control over our reactions in challenging situations.
- Intuition and Gut Feelings: Our intuition and gut feelings are powerful sources of insight that can guide us through uncertain or potentially manipulative circumstances. Often, we may experience a gut feeling that something is not right, or we might sense a certain level of discomfort around certain individuals or situations. Honoring these intuitive cues is essential because they serve as

valuable early warning signals. Intuition, while not always logical, is based on our subconscious processing of information and past experiences. By paying attention to our intuition, we can proactively distance ourselves from situations that may have hidden motives or manipulative elements.

- Navigating Emotional Manipulation: Emotional intelligence is the capacity to understand and manage our emotions effectively, as well as to comprehend and empathize with the emotions of others. Developing emotional intelligence provides us with the tools to navigate emotional manipulation with clarity and rationality. When we are emotionally intelligent, we can recognize when others are attempting to manipulate our feelings, as well as acknowledge and process our own emotions without impulsively reacting to them. Emotional intelligence empowers us to detach emotionally from manipulative tactics and respond in a calm, collected manner, making it harder for manipulators to succeed in their efforts.

In summary, by cultivating self-awareness, honoring our intuition and gut feelings, and developing emotional intelligence, we build a strong defense against manipulation. These practices equip us with a deeper understanding of ourselves and others, allowing us to navigate potential manipulation attempts with greater clarity, resilience, and emotional control. By empowering ourselves with these skills, we can make more informed decisions and protect our well-being and autonomy in various life situations.

Emotional Self-Regulation and Empathy

Emotional self-regulation and empathy form pillars of emotional intelligence, assisting us in maintaining our emotional balance while understanding others' perspectives. In this section, we explore the significance of these traits in our defense against manipulation.

- Emotional Resilience: Emotional resilience refers to our ability to adapt and bounce back from challenging or emotionally distressing situations. It involves mastering emotional self-regulation, which means having control over our emotions rather than allowing them to control us. When we are emotionally resilient, we are better equipped to withstand emotional manipulation and maintain a clear focus on our well-being and values. Manipulators often try to evoke intense emotions to cloud our judgment and exploit our vulnerabilities. However, by cultivating emotional resilience, we can recognize and manage these emotions effectively, making it harder for manipulators to gain control over us.

- Empathy and Perspective-Taking: Empathy is the ability to understand and share the feelings of others. It plays a crucial role in identifying genuine connections and distinguishing them from manipulative tactics. Manipulators may use charm and charisma to feign empathy and create a false sense of understanding, making it challenging to recognize their true intentions. By honing our empathy and perspective-taking skills, we can discern whether someone is genuinely empathetic or using it as a manipulative tool. Understanding others' feelings and motivations helps us develop a deeper level of discernment in our interactions and relationships, enabling us to establish healthier and more authentic connections.
- Setting Emotional Boundaries: Emotional intelligence involves recognizing, understanding, and managing our emotions and the emotions of others. When we have developed emotional intelligence, we can establish and enforce emotional boundaries effectively. Emotional boundaries are essential for protecting our mental and emotional well-being from manipulation. Manipulators may try to exploit our emotions or use guilt-tripping tactics to control our behavior. By having clear emotional boundaries, we can prevent emotional manipulation from infiltrating our lives. Emotional boundaries also enable us to communicate our needs and limits assertively, safeguarding our emotional well-being and autonomy.

In summary, emotional resilience allows us to regulate our emotions and maintain focus despite manipulative attempts. Empathy and perspective-taking help us discern genuine connections from manipulative tactics, strengthening our ability to build authentic relationships. Developing emotional intelligence empowers us to set and maintain healthy emotional boundaries, protecting us from emotional manipulation and fostering healthier interactions with others. By cultivating these aspects, we can create a foundation of emotional strength, authenticity, and empowerment that safeguards us against manipulation and promotes overall well-being.

Embracing Vulnerability Without Being Exploited

Embracing vulnerability is a courageous act, but it can make us susceptible to manipulation if not managed wisely. In this section, we explore how emotional intelligence helps us embrace vulnerability without being exploited.

- Discerning Trustworthy Individuals: Emotional intelligence plays a vital role in helping us identify trustworthy individuals with whom we can form genuine and authentic connections. When we possess emotional intelligence, we are better equipped to understand and recognize the emotions, intentions, and nonverbal cues of others. This heightened awareness enables us to gauge whether someone is sincere and reliable or potentially manipulative. Trust is a fundamental aspect of any relationship, and emotional intelligence assists us in building trust with individuals who genuinely care for our well-being, allowing us to share our vulnerabilities and experiences without fear of manipulation or exploitation.

- Assertiveness and Boundaries: Emotional intelligence empowers us to assertively communicate our boundaries and expectations in relationships. By understanding and managing our emotions effectively, we can express our needs and limits with confidence and clarity. This assertiveness is crucial in protecting ourselves from manipulation, as manipulators may attempt to exploit our inability to communicate our boundaries clearly. With emotional intelligence, we can recognize when someone is attempting to push our boundaries and respond assertively, ensuring that our emotional and mental well-being remains safeguarded.
- Learning from Mistakes: Emotional intelligence fosters resilience and the ability to learn from past experiences, including instances where we may have been vulnerable to manipulation. When we possess emotional intelligence, we can reflect on our emotions, actions, and decisions in a balanced and non-judgmental manner. This reflective approach allows us to understand the factors that may have contributed to our vulnerabilities and manipulation in the past. By learning from these experiences, we can develop strategies to prevent similar vulnerabilities from arising in the future. Emotional intelligence, therefore, acts as a protective shield, enabling us to grow and evolve from our mistakes, ensuring that we become less susceptible to manipulation as we continue to develop our emotional resilience.

In summary, emotional intelligence is a powerful tool that supports us in navigating relationships and interactions with others. It aids in discerning trustworthy individuals, allowing us to form authentic connections with those who genuinely care for our well-being. Emotional intelligence also empowers us to assertively communicate boundaries, protecting us from potential manipulation. Moreover, emotional intelligence fosters resilience and the ability to learn from past experiences, helping us evolve and grow as individuals, and reducing our vulnerability to manipulation in the future. By cultivating emotional intelligence, we can navigate life's complexities with greater awareness, authenticity, and self-protection.

Conclusion

Emotional intelligence serves as a vital defense in the face of manipulation, empowering us to navigate emotional minefields with resilience and discernment. By strengthening emotional intelligence, practicing emotional self-regulation, and embracing empathy and vulnerability wisely, we become equipped to resist manipulation and protect our emotional well-being. Together, we foster a community that values emotional intelligence, empathy, and assertiveness, creating a society where manipulation finds no fertile ground to take root. As we harness the armor within, fortified by emotional intelligence, we inspire others to do the same, contributing to a collective consciousness that values emotional integrity and genuine connections. Guided by emotional intelligence, we shape a world where individuals stand tall in their emotional strength, forging a future where manipulation is met with awareness, empathy, and the power to defend against it.

CHAPTER 29

LOVE BOMBING AND ITS EFFECTS

Love Bombing: The Seductive Trap and Its Impact

Introduction

Delving into the concept of love bombing, a manipulative tactic that involves overwhelming individuals with excessive affection and attention is explored. This chapter sheds light on the purpose and effects of love bombing, examining its presence in romantic relationships, friendships, and even in the context of manipulative cults. Additionally, the process of recovering from the aftermath of the love bombing will be addressed.

Understanding Love Bombing and Its Purpose

Love bombing is a psychological manipulation tactic designed to create a sense of dependency and emotional attachment by showering individuals with extreme love and admiration. In this section, we explore the purpose and mechanisms behind love bombing.

- Grooming and Manipulation: Love bombing is a manipulative technique used by individuals with dark intentions to groom and control others. It involves an overwhelming display of affection, attention, and flattery directed towards the targeted individual. The goal of love bombing is to create a false sense of intimacy and connection, making the victim feel special, desired, and emotionally attached to the manipulator. By bombarding the individual with excessive positive reinforcement, the manipulator aims to lower their defenses and establish a deep emotional bond.
- Emotional Dependency: Love bombing seeks to foster emotional dependency in the targeted individual. By continuously showering them with affection and attention, the manipulator encourages the victim to rely on this positive reinforcement for their emotional well-being. Over time, the individual becomes emotionally dependent on the manipulator, seeking validation and affirmation from them. This emotional dependency weakens the victim's ability to see the manipulator's true intentions and further entrenches them in the manipulative relationship.

- Erosion of Boundaries: Love bombing aims to erode the targeted individual's personal boundaries and critical thinking. The overwhelming affection and attention can cloud the victim's judgment, making them more susceptible to accepting behaviors or requests that they would otherwise find unacceptable. As the manipulator continues to exert control through love bombing, the victim's ability to assert their boundaries weakens, and they may become more compliant and accommodating to the manipulator's wishes.

In summary, love bombing is a manipulative strategy that involves showering the targeted individual with excessive affection and attention to groom them and create emotional dependency. The manipulator aims to weaken the individual's critical thinking and erode their personal boundaries, making them more compliant and vulnerable to manipulation. By understanding these tactics, individuals can be more vigilant and aware of potential manipulative behaviors in their relationships, thus protecting themselves from exploitation and harm. It is essential to cultivate self-awareness and emotional resilience to recognize and resist these manipulative tactics and build healthier, more authentic connections with others.

Love Bombing in Romantic Relationships, Friendships, and Cults

Love bombing can manifest in various relationships, extending beyond romantic entanglements into friendships and even manipulative cults. In this section, we examine the presence of love bombing in different contexts.

- Romantic Relationships: Love bombing is a deceptive tactic often employed by manipulative partners to entice and captivate their romantic interests. In the initial stages of a relationship, the manipulator overwhelms their target with an extravagant display of affection, attention, and flattery. They shower the individual with gifts, compliments, and grand gestures, creating an illusion of a perfect and intensely passionate romance. The manipulator aims to evoke feelings of euphoria and emotional dependence in the target, making them feel valued and cherished.

- However, as the relationship progresses, the manipulator may gradually reveal their true intentions, and the excessive affection may diminish. This shift in behavior can leave the target confused and vulnerable, as they have become emotionally dependent on the manipulator's love and attention. The manipulator may use this dependency to gain control over the individual and exploit their vulnerabilities for their benefit.

- Friendships and Social Circles: Love bombing is not limited to romantic relationships; it can also be employed in friendships and social circles. In these situations, the manipulator may utilize love bombing to establish emotional bonds with their friends or social group. They might go above and beyond to be extremely supportive, caring, and accommodating, making others feel valued and appreciated. This behavior aims to foster a strong emotional connection and loyalty from their friends.
- By love bombing their social circle, the manipulator seeks to create a favorable environment where they can maintain influence and control. The individuals in the group may feel indebted to the manipulator for their unwavering support and kindness, making it harder for them to question the manipulator's intentions or actions. The manipulator can then exploit this emotional attachment to achieve their own objectives or manipulate group dynamics to their advantage.
- Manipulative Cults: Love bombing is also a common recruitment tactic used by cult-like organizations to lure individuals into their ranks. In this context, the manipulator targets vulnerable individuals who may be seeking a sense of belonging, purpose, or meaning in their lives. The manipulative cult showers these potential recruits with love, affection, and a strong sense of community. The recruits are made to feel special and chosen, creating a powerful emotional bond.
- The cult's love bombing tactics create an intense emotional experience for the recruits, often leaving them feeling deeply connected to the group and its ideologies. This emotional attachment can blind them to the potential dangers and manipulation within the cult. As they become emotionally dependent on the cult and its members, they may become more susceptible to further manipulation and control by the cult's leaders.

In summary, love bombing is a manipulative tactic that can be utilized in various contexts, including romantic relationships, friendships, and even by manipulative cults. The manipulator overwhelms their target with excessive affection, attention, and flattery to establish emotional bonds and dependency. By understanding these tactics, individuals can be more vigilant in recognizing potential manipulative behaviors and protecting themselves from exploitation and harm in their relationships and social interactions.

Recovering from the Aftermath of Love Bombing

The aftermath of love bombing can leave individuals emotionally scarred and disoriented. In this section, we address the process of recovering from the effects of love bombing.

- Recognizing Manipulation: Love bombing is a manipulative technique where an individual, often with dark and deceitful intentions, bombards their target with excessive affection, attention, and flattery. This tactic is employed in various contexts, such as romantic relationships, friendships, and even by manipulative cults. It aims to overwhelm the target emotionally and create an illusion of intense connection and attraction. By recognizing the signs of love bombing, such as excessive flattery, rushing into commitments, and a lack of genuine depth in the relationship, individuals can develop awareness of the manipulation and regain clarity about the authenticity of the connection.
- Rebuilding Self-Trust: After experiencing love bombing and manipulation, individuals may doubt their ability to judge the sincerity of others and their own intuition. Rebuilding self-trust is crucial to regain confidence in one's judgment and decision-making. This involves reflecting on past experiences and understanding how manipulation occurred, recognizing any vulnerabilities that were exploited, and learning from the lessons. Engaging in self-compassion and forgiveness for any mistakes made during the manipulation process can also aid in rebuilding self-trust. With time and practice, individuals can gradually learn to trust their instincts and judgment again, enabling them to protect themselves from future manipulation.
- Establishing Boundaries: Setting and enforcing healthy boundaries is an essential aspect of protecting oneself from manipulation and exploitation. Love bombing often involves the manipulator pushing past the target's boundaries, disregarding their comfort levels, and moving the relationship too quickly. Learning to establish clear and healthy boundaries is a protective measure to prevent such manipulation. Individuals need to recognize their own needs, values, and limits, and assertively communicate them to others. By establishing boundaries and being consistent in enforcing them, individuals create a safe space for themselves where manipulators are less likely to exploit vulnerabilities.

In summary, recognizing manipulation tactics used during love bombing, rebuilding self-trust, and establishing boundaries are key steps in protecting oneself from emotional manipulation and exploitation. Developing awareness of manipulative behaviors enables individuals to discern genuine connections from deceitful tactics. Rebuilding self-trust empowers individuals to trust their instincts and judgment once again. Lastly, setting and enforcing healthy boundaries fosters a sense of personal agency and creates a protective barrier against potential manipulation in relationships and social interactions.

Conclusion

Love bombing is a powerful and insidious form of manipulation that can have lasting effects on individuals. By understanding its purpose and mechanisms, recognizing its presence in various relationships, and taking steps to recover from its aftermath, we empower ourselves to break free from the seductive trap of love bombing. Together, we foster a community that values genuine connections built on trust, empathy, and respect. As we become vigilant against love bombing and its effects, we create a world where emotional integrity and autonomy are celebrated, paving the way for healthier relationships and a more empowered society.

CHAPTER 30

THE DARK SIDE OF PERSUASION IN MARKETING

The Subtle Art of Influence: Unraveling Manipulative Marketing Techniques

Introduction

There is a dark side of persuasion in marketing, where businesses employ manipulative tactics to sway consumer behavior. This chapter delves into the world of manipulative advertising and marketing techniques, shedding light on the intricacies of consumer psychology and decision-making. By becoming critical consumers and avoiding manipulation, we empower ourselves to make informed choices in a world filled with persuasive messages.

Manipulative Advertising and Marketing Techniques

In the pursuit of profit, some marketers resort to manipulative techniques to influence consumers' perceptions and decisions. In this section, we explore the deceptive practices employed in marketing.

- Emotional Appeals: Emotional appeals are marketing strategies designed to evoke specific emotions in consumers to create positive associations with products or services. Marketers use various techniques, such as storytelling, sentimental imagery, or relatable messaging, to tap into consumers' feelings and values. By eliciting emotions like joy, nostalgia, or empathy, they aim to establish an emotional connection with the audience. This emotional resonance can lead to increased brand loyalty and a more memorable and persuasive advertising experience.
- False Scarcity: False scarcity is a psychological tactic used by marketers to create a perception of limited availability or urgency around a product or offer. By suggesting that a product is in short supply or that a time-limited deal is expiring soon, marketers aim to trigger a fear of missing out (FOMO) in consumers. This fear compels individuals to make impulsive purchasing decisions to secure the product or deal before it disappears. However, in many cases, the scarcity is artificial, and the product may

not actually be limited in quantity or time. False scarcity plays on our instinctive desire to avoid loss and gain an advantage, making it an effective manipulation technique in marketing.

- Celebrity Endorsements: Celebrity endorsements leverage the popularity and influence of well-known individuals to promote products or services. When consumers see a celebrity they admire endorsing a product, it creates a sense of trust and credibility. This association between the celebrity's positive image and the product can influence consumer preferences and purchasing decisions. Consumers may feel that if a product is good enough for a celebrity they admire, it must be of high quality and worth trying. Celebrity endorsements are especially impactful in industries like fashion, beauty, and fitness, where image and prestige play significant roles in consumer choices.

In summary, emotional appeals in marketing use emotions to create a strong bond between consumers and products, building brand loyalty and resonance. False scarcity exploits the fear of missing out, encouraging impulsive buying decisions. Celebrity endorsements capitalize on the credibility and popularity of well-known individuals to influence consumer choices. Understanding these marketing tactics empowers consumers to make more informed decisions and recognize when emotions or false perceptions are being used to sway their choices.

Consumer Psychology and Decision-Making

Consumer psychology plays a significant role in how we respond to marketing messages and make purchasing decisions. In this section, we explore the psychological factors that marketers exploit.

- Cognitive Biases: Cognitive biases are inherent mental shortcuts or patterns of thinking that often lead to systematic errors in judgment and decision-making. These biases can influence our perceptions, beliefs, and choices without us being fully aware of them. Examples of common cognitive biases include confirmation bias, where we tend to favor information that confirms our existing beliefs, and availability bias, where we rely on readily available information rather than seeking out more comprehensive data. Understanding cognitive biases is essential for consumers to recognize and mitigate their impact on decision-making, enabling them to make more rational and informed choices.

- Social Proof and FOMO: Social proof is a psychological phenomenon where individuals look to others' actions and behaviors to determine the appropriate course of action in a given situation. It operates on the principle that if many people are doing something, it must be the right or desirable thing to do. Marketers leverage social proof by showcasing positive customer reviews, testimonials, or displaying the popularity of a product to create a sense of credibility and trust. Additionally, the Fear Of Missing Out (FOMO) taps into the human desire to be part of something exciting and not miss out on rewarding experiences. By presenting limited-time offers or emphasizing scarcity, marketers can trigger FOMO, prompting consumers to act quickly and make impulsive decisions.
- The Power of Persuasion: Persuasion is a communication strategy that aims to influence attitudes, beliefs, and behaviors. Various psychological principles underpin persuasive techniques, including:
    1. Reciprocity: The principle of reciprocity suggests that people tend to feel obligated to return favors or concessions. Marketers often use this tactic by offering free samples, gifts, or discounts, creating a sense of indebtedness, which may increase the likelihood of a purchase.
    2. Authority: People tend to comply with authority figures or those perceived as experts. Marketers utilize authority figures or endorsements by experts to enhance the credibility of their products and influence consumer decisions.
    3. Liking: People are more receptive to persuasion from individuals they like or relate to. Marketers may use relatable spokespeople, influencers, or likeable characters in advertisements to enhance product appeal and create positive associations.

By understanding the power of persuasion and being aware of cognitive biases like social proof and FOMO, consumers can make more conscious and informed choices. They can critically assess marketing messages, recognize when psychological principles are being used to influence them, and make decisions that align better with their actual needs and preferences.

Becoming a Critical Consumer and Avoiding Manipulation

To shield ourselves from manipulative marketing tactics, we must develop a critical eye and hone our decision-making skills. In this section, we explore strategies to become savvy consumers.

- Media Literacy: Media literacy refers to the ability to analyze, evaluate, and interpret media messages critically. In the context of marketing, media literacy helps consumers recognize and understand the tactics used to influence their perceptions and behaviors. By promoting media literacy, consumers become more adept at identifying manipulative marketing techniques, such as emotional appeals, false scarcity, and celebrity endorsements. They learn to question the motives behind advertisements and consider the potential biases that may influence the content they consume.
- Fact-Checking: Fact-checking is a crucial skill that empowers consumers to verify the accuracy and reliability of claims and promises made by advertisers. With the vast amount of information available in the digital age, fact-checking helps consumers distinguish between genuine information and misinformation or exaggerated claims. By fact-checking, consumers can make informed decisions and avoid falling prey to deceptive marketing practices.
- Conscious Consumerism: Conscious consumerism involves making purchasing decisions that align with personal values and ethical considerations. It goes beyond just buying products; it entails supporting businesses that prioritize transparency, sustainability, and social responsibility. By embracing conscious consumerism, individuals become more selective about the products and brands they support, seeking out companies that align with their values. This approach encourages businesses to prioritize ethical practices and motivates the industry as a whole to move towards more sustainable and socially conscious practices.
- When consumers develop media literacy, practice fact-checking, and embrace conscious consumerism, they become more empowered and resilient against manipulative marketing. They can decipher marketing messages, identify potential red flags, and make choices that align with their values and well-being. Additionally, conscious consumerism encourages businesses to adopt ethical practices and foster a more transparent and responsible marketplace. Ultimately, these practices contribute to a more informed and responsible society, where individuals can make choices that positively impact themselves, others, and the environment.

Conclusion

The dark side of persuasion in marketing lurks in the shadows, attempting to influence our choices without our conscious awareness. By understanding manipulative advertising and marketing techniques, recognizing the role of consumer psychology in decision-making, and becoming critical consumers, we reclaim control over our choices. Together, we foster a community that values transparency, ethics, and informed decision-making, creating a society where consumers are empowered to make choices that align with their values and needs. As we navigate the maze of manipulative marketing with discernment and awareness, we contribute to a world where honesty and authenticity prevail, paving the way for a more responsible and conscious marketplace.

PART VI: SOCIETY'S VULNERABILITIES

CHAPTER 31

MEDIA MANIPULATION AND PROPAGANDA

The Puppeteers of Perception: Unveiling Media Manipulation and Propaganda

Introduction

Delving into the vulnerabilities of society, we are focusing on the role of media manipulation and propaganda in shaping public opinion. This chapter exposes the powerful influence of media on our perceptions, identifying biased and manipulative content, and advocating for media literacy and responsible consumption to safeguard against misinformation.

The Role of Media in Shaping Public Opinion

Media wields immense power in shaping public opinion, influencing how we perceive the world and its events. In this section, we explore the pivotal role of media in shaping our collective understanding.

- Gatekeeping and Agenda Setting: Gatekeeping refers to the process of selecting and controlling the information that is presented to the public through media channels. Agenda setting, on the other hand, is the process by which media outlets prioritize certain news stories and topics, influencing the public's perception of what issues are important. Both gatekeeping and agenda-setting play a significant role in shaping the narratives that reach the audience. Media gatekeepers, such as editors and news producers, have the power to decide which stories get published or aired, and which ones are excluded. This can lead to the amplification or suppression of certain information, impacting public understanding and awareness of important issues.
- Framing and Bias: Media framing refers to the way in which news stories are presented to emphasize certain aspects and downplay others. The framing of news can shape how audiences perceive and interpret information, influencing their opinions and attitudes. Additionally, media bias refers to the inherent prejudice or partiality that may be present in media content. Bias can manifest

in various forms, including political, ideological, or corporate biases. When media outlets have biases, it can lead to a skewed representation of events, influencing public perception and contributing to polarization.

- The Impact of Social Media: Social media platforms have revolutionized the way information is disseminated and consumed. They offer a vast and accessible space for sharing news, opinions, and ideas. Social media plays a significant role in shaping public discourse, as it allows information to spread rapidly and reach a wide audience. However, the decentralized nature of social media can also lead to the spread of misinformation, echo chambers, and the reinforcement of pre-existing beliefs. The viral nature of social media content can amplify certain narratives, even if they lack factual accuracy. As a result, social media has both positive and negative impacts on public discourse, and its role in shaping opinions and influencing public understanding continues to be a subject of ongoing research and debate.

In summary, gatekeeping and agenda-setting influence which information reaches the public, framing and bias impact how that information is presented and interpreted, and social media has transformed the way information is disseminated and discussed. Understanding these dynamics is crucial for media consumers to be informed and critical thinkers, enabling them to navigate the vast and complex landscape of information in the modern digital age.

Identifying Biased and Manipulative Media Content

Identifying biased and manipulative media content is crucial to becoming informed and discerning consumers of information. In this section, we examine techniques used in media manipulation.

- Sensationalism and Clickbait: Sensationalism and clickbait are manipulative techniques used in media to attract attention and increase viewership or readership. Sensationalism involves presenting news stories or information in an exaggerated or shocking manner to provoke emotional reactions from the audience. It aims to grab attention quickly and may focus on the dramatic or sensational aspects of a story rather than its factual accuracy or context. Clickbait, on the other hand, refers to eye-catching or intriguing headlines or thumbnails that entice users to click on a link or article. However, the content often fails to deliver on the promise made in the headline, leading to disappointment or frustration for the audience. Both sensationalism and clickbait exploit people's curiosity and emotions, potentially compromising the accuracy and depth of information presented.

- False Equivalency: False equivalency is a deceptive tactic used in media to create a sense of balance or fairness in reporting, but it can distort the truth and create a misleading narrative. It involves presenting two contrasting perspectives or arguments as if they hold equal validity or merit, even when evidence overwhelmingly supports one side. By doing so, false equivalency can create confusion and lead audiences to question established facts or scientific consensus. This tactic is particularly prevalent in controversial or divisive topics, where giving undue attention to fringe or discredited viewpoints can undermine the public's understanding of critical issues.
- Selective Storytelling: Selective storytelling refers to the deliberate choice of which stories or aspects of a story to highlight or omit in media reporting. This editorial decision-making can significantly influence public sentiment and opinions. When certain information is omitted or downplayed, it may create a biased or one-sided narrative that skews the audience's understanding of events. Selective storytelling can be influenced by various factors, such as media bias, ideological preferences, or commercial interests. It can lead to an incomplete or distorted perception of events and issues, hindering the public's ability to make well-informed decisions.

In summary, sensationalism and clickbait aim to capture attention through emotional appeals, often at the expense of accuracy and context. False equivalency misrepresents differing viewpoints as equally valid, undermining public understanding of complex issues. Selective storytelling influences public sentiment by shaping the narrative around chosen elements of a story while omitting others. Recognizing these manipulative tactics is essential for media consumers to approach information critically, seek multiple perspectives, and cultivate media literacy skills to navigate the ever-evolving media landscape responsibly.

Media Literacy and Responsible Consumption

To safeguard against media manipulation, developing media literacy and adopting responsible consumption practices is essential. In this section, we explore strategies to become media-savvy individuals.

- Fact-Checking and Verification: Fact-checking and verification are essential practices in media literacy that involve independently confirming the accuracy and reliability of information before accepting it as true. In today's digital age, information spreads rapidly through various media channels, making it crucial to verify the authenticity of claims, statistics, and news stories. Fact-checking involves cross-referencing information with credible sources, examining evidence, and evaluating the credibility of the authors or organizations behind the information. By engaging in fact-checking, individuals can avoid spreading misinformation and make well-informed decisions based on reliable information.

- Critical Thinking: Critical thinking is the ability to objectively analyze and evaluate information, arguments, and claims presented in media content. It involves questioning assumptions, biases, and logical fallacies that may be present in the information. Critical thinkers seek evidence, consider different viewpoints, and assess the credibility and expertise of the sources. By cultivating critical thinking skills, individuals become better equipped to discern credible information from biased or misleading content. They can also identify manipulative tactics, such as emotional appeals, false equivalencies, and selective storytelling, which may attempt to sway opinions without presenting sound evidence.
- Diverse Media Sources: Accessing diverse media sources is crucial to gaining a comprehensive understanding of events and perspectives. Consuming content from a variety of reputable news outlets with different political leanings, geographical locations, and cultural backgrounds helps individuals avoid echo chambers and filter bubbles, where they only encounter information that aligns with their preexisting beliefs. Exposure to diverse viewpoints promotes open-mindedness, empathy, and a more balanced worldview. It allows individuals to see the complexities of various issues and fosters a deeper understanding of the broader social, political, and economic landscape.

In summary, fact-checking and verification are vital for ensuring the accuracy of information. Critical thinking enables individuals to analyze media content objectively, identify biases, and recognize manipulative tactics. Emphasizing the importance of diverse media sources encourages people to seek a well-rounded perspective on events and issues. By combining these practices, individuals can become more discerning and responsible media consumers, contributing to a more informed and engaged society.

Conclusion

Media manipulation and propaganda present society with vulnerabilities that can sway public opinion and influence the course of history. By understanding the role of media in shaping public perceptions, identifying biased and manipulative content, and promoting media literacy and responsible consumption, we safeguard against misinformation and deceit. Together, we foster a community that values critical thinking, open-mindedness, and discernment, creating a society where truth and accurate information are celebrated. As we navigate the media landscape with awareness and responsibility, we contribute to a world where information is a catalyst for progress and understanding, paving the way for an informed and enlightened society.

CHAPTER 32

POLITICAL MANIPULATION AND POPULISM

The Perils of Populism: Unmasking Political Manipulation and Preserving Democratic Values

Introduction

Examining the dangers of political manipulation and its connection to the rise of populism. This chapter delves into the tactics employed in political manipulation, explores the appeal of populism, and emphasizes the importance of preserving democratic values in the face of manipulative influences.

Understanding Political Manipulation Tactics

Political manipulation involves the strategic use of tactics to influence public opinion and behavior for political gain. In this section, we explore the various tactics used in political manipulation.

- Fear-Mongering: Fear-mongering is a manipulative tactic used to evoke fear and anxiety in individuals or the general public, often with the aim of influencing their sentiments and decision-making. This strategy is frequently employed in various contexts, such as political campaigns, advertising, and media, to create a sense of urgency or threat that compels people to act in a specific way. By triggering fear, manipulators can sway public opinion, garner support for certain policies or candidates, and even drive consumer behavior. Recognizing fear-mongering is crucial for media literacy, as it allows individuals to approach fear-inducing messages with critical thinking and emotional resilience, ensuring they are not unduly influenced by exaggerated or unfounded fears.
- Disinformation and Fake News: Disinformation refers to the deliberate spread of false or misleading information with the intent of deceiving the public. Fake news, a subset of disinformation, includes fabricated stories presented as factual news to mislead readers or viewers. Disinformation and fake news can have a significant impact on political discourse, public opinion, and social cohesion. When false information

circulates widely, it can lead to confusion, polarization, and erosion of trust in credible sources. Media consumers must be vigilant in fact-checking and verifying the authenticity of news stories before sharing or accepting them as accurate. This critical practice not only safeguards individuals from misinformation but also helps maintain the integrity of public discourse and democratic processes.

- Polarization and Divisiveness: In the realm of politics, polarization refers to the increasing ideological divide between different groups or individuals. Manipulative politicians may exploit this polarization by emphasizing divisions and promoting an "us versus them" mentality to consolidate support within their base. By perpetuating hostility and exacerbating differences, these politicians create an atmosphere of divisiveness that can hinder constructive dialogue and compromise. The result is often a fractured society, where people become entrenched in their beliefs and are less receptive to opposing viewpoints. Recognizing this manipulation tactic empowers individuals to seek common ground and foster a more cohesive and inclusive society.

In summary, understanding fear-mongering helps individuals resist being swayed by emotionally charged messages. Being aware of disinformation and fake news enables media consumers to uphold the credibility of information and preserve trust in reliable sources. Recognizing the effects of polarization and divisiveness empowers people to foster constructive dialogue and promote unity in their communities and political discourse. These practices collectively contribute to a more informed and engaged citizenry, capable of navigating the complexities of the media landscape and making well-informed decisions.

The Rise of Populism and Its Appeal

Populism is a political ideology that seeks to appeal to the interests and emotions of ordinary people. In this section, we explore the rise of populism and its appeal to a broad audience.

- Economic Anxiety: Economic anxiety refers to the feelings of uncertainty and insecurity individuals experience about their financial well-being. When people face economic hardships, such as job loss, stagnant wages, or rising costs of living, they may become susceptible to the appeal of populist leaders. Populist leaders often capitalize on these anxieties, promising to address economic concerns and uplift the working class. By offering seemingly simple solutions to complex economic problems, they create a sense of hope and empowerment among those who feel economically marginalized. Understanding the link between economic anxiety and the attraction to populist leaders is crucial for policymakers and politicians to address the root causes of these anxieties and build policies that promote economic stability and inclusive growth.

- Simple Solutions: Populist leaders often present straightforward solutions to multifaceted and intricate issues, resonating with those who feel overwhelmed or disillusioned by mainstream politics. The allure of simple solutions lies in their apparent ease of implementation and directness. However, in reality, complex problems rarely have simple fixes. Simplistic approaches can lead to unintended consequences and fail to address the underlying complexities of issues. Recognizing the appeal of simple solutions offered by populist leaders helps individuals critically evaluate proposed policies and demand evidence-based approaches to governance that tackle problems comprehensively.
- Anti-Establishment Sentiment: Populist movements often thrive on anti-establishment sentiment, capitalizing on public dissatisfaction with traditional political elites and institutions. Citizens who feel disconnected or disillusioned with the existing political order may be drawn to the promise of change offered by populist leaders. These leaders position themselves as outsiders who will challenge the status quo and bring about a new era of governance. However, the rejection of established institutions can also lead to destabilizing political environments and undermine democratic norms. Acknowledging the potency of anti-establishment sentiment allows societies to address the legitimate concerns driving these sentiments while also safeguarding the principles of democratic governance and institutions.

In summary, understanding economic anxiety sheds light on the factors that make populist leaders appealing to certain segments of the population. Recognizing the allure of simple solutions helps individuals engage critically with proposed policies and demand comprehensive approaches to address complex challenges. Being aware of the strength of anti-establishment sentiment enables societies to address legitimate grievances while safeguarding democratic institutions. By understanding these dynamics, policymakers, and citizens can work together to foster inclusive governance that addresses the root causes of economic anxieties and builds a resilient and inclusive political landscape.

Preserving Democratic Values Against Manipulation

The rise of populism and political manipulation poses a threat to democratic values and institutions. In this section, we examine the importance of preserving democratic principles and resisting manipulation.

- Strengthening Media Freedom: Media freedom is a fundamental pillar of democracy, as it allows for the free flow of information, diverse perspectives, and open debate. When media outlets are independent and free from government interference or control, they can play a crucial role in holding politicians accountable. They can investigate and report on government actions, policies, and decisions, ensuring transparency and providing citizens with essential information to make informed choices. Additionally, robust and independent media acts as a check against misinformation and disinformation, promoting fact-checking and accuracy in reporting. Advocating for media freedom is essential to safeguarding democratic principles and ensuring the public's right to access unbiased and reliable information.
- Political Education: Political education empowers citizens with the knowledge and skills to critically assess political rhetoric, policies, and candidates. When citizens are well-informed about the political process, they can make educated decisions during elections and engage in informed discussions about public issues. Political education helps individuals recognize manipulative tactics, such as fear-mongering or misleading statistics and encourages them to seek objective sources of information. It fosters a culture of critical thinking, where citizens are encouraged to question assumptions, evaluate evidence, and engage in civil discourse. By promoting political education, societies can nurture an informed and active citizenry that actively participates in shaping the direction of their communities and countries.
- Engaged Citizenship: Encouraging engaged citizenship involves motivating individuals to take an active role in democratic processes and decision-making. This includes voting in elections, participating in community initiatives, attending public meetings, and voicing opinions to elected representatives. Engaged citizens stay informed about current events, seek diverse perspectives, and actively contribute to public discussions. They recognize their collective power to influence change and advocate for policies that align with their values and priorities. Engaged citizenship

strengthens democracy by ensuring that the government remains accountable to the people it serves and that policies reflect the needs and aspirations of the broader population.

In summary, advocating for media freedom is crucial to maintaining an open and transparent democratic society, as it ensures access to unbiased information and helps counter misinformation. Political education equips citizens with the critical thinking skills to navigate complex political landscapes and make informed decisions. Encouraging engaged citizenship fosters an active and participatory democracy, where citizens are empowered to shape the future of their communities and countries. Together, these pillars contribute to the strength and resilience of democratic governance, promoting inclusive decision-making and safeguarding the rights and interests of all citizens.

Conclusion

Political manipulation and the rise of populism challenge the foundation of democratic values and institutions. By understanding the tactics of political manipulation, recognizing the appeal of populism, and prioritizing the preservation of democratic principles, we fortify the resilience of our democratic systems. Together, we foster a community that values critical thinking, informed decision-making, and democratic participation, creating a society where the voices of the people are heard and the power of manipulation is diminished. As we safeguard against political manipulation and uphold democratic values, we contribute to a world where transparency, integrity, and fairness prevail, paving the way for a stronger and more vibrant democracy.

CHAPTER 33

EXPLOITATION OF FEAR AND ANXIETY

The Shadow of Manipulation: Unraveling Fear and Anxiety-Based Tactics

Introduction

The unsettling world of fear and anxiety-based manipulation examines how emotions are exploited, particularly in times of crisis. This chapter explores the impact of fear-mongering on society and advocates for cultivating resilience in the face of manipulation.

Manipulating Emotions in Times of Crisis

In times of crisis, emotions run high, making individuals more susceptible to manipulation. In this section, we explore how fear and anxiety are tactically exploited during times of uncertainty and distress.

- Amplifying Threats: Fear-mongering is a manipulative strategy used by certain individuals or groups to exploit emotions and create a heightened sense of fear and anxiety among the public. By exaggerating or sensationalizing potential threats, fear-mongers aim to trigger strong emotional reactions, which can lead to impulsive decision-making and a willingness to follow their proposed solutions. This tactic is commonly employed in various contexts, such as in politics, media, and advertising, to influence public sentiment and garner support for specific agendas. By revealing how fear-mongers amplify threats, we can develop a greater awareness of when emotional manipulation is at play, enabling us to critically assess information and make more rational and informed decisions.
- The Illusion of Control: Manipulation tactics often prey on individuals' desire for control, particularly in times of uncertainty or chaos. By offering seemingly straightforward solutions or promises of restoring stability, manipulators create an illusion of control, leading people to believe that by following them, they can protect themselves from perceived threats. This illusion can be especially compelling during times of crisis or social unrest when individuals may feel

vulnerable or uncertain about the future. Understanding how the illusion of control operates allows us to recognize when we are being manipulated by false assurances and encourages us to seek more comprehensive and evidence-based approaches to address complex challenges.

- Emotional Contagion: Emotional contagion refers to the spread of emotions, such as fear and anxiety, from one individual to others within a social group or community. Fear-mongers capitalize on emotional contagion by strategically disseminating alarming information or narratives through various channels, including social media and traditional media outlets. As fear spreads rapidly and infectiously, it can influence public perceptions, behaviors, and decision-making. By analyzing how emotional contagion operates, we can become more discerning consumers of information, recognizing when emotional reactions are being manipulated and taking steps to verify and contextualize the information we receive. Additionally, fostering emotional resilience and self-awareness can help mitigate the effects of emotional contagion, allowing us to make more balanced and rational choices.

In summary, by thoroughly examining each aspect of fear-mongering, including the amplification of threats, the illusion of control, and emotional contagion, we can become more adept at recognizing and resisting manipulative tactics. This awareness empowers us to think critically, question information presented to us, and make decisions based on evidence, reason, and empathy. Moreover, it helps us cultivate emotional resilience and fortitude, enabling us to navigate challenging times with greater clarity and agency. By promoting informed and thoughtful responses to fear-mongering, we can contribute to a more informed and resilient society that values truth, compassion, and a commitment to the common good.

Fear-Mongering and Its Impact on Society

Fear-mongering can have far-reaching consequences on society's collective psyche and decision-making. In this section, we examine the impact of fear-based manipulation.

- Division and Polarization: Fear-mongering can have a profound impact on communities and societies by exacerbating existing divisions and polarizing different groups. When fear is strategically amplified, it can lead individuals to adopt more extreme and rigid positions, making it challenging to find common ground or engage in productive dialogue. Fear-driven narratives often target specific demographics or ideologies, portraying them as threats or enemies, which can further deepen societal divisions. As people become emotionally charged and driven by fear, it becomes increasingly difficult to foster empathy and understanding among opposing viewpoints. Consequently, fear-mongering can fracture social cohesion, hamper cooperation, and hinder progress towards collective solutions to shared challenges.

- Erosion of Trust: Fear-based tactics employed by manipulators can erode trust in institutions and leadership. When individuals are repeatedly exposed to fear-inducing messages or misleading information, they may develop skepticism and doubt towards sources of authority. This erosion of trust can have severe consequences, leading to a lack of confidence in public institutions, media, and elected officials. Moreover, when people feel betrayed or misled, they may become disengaged from civic processes, further undermining the functioning of democratic societies. Recognizing the impact of fear-mongering on trust allows us to be more discerning consumers of information and encourages us to seek reliable and verifiable sources.
- Paralysis and Inaction: Fear can trigger a "fight or flight" response, and in some cases, it may lead to a state of paralysis and inaction. When individuals are overwhelmed by fear, they may become immobilized, unable to take decisive action or make informed decisions. Fear-mongering can exploit this psychological response by presenting complex issues as insurmountable threats, leaving people feeling powerless and discouraged from engaging in meaningful problem-solving. Consequently, fear can hinder collective efforts to address societal challenges, perpetuating a sense of helplessness and despair. By understanding how fear can lead to paralysis, we can work towards fostering resilience and empowerment, encouraging active participation in finding constructive solutions.

In summary, fear-mongering is a manipulative tactic that can have far-reaching consequences on individuals and societies. By exploring the effects of fear-mongering, such as division and polarization, erosion of trust, and paralysis and inaction, we can cultivate greater awareness and agency. This awareness enables us to recognize when fear-based tactics are being used to manipulate public sentiment and empower us to respond with critical thinking, empathy, and constructive action. By fostering open dialogue, promoting media literacy, and nurturing a sense of community, we can work towards building a society that values understanding, cooperation, and resilience in the face of fear-based manipulation.

Cultivating Resilience in the Face of Fear-Based Manipulation

Cultivating resilience is crucial in protecting ourselves from fear-based manipulation. In this section, we explore strategies to build resilience against fear and anxiety-based tactics.

- Media Literacy and Critical Thinking: Media literacy involves developing the ability to analyze, evaluate, and critically interpret media content. By promoting media literacy, individuals become more discerning consumers of information, enabling them to distinguish between reliable and unreliable sources. Critical thinking complements media literacy by encouraging individuals to question, analyze, and challenge the information presented to them. Through critical thinking, people can identify biases, misinformation, and propaganda, reducing their susceptibility to manipulation. Understanding the importance of media literacy and critical thinking empowers individuals to make informed decisions and participate in democratic processes with greater discernment.
- Emotional Intelligence and Self-Awareness: Emotional intelligence refers to the capacity to recognize, understand, and manage one's emotions and the emotions of others. Self-awareness is a fundamental component of emotional intelligence, allowing individuals to reflect on their emotional responses and triggers. By emphasizing emotional intelligence and self-awareness, people can better regulate their emotions, making them less susceptible to fear-based manipulation. Recognizing emotions and understanding their origins helps individuals maintain a rational perspective, preventing emotional hijacking by manipulative tactics. Emotional intelligence also enables individuals to identify and address emotional vulnerabilities that manipulators might exploit.
- Community Solidarity: Encouraging community support and solidarity is vital in countering fear-based manipulation. When people come together as a collective, they are better equipped to challenge manipulative narratives and address shared concerns. Community solidarity provides a sense of belonging, reducing feelings of isolation and vulnerability that manipulators often exploit. It fosters open dialogue and cooperation, encouraging diverse perspectives and collaborative problem-solving. By building strong community bonds, individuals can collectively resist fear-mongering tactics and work towards a more cohesive and resilient society.

In summary, media literacy and critical thinking empower individuals to be more discerning consumers of information, reducing susceptibility to misinformation and propaganda. Emotional intelligence and self-awareness enable individuals to regulate emotions and recognize manipulation attempts, enhancing their ability to make rational decisions. Community solidarity fosters a sense of belonging and cooperation, providing a supportive environment to counter fear-based manipulation. By promoting these qualities and skills, we can cultivate a more informed, resilient, and united society that is less vulnerable to manipulation and fear-based tactics.

Conclusion

The exploitation of fear and anxiety in manipulation casts a shadow on society, influencing decision-making and eroding trust. By understanding the tactics of fear-mongering, recognizing its impact on society, and cultivating resilience, we empower ourselves and our communities to resist manipulation and preserve our emotional well-being. Together, we foster a community that values emotional intelligence, critical thinking, and unity, creating a society where fear-based manipulation finds little foothold. As we rise above the shadows of manipulation with resilience and discernment, we contribute to a world where empathy, trust, and rationality prevail, paving the way for a more emotionally resilient and compassionate society.

CHAPTER 34

WORKPLACE MANIPULATION AND TOXIC ENVIRONMENTS

Navigating the Labyrinth: Unraveling Workplace Manipulation and Cultivating a Healthy Environment

Introduction

The complex world of workplace manipulation and toxic environments is where manipulative dynamics can significantly impact employees' well-being and productivity. This chapter explores the tactics of workplace manipulation, offers strategies to deal with toxic coworkers and superiors, and emphasizes the importance of creating a healthy work environment.

Manipulative Dynamics in the Workplace

Workplaces can harbor manipulative dynamics that erode trust, create hostility, and hinder professional growth. In this section, we explore various manipulative tactics that can manifest in the workplace.

- Office Politics: Office politics refers to the complex social dynamics and power struggles that occur in the workplace. It involves the informal alliances, rivalries, and manipulative behaviors that employees engage in to gain influence, recognition, or advancement. While some level of office politics is inevitable in any organization, it can become toxic when it undermines collaboration and teamwork. Employees may prioritize personal gains over the collective goals of the organization, leading to a breakdown in communication and trust. Recognizing the existence and potential consequences of office politics is essential for fostering a healthy and productive work environment.
- Gaslighting in the Workplace: Gaslighting is a manipulative tactic used by some individuals to make others doubt their perceptions, memories, or sanity. In the workplace, gaslighting can be particularly insidious, as it can lead to self-doubt and confusion among employees. Gaslighters may undermine their colleagues' confidence, create false narratives, or discredit their ideas to maintain control or gain an advantage. The psychological impact of gaslighting

996awards, or rewards. Genuine appreciation shows employees that their efforts are recognized and valued by their peers and leaders. It creates a culture of positivity and encourages employees to continue performing at their best. When employees feel appreciated, they are more likely to be engaged in their work and have a higher level of job satisfaction, leading to increased productivity and reduced turnover.

- Conflict Resolution: Conflict is a natural part of any workplace, as employees may have different perspectives, preferences, or goals. Effective conflict resolution involves addressing workplace issues in a constructive and respectful manner. It includes active listening, understanding each party's viewpoint, and finding common ground. It is essential to approach conflicts with a focus on finding solutions rather than assigning blame. Conflict resolution strategies may involve mediation, facilitated discussions, or collaboration to find win-win solutions. Resolving conflicts in a healthy and timely manner prevents issues from escalating and negatively impacting team dynamics. It also promotes a culture of open communication and trust, where employees feel safe expressing concerns and working together to overcome challenges.

Conclusion

Workplace manipulation and toxic environments can have detrimental effects on employees' mental health and job satisfaction. By understanding the dynamics of workplace manipulation, developing strategies to deal with toxic coworkers and superiors, and prioritizing the creation of a healthy work environment, we empower ourselves to navigate the labyrinth of workplace challenges with resilience and professionalism. Together, we foster a community that values transparency, empathy, and collaboration, creating workplaces where employees feel supported, appreciated, and motivated to thrive. As we strive for healthy work environments with integrity and respect, we contribute to a world where workplaces become nurturing spaces for personal growth and professional success.

CHAPTER 35

CYBER MANIPULATION AND ONLINE SCAMS

Unmasking the Virtual Intrigue: Safeguarding Against Cyber Manipulation and Online Scams

Introduction

The world of cyber manipulation and online scams is where individuals fall victim to cunning social engineering tactics in the digital realm. This chapter sheds light on the tactics employed by cyber manipulators, offers strategies to protect oneself from online scams and fraud, and emphasizes the importance of cybersecurity and digital self-defense.

Cyber Manipulation and Social Engineering

Cyber manipulation and social engineering target the vulnerabilities of individuals in the virtual world. In this section, we explore the tactics used by cyber manipulators to deceive and exploit.

- Phishing Attacks: Phishing attacks are deceptive tactics used by cybercriminals to trick individuals into divulging sensitive information, such as login credentials, credit card details, or personal data. These attacks typically occur through emails, messages, or websites that appear to be from legitimate sources. Cybercriminals often use persuasive language and urgency to create a sense of urgency and fear, prompting the recipient to take immediate action. For example, they may claim that the recipient's account has been compromised and that they need to verify their information urgently. Unsuspecting individuals who fall victim to phishing attacks may unknowingly provide their sensitive information, which can lead to identity theft, financial loss, or other cybercrimes. Recognizing the signs of phishing attacks, such as suspicious email addresses, spelling errors, and urgent requests for personal information, is crucial to protecting oneself from such scams.
- Social Media Manipulation: Cyber manipulators leverage social media platforms to gather personal data and influence individuals' behavior. They may use tactics like creating fake accounts, posing as trustworthy

entities, or using psychological techniques to exploit users' vulnerabilities. By analyzing the content individuals engage with, cyber manipulators can gain insights into their preferences, interests, and beliefs. Armed with this information, they can tailor targeted content, advertisements, or misinformation to manipulate users' perceptions and decision-making. For instance, they may use divisive content to provoke emotional reactions and polarize communities. Raising awareness about social media manipulation, being cautious about sharing personal information online, and fact-checking information before sharing or acting upon it can help mitigate the risks associated with this type of cyber manipulation.

- Identity Theft: Identity theft involves stealing personal information, such as Social Security numbers, financial data, or personal documents, with the intent to impersonate an individual and commit fraudulent activities. Cybercriminals employ various methods to perpetrate identity theft, including hacking into databases, phishing for sensitive information, or using malware to capture keystrokes. Once they have acquired an individual's personal data, they can open fraudulent accounts, make unauthorized transactions, or commit other crimes in the victim's name. Preventing identity theft requires safeguarding personal information, using strong and unique passwords, regularly monitoring financial accounts, and being cautious about sharing sensitive data. It is also essential to promptly report any suspicious activities or signs of identity theft to relevant authorities to mitigate potential damages and protect one's identity.

Protecting Yourself from Online Scams and Fraud

To safeguard against online scams and fraud, individuals must be vigilant and informed. In this section, we explore strategies to protect oneself from falling victim to cyber manipulations.

- Cyber Awareness: Cyber awareness involves educating individuals about common online scams and tactics used by cyber manipulators to deceive and exploit unsuspecting internet users. By raising awareness, individuals can become more vigilant and informed about potential threats, enabling them to recognize and avoid falling victim to cyber manipulation. Some common cyber manipulations include phishing attacks, social engineering, and identity theft. Cyber awareness initiatives may include workshops, training programs, and educational materials that highlight the red flags and warning signs of cyber manipulation, as well as best practices for online safety.

- Verification and Authentication: Verifying and authenticating online requests and messages is a crucial step in protecting oneself from cyber manipulation. Cyber manipulators often use deceptive techniques to create the illusion of legitimacy, such as crafting emails that appear to be from trusted organizations or individuals. To counter this, individuals should always verify the authenticity of requests before providing sensitive information or taking any action. This can be done by independently contacting the supposed sender through official channels or using multi-factor authentication methods to ensure secure access to online accounts. By adopting verification and authentication measures, individuals can reduce the risk of falling prey to phishing attempts and other cyber manipulations.
- Privacy Settings and Data Protection: Strengthening privacy settings and practicing data protection is essential in safeguarding personal information and preventing data breaches. Cyber manipulators may use social media platforms or other online channels to gather personal data and use it for malicious purposes. By adjusting privacy settings on social media accounts and other online platforms, individuals can limit the amount of personal information visible to the public and reduce the chances of unauthorized access. Additionally, practicing data protection involves implementing strong and unique passwords, regularly updating software and applications, and being cautious about sharing sensitive information online. Taking these proactive measures can help individuals protect their personal data and minimize the risk of falling victim to cyber manipulation and identity theft.

Cybersecurity and Digital Self-Defense

Cybersecurity plays a vital role in defending against cyber manipulations and online scams. In this section, we emphasize the significance of digital self-defense.

- Antivirus and Firewall Protection: Antivirus and firewall protection are fundamental cybersecurity measures that aim to defend computer systems and networks against malicious software (malware) and cyber threats. Antivirus software scans and detects potential threats, such as viruses, worms, and trojans, on a computer or network, and removes or quarantines them to prevent damage. Firewalls act as a barrier between a trusted internal network and external networks (like the Internet) to control incoming and outgoing traffic and block unauthorized access to sensitive data. By implementing robust antivirus and firewall protection, individuals and organizations can significantly reduce the risk of cyberattacks and unauthorized access to their systems and data.

- Two-Factor Authentication: Two-factor authentication (2FA) is an additional layer of security that requires users to provide two forms of identification before gaining access to an account or system. Typically, this involves something the user knows (like a password) and something they have (like a smartphone for receiving a unique code). 2FA adds an extra level of protection against cyber manipulators who may have obtained or guessed a user's password. Even if the password is compromised, the second authentication factor acts as a barrier to prevent unauthorized access. By using 2FA, individuals can significantly enhance their account security and protect sensitive information from being exploited by cyber manipulators.
- Continuous Education: Cyber threats are constantly evolving, with new tactics and techniques emerging regularly. Continuous education and staying updated on the latest cybersecurity threats and protection measures are crucial in maintaining a robust defense against cyber manipulators. Cybersecurity awareness training and education programs provide individuals with the knowledge and skills needed to identify potential threats, avoid common pitfalls, and respond appropriately to suspicious activities. Moreover, staying informed about the latest cybersecurity trends and best practices empowers individuals to adapt their protection strategies to new and emerging threats. Continuous education is a vital component of a proactive approach to cybersecurity, ensuring that individuals are well-equipped to defend themselves and their organizations against cyber manipulations and cyberattacks.

Conclusion

Cyber manipulation and online scams pose significant risks in the digital age. By understanding the tactics of cyber manipulators, adopting protective strategies against online scams and fraud, and prioritizing cybersecurity and digital self-defense, we empower ourselves to navigate the virtual realm with resilience and vigilance. Together, we foster a community that values cyber awareness, data protection, and online safety, creating a digital landscape where individuals can confidently interact and transact without fear of manipulation or exploitation. As we fortify our digital defenses and promote a culture of cybersecurity, we contribute to a world where the virtual space becomes a secure and trustworthy environment for all users.

PART VII: UNCONVENTIONAL MINDS

CHAPTER 36

GENIUS AND PSYCHOPATHY

Unraveling the Paradox: Exploring the Nexus between Genius and Psychopathy

Introduction

The enigmatic realm of unconventional minds is where exceptional talent can sometimes be associated with unconventional traits. This chapter unravels the intricate connection between genius and psychopathy, shedding light on the dark side of exceptional talent and the importance of balancing creativity with mental well-being.

The Association between Genius and Psychopathy

Throughout history, there have been instances where genius and psychopathy have been linked. In this section, we explore the intriguing association between extraordinary talent and unconventional mental traits.

- Cognitive Empathy and Cold Rationality: Cognitive empathy refers to the ability to understand and perceive the emotions and perspectives of others without necessarily sharing or experiencing those emotions. Some geniuses may exhibit high levels of cognitive empathy, allowing them to analyze situations objectively and from multiple viewpoints. This capacity for cognitive empathy can be beneficial in problem-solving and decision-making, as it enables them to consider various factors and make rational, well-informed choices. However, these individuals may struggle with emotional empathy, which involves emotionally connecting and resonating with others' feelings. As a result, their decisions and actions may be perceived as lacking in warmth or emotional understanding, leading to potential challenges in interpersonal relationships.
- Risk-Taking and Rule-Breaking: Certain geniuses may demonstrate a penchant for risk-taking and a willingness to challenge established norms and conventions. This propensity can be linked to their ability to think outside the box and explore unconventional ideas. By taking risks and questioning

traditional boundaries, these individuals may push the boundaries of knowledge and innovation, leading to groundbreaking discoveries and advancements. However, risk-taking can also expose them to failures and setbacks, as not all unconventional ideas may prove successful. Additionally, their propensity for rule-breaking may sometimes lead to conflicts with established authorities or societal expectations.

- Unconventional Thinking: Unconventional thinking patterns are often associated with both genius and psychopathic tendencies. Geniuses often possess the ability to think creatively and divergently, considering ideas and connections that others might overlook. This unconventional thinking allows them to explore uncharted territories and develop novel solutions to complex problems. On the other hand, psychopaths may also exhibit unconventional thinking, but their motivations are driven by self-interest and a disregard for moral or ethical considerations.
- It is important to note that while unconventional thinking is a common trait among geniuses, not all geniuses exhibit psychopathic tendencies. Genius is generally associated with extraordinary intellectual abilities and creative insights that lead to positive contributions to society, while psychopathy involves harmful and manipulative behaviors that disregard the well-being of others. Unconventional thinking in geniuses often stems from curiosity, a desire to challenge the status quo, and a genuine interest in problem-solving and innovation. In contrast, psychopathic tendencies involve manipulative and exploitative behavior, often motivated by personal gain and a lack of empathy for others.

In summary, the combination of cognitive empathy, cold rationality, risk-taking, and unconventional thinking can shape the behavior and contributions of geniuses in society. While these traits can lead to remarkable achievements and innovations, it is essential to differentiate them from harmful and manipulative behaviors associated with psychopathy. Understanding and appreciating these nuances can help us better grasp the complexities of genius and its impact on various aspects of human life.

The Dark Side of Exceptional Talent

While exceptional talent can be awe-inspiring, it may come with a dark side that warrants scrutiny. In this section, we delve into the potential negative aspects of exceptional talent.

- Unstable Relationships: The unconventional minds of geniuses, while instrumental in their creative and intellectual pursuits, can present challenges in forming and maintaining stable relationships. Their unique thought patterns and intense focus on their work may lead them to prioritize their passions over interpersonal connections. As a result, they may struggle to relate to others on a more conventional level, leading to feelings of isolation or difficulty in understanding and empathizing with the emotions and needs of their loved ones. Additionally, the intensity and single-mindedness of their pursuits may leave little room for nurturing and sustaining relationships, resulting in a higher likelihood of unstable or short-lived connections.
- Self-Destructive Behaviors: The unconventional thinking of geniuses can make them susceptible to self-destructive behaviors and impulses. The relentless pursuit of their ideas and goals may lead them to neglect self-care or engage in risky behaviors without fully considering the consequences. Their ability to see beyond conventional boundaries might also incline them towards experimentation or exploration which can be detrimental to their well-being. Moreover, the burden of their exceptional abilities and the pressure to continuously innovate can lead to stress and mental health challenges, further contributing to self-destructive tendencies.
- Ethical Boundaries: Unconventional thinking can sometimes blur ethical boundaries for geniuses. Their relentless pursuit of knowledge and innovation might lead them to question societal norms and rules, potentially challenging existing ethical frameworks. While this can be beneficial in promoting progress and questioning outdated practices, it also raises concerns about the potential consequences of pushing ethical boundaries too far. Some geniuses might justify their actions or ideas based on the greater good they believe they are serving, but this could lead to unintended negative consequences or ethical dilemmas.
- Understanding these aspects of unconventional thinking among geniuses is crucial for appreciating the complexities of their contributions to society. While their exceptional abilities and unconventional perspectives drive groundbreaking discoveries and advancements, they can also pose challenges in forming meaningful relationships and adhering to ethical standards. Encouraging a supportive environment that addresses their unique needs while promoting self-awareness, emotional well-being, and ethical considerations can help geniuses channel their brilliance in positive and constructive ways. It is important to celebrate their achievements while also recognizing and supporting their personal growth and interpersonal connections.

Balancing Creativity and Mental Well-Being

Nurturing exceptional talent while safeguarding mental well-being is crucial for the holistic development of unconventional minds. In this section, we explore strategies to strike a balance between creativity and mental health.

- Emotional Self-Awareness: Emotional self-awareness is a critical skill for geniuses as it enables them to understand and manage the unique emotional challenges that often accompany exceptional talent. While their brilliance and unconventional thinking bring about groundbreaking ideas and innovations, they may also experience heightened emotional intensity and sensitivity. The pressure to continuously excel and the burden of expectations can lead to stress, anxiety, and feelings of isolation. By promoting emotional self-awareness, geniuses can recognize and acknowledge their emotions, identify triggers, and develop coping mechanisms to navigate the emotional complexities that arise from their exceptional abilities.
- Supportive Environments: Creating and fostering supportive environments is crucial for geniuses to thrive without compromising their well-being. Traditional education systems or workplaces may not always be equipped to accommodate their unconventional thinking and unique needs. Providing an environment that encourages exploration, creative expression, and intellectual freedom can help geniuses unleash their full potential. A supportive environment should also promote work-life balance, understanding that geniuses may be deeply invested in their work and need spaces to recharge and nurture their emotional well-being. By surrounding geniuses with mentors, peers, and institutions that appreciate their exceptional talents and offer appropriate support, they can flourish both professionally and personally.
- Seeking Professional Help: Encouraging geniuses to seek professional help and support for their mental health concerns is essential. The pressure and demands of their exceptional abilities can take a toll on their mental well-being. Some geniuses might hesitate to seek help, fearing that it could be seen as a sign of weakness or vulnerability. However, providing them with a safe and non-judgmental space to discuss their emotions and experiences can be transformative. Mental health professionals experienced in working with gifted individuals can offer specialized support tailored to their unique needs. Addressing mental health challenges early on can lead to better overall well-being and prevent potential burnout or emotional crises.

- Recognizing the importance of emotional self-awareness, supportive environments, and seeking professional help for geniuses is crucial in nurturing their exceptional talents and potential contributions to society. By promoting emotional well-being alongside intellectual development, we can ensure that geniuses can thrive in their pursuits without sacrificing their mental and emotional health. By embracing a holistic approach that addresses the emotional complexities of exceptional talent, we can create a more inclusive and supportive world for geniuses to flourish.

Conclusion

The nexus between genius and psychopathy presents a paradoxical dimension of human nature. By exploring the association between exceptional talent and unconventional traits, recognizing the dark side of genius, and prioritizing the balance between creativity and mental well-being, we empower unconventional minds to reach their fullest potential. Together, we foster a community that values the nurturing of talent while prioritizing mental health and emotional well-being. As we nurture and support unconventional minds, we contribute to a world where genius is celebrated, creativity flourishes, and mental well-being is prioritized, creating a society that cherishes both the brilliance and the humanity of exceptional individuals.

CHAPTER 37

CULTIVATING EMPATHY IN A MANIPULATIVE WORLD

The Compassionate Revolt: Empathy as an Antidote to Manipulation

Introduction

We explore the transformative power of empathy as a potent antidote to manipulation in a world often fraught with deceit. This chapter highlights the importance of cultivating empathy, fostering empathetic relationships and connections, and embracing collective empathy to counteract the influences of manipulation.

Empathy as an Antidote to Manipulation

Empathy acts as a powerful shield against manipulation, as it allows individuals to understand and connect with others on a deeper level. In this section, we explore how empathy can counteract manipulation.

- Emotional Resonance: Emotional resonance refers to the deep connection and understanding we experience when we empathize with others' emotions. Empathy enables us to put ourselves in someone else's shoes, sharing in their joys, sorrows, and struggles. This emotional connection is powerful, as it allows us to relate to and support others on a profound level. When we have emotional resonance with someone, we become more attuned to their feelings and experiences, making it difficult for manipulators to exploit us emotionally. By recognizing and understanding the emotions of others, we can better protect ourselves from emotional manipulation.

- Recognizing Vulnerabilities: Empathy helps us recognize vulnerabilities in others, such as their insecurities, fears, and needs. When we empathize with someone, we become more perceptive to their emotional state and can identify when they might be in a vulnerable position. Manipulators often prey on these vulnerabilities to exert control and influence over their targets. By recognizing vulnerabilities, we can be more cautious and vigilant in our interactions, ensuring that we do not fall victim to manipulation.

- Empathy and Critical Thinking: Contrary to a common misconception, cultivating empathy does not hinder critical thinking; in fact, it enhances our ability to discern authentic emotions from manipulative tactics. When we empathize with others, we develop a deeper understanding of their emotional experiences. This heightened emotional intelligence allows us to differentiate between genuine expressions of emotions and calculated manipulations. Empathy helps us consider the context, motivations, and intentions behind others' behaviors, enabling us to think critically and make informed judgments about the situation. In essence, empathy serves as a complement to critical thinking, empowering us to navigate social interactions more effectively and avoid falling prey to emotional manipulation.

In summary, emotional resonance facilitated by empathy plays a vital role in protecting ourselves from emotional manipulation. By understanding and connecting with others on an emotional level, we can better identify potential manipulation attempts and safeguard our emotional well-being. Moreover, empathy empowers us to recognize vulnerabilities in others and enhances our critical thinking skills, allowing us to discern authentic emotions from manipulative tactics. Embracing empathy as a tool for understanding and connecting with others strengthens our emotional resilience and fosters healthier relationships.

Developing Empathetic Relationships and Connections

Fostering empathetic relationships is essential in building a resilient defense against manipulation. In this section, we explore strategies to develop empathetic connections with others.

- Active Listening: Active listening is a communication skill that involves fully concentrating, understanding, responding, and remembering what the other person is saying. When we engage in active listening, we are fully present in the conversation, giving our undivided attention to the speaker. By doing so, we demonstrate that we value and respect their thoughts and feelings. Active listening goes beyond simply hearing the words; it involves empathetically understanding the speaker's perspective and emotions. Through active listening, we create a safe and open space for the other person to share their experiences and concerns.
- Perspective-Taking: Perspective-taking is the ability to put ourselves in someone else's shoes and view a situation from their point of view. It requires empathy and an open mind to consider different beliefs, values,

and life experiences. By practicing perspective-taking, we gain a deeper understanding of others' thoughts and feelings, which in turn fosters compassion and empathy. This skill is especially valuable in resolving conflicts, as it allows us to see beyond our own biases and preconceived notions. Perspective-taking nurtures a sense of connectedness with others, leading to more harmonious relationships and improved communication.

- Emotional Support: Providing emotional support involves offering comfort, understanding, and validation to someone in distress or facing challenges. It requires empathy, active listening, and genuine concern for the well-being of others. When we offer emotional support, we create a sense of safety and trust, encouraging others to open up about their feelings and experiences. This support can be a source of strength for individuals during difficult times, knowing that they have someone who cares and is willing to listen without judgment. By offering emotional support, we reinforce our empathetic bonds with others, fostering a sense of belonging and interconnectedness.

In summary, active listening is a foundational element of effective communication, as it allows us to understand and validate others' perspectives and experiences. Perspective-taking enhances our empathy and compassion by helping us see situations through the eyes of others. Offering emotional support is an essential way to strengthen empathetic connections, as it provides comfort and understanding during challenging times. These skills collectively contribute to fostering meaningful and supportive relationships, promoting emotional well-being, and creating a more empathetic and compassionate society.

The Power of Collective Empathy

Collective empathy amplifies the transformative impact of individual empathy, creating a more compassionate and understanding society. In this section, we explore the significance of collective empathy.

- Building Empathetic Communities: Cultivating empathetic communities involves creating environments where individuals feel safe, supported, and understood. In empathetic communities, people show genuine concern for each other's well-being and actively listen to one another's experiences and emotions. This fosters a sense of belonging and interconnectedness, encouraging individuals to offer empathy and compassion to those in need. Empathetic communities prioritize kindness, understanding, and inclusivity, promoting a culture of support and upliftment.

- Promoting Empathy in Education: Integrating empathy education in schools is crucial for nurturing a more empathetic generation. By incorporating empathy into the curriculum, students learn about understanding others' perspectives, recognizing emotions, and developing compassion. Empathy education teaches children to appreciate diversity, embrace differences, and resolve conflicts peacefully. It empowers them to communicate effectively, foster healthy relationships, and be responsible and caring members of society. Promoting empathy in education lays the foundation for a more compassionate and harmonious world.
- Empathy in Leadership: Encouraging empathetic leadership is essential for fostering a positive and supportive organizational culture. Empathetic leaders are attuned to the emotions and needs of their team members, creating a work environment where everyone feels valued and heard. They prioritize open communication, actively listen to their employees' concerns, and offer support during challenging times. Empathetic leaders also lead by example, displaying kindness, integrity, and compassion. This not only boosts employee morale and satisfaction but also enhances team collaboration and overall productivity.

In summary, building empathetic communities involves creating spaces where individuals support and uplift each other, fostering a sense of belonging and interconnectedness. Promoting empathy in education lays the groundwork for nurturing a more compassionate and understanding generation. Encouraging empathetic leadership in organizations fosters a positive and supportive work culture, benefiting both employees and the overall success of the company. By embracing empathy at various levels of society, we create a more empathetic world where understanding, compassion, and kindness thrive.

Conclusion

In a manipulative world, empathy stands as a beacon of hope and resilience. By recognizing empathy as an antidote to manipulation, developing empathetic relationships and connections, and embracing collective empathy, we embark on a compassionate revolt against deceit and exploitation. Together, we foster a community that values empathy, understanding, and compassion, creating a society where manipulation finds less fertile ground to thrive. As we cultivate empathy in ourselves and others, we contribute to a world where genuine connections flourish, empathy becomes a cornerstone of our interactions, and the light of compassion drives out the shadows of manipulation.

CHAPTER 38

BENEVOLENT MANIPULATION AND INFLUENCE

The Power of Positive Persuasion: Embracing Benevolent Manipulation and Influence

Introduction

The concept of benevolent manipulation and influence is where leaders utilize ethical persuasion to bring about positive change. This chapter highlights the importance of recognizing positive manipulation in leadership, understanding ethical persuasion techniques, and empowering others through benevolent influence.

Recognizing Positive Manipulation in Leadership

Benevolent manipulation in leadership involves using influence for positive and constructive outcomes. In this section, we explore how leaders can employ benevolent manipulation for the greater good.

- Visionary Leadership: Visionary leadership is about inspiring and motivating others through a compelling vision for the future. Visionary leaders have a clear and inspiring picture of what they want to achieve and communicate it effectively to their team or followers. They articulate the vision in a way that resonates with others, creating a sense of purpose and direction. This type of leadership encourages individuals to align their efforts towards a common goal, fostering teamwork and collective achievement.
- Influence without Coercion: Benevolent influence is about persuading or guiding others in a positive and respectful manner, allowing them to make their choices freely. It involves providing information, support, and encouragement, allowing individuals to make informed decisions without feeling pressured or coerced. Unlike coercive manipulation, which uses deception, threats, or undue influence to control others, benevolent influence respects individual autonomy and values their ability to make independent choices.
- Empowering Others: Empowering others means giving them the tools, knowledge, and support they need to make informed decisions and take

charge of their own lives. It involves fostering self-confidence, providing resources, and creating an environment where individuals feel capable and valued. Positive manipulation, in this context, refers to the act of guiding and empowering others in a way that enhances their well-being and helps them reach their full potential.

In summary, visionary leadership involves inspiring and motivating others through a compelling vision for the future. It focuses on benevolent influence, where choices are freely made and individuals are empowered to make informed decisions. Positive manipulation comes into play when leaders empower others in a way that fosters growth, well-being, and self-determination. By understanding these concepts, leaders can create a positive and empowering environment that brings out the best in their team and followers.

Ethical Persuasion for Positive Change

Ethical persuasion techniques can be powerful tools for bringing about positive change. In this section, we explore strategies for employing ethical persuasion in various contexts.

- Honesty and Transparency: In the context of persuasion, honesty and transparency are essential principles that leaders and communicators should uphold. Being honest means providing accurate information without distortion or deception. Transparency involves being open and candid about intentions, motives, and potential outcomes. When leaders demonstrate honesty and transparency, they build trust and credibility with their audience, which is vital for effective persuasion. People are more likely to be persuaded by someone they trust and believe is being forthright with them.
- Appealing to Values: Successful persuasion often involves connecting with individuals on a personal level by appealing to their values and beliefs. People are more receptive to messages that align with their core values and resonate with their sense of identity. Leaders who understand the values of their audience can frame their messages in a way that addresses those values, making their arguments more persuasive and impactful. This approach demonstrates empathy and understanding, which can create a stronger emotional connection with the audience.
- Providing Evidence and Data: Utilizing evidence and data is a powerful strategy in persuasion, as it appeals to the logical and rational side of decision-making. Presenting well-researched facts and data can support the credibility of the message and reinforce the persuader's position. Data-driven

arguments can appeal to people's sense of reason and logic, providing a solid foundation for their beliefs and actions. However, it's crucial to ensure that the evidence presented is accurate, relevant, and from reliable sources to maintain trust and avoid manipulation.

In summary, effective persuasion involves honesty and transparency to build trust and credibility with the audience. Understanding and appealing to the values of individuals can create a strong emotional connection and make the message more relatable. Supporting arguments with evidence and data enhances the persuader's position and appeals to the audience's logical reasoning. By employing these strategies, leaders can conduct persuasive communication that respects the audience's autonomy and encourages them to make informed decisions.

Empowering Others through Benevolent Influence

Benevolent influence goes beyond achieving personal goals; it aims to empower and uplift others. In this section, we explore how leaders can use their influence to empower individuals and communities.

- Mentoring and Coaching: Mentoring and coaching involve individuals with more experience and knowledge guiding and supporting others in their personal and professional growth. As mentors, they share their wisdom, insights, and expertise, while as coaches, they help individuals identify and overcome challenges, set goals, and develop skills. By taking on these roles, mentors and coaches provide valuable guidance and encouragement, enabling others to reach their full potential.
- Recognizing Strengths: Effective mentors and coaches have the ability to identify the unique strengths and talents of their mentees or coachees. By recognizing and nurturing these strengths, they empower individuals to believe in their capabilities and build self-confidence. This process involves creating opportunities for individuals to showcase and develop their strengths, fostering a sense of accomplishment and competence.
- Encouraging Collaboration: Mentoring and coaching environments that promote collaboration and teamwork foster a supportive and empowering atmosphere. When individuals work together, they can share knowledge, skills, and experiences, enhancing their collective growth. Collaboration encourages open communication, a sense of belonging, and mutual support, which contributes to a positive and enriching learning experience for all involved.

In-depth Explanation:

- Mentoring and coaching are powerful tools for personal and professional development. In these roles, individuals who have accumulated valuable experience and knowledge take on the responsibility of guiding and supporting others on their journey of growth. Mentors and coaches serve as role models, offering guidance, feedback, and encouragement to help their mentees or coachees develop their skills and achieve their goals.
- Recognizing strengths is an essential aspect of effective mentoring and coaching. By identifying the unique strengths and talents of their mentees or coachees, mentors and coaches can provide targeted support and opportunities for growth. This recognition empowers individuals to believe in their abilities, boosting their self-confidence and motivation to tackle challenges. When individuals are aware of their strengths and how to leverage them, they become more resilient and willing to take on new opportunities.
- Encouraging collaboration is another key element in mentoring and coaching. A collaborative environment fosters a sense of community and shared learning, where mentees or coachees can benefit from each other's experiences and perspectives. Collaboration encourages open communication and mutual support, creating a safe space for individuals to share ideas, seek advice, and learn from one another. By working together, individuals not only enhance their own growth but also contribute to the development of their peers.

In summary, mentoring and coaching play crucial roles in nurturing personal and professional growth. By recognizing and nurturing strengths and encouraging collaboration, mentors and coaches create a supportive and empowering environment where individuals can thrive and reach their full potential. Through these practices, mentors and coaches contribute to the growth and success of those they support, fostering a cycle of continuous learning and development.

Conclusion

Benevolent manipulation and influence serve as tools for leaders to bring about positive change and foster growth in others. By recognizing the potential of positive manipulation in leadership, understanding ethical persuasion techniques, and empowering others through benevolent influence, we create a world where leadership is guided by compassion, integrity, and a genuine desire to uplift others. Together, we foster a community that values benevolent leadership, ethical persuasion, and empowerment, creating a society where positive change and collective progress become attainable aspirations. As we embrace benevolent manipulation and influence, we contribute to a world where leaders are revered for their impact on others' lives, and the ripple effects of positive influence continue to spread, inspiring a brighter and more compassionate future for all.

CHAPTER 39

EMPATHETIC PARENTING AND CHILDHOOD DEVELOPMENT

Compassionate Roots: Cultivating Empathy in Children through Parenting

Introduction

The profound influence of empathetic parenting on childhood development is paramount. This chapter explores the significance of nurturing empathy in children, the potential impact of parental manipulation, and strategies to raise emotionally intelligent and resilient kids through compassionate guidance.

Nurturing Empathy in Children

Empathy is a crucial skill that forms the foundation of healthy relationships and emotional intelligence. In this section, we explore the importance of fostering empathy in children.

- Modeling Empathy: Parents play a critical role in shaping their children's social and emotional development, and one powerful way they do this is through modeling empathy. Children learn by observing the behavior of their parents and caregivers, and when they witness empathetic responses to others' emotions and needs, they internalize these behaviors. When parents demonstrate understanding, compassion, and kindness towards others, they provide a valuable model for their children to emulate in their own interactions.
- Teaching Perspective-Taking: Perspective-taking is the ability to understand and consider other people's feelings, thoughts, and perspectives. Parents can actively teach perspective-taking to their children by engaging in activities that encourage them to see situations from different viewpoints. This can include reading books with diverse characters and discussing their feelings and experiences, or engaging in role-playing exercises where children take on different roles to understand how others may feel in various situations. By teaching perspective-taking, parents help children develop a deeper understanding of others' emotions and needs, which lays the foundation for empathy.

- Encouraging Empathetic Actions: Parents can foster empathy in their children by reinforcing and encouraging empathetic actions. This involves praising and positively reinforcing instances where children display empathy, such as sharing toys with a friend who is feeling sad or comforting a sibling who is upset. By acknowledging and celebrating empathetic behavior, parents reinforce its importance and encourage children to continue engaging in such actions. Additionally, parents can engage in discussions with their children about the positive impact of empathy and how it can strengthen relationships and create a more caring and compassionate community.

  In-depth Explanation:

- Modeling Empathy: Parents are powerful role models for their children, and their behavior significantly influences how children perceive and respond to the world around them. When parents demonstrate empathy in their interactions with others, whether it's comforting a friend in distress, showing kindness to a stranger, or actively listening to a family member's feelings, they set an example for their children to follow. Children learn to recognize and understand emotions by observing how their parents respond to various situations. When parents consistently display empathy, children internalize this behavior and are more likely to exhibit empathetic responses in their own interactions.
- Teaching Perspective-Taking: Perspective-taking is a crucial aspect of empathy as it enables individuals to put themselves in someone else's shoes and understand their emotions and experiences. Parents can actively foster this skill in their children by engaging in activities that encourage them to see the world from different perspectives. Reading books or watching movies with diverse characters and discussing their feelings and experiences can help children develop a broader understanding of emotions and situations beyond their own. Role-playing exercises, where children take on different roles in imaginary scenarios, allow them to practice seeing situations from various viewpoints, which enhances their ability to empathize with others.
- Encouraging Empathetic Actions: Reinforcing empathetic actions in children's interactions with others reinforces the value of empathy and encourages its expression in their daily lives. Parents can provide positive reinforcement and praise when they witness their children engaging in empathetic behaviors, such as sharing, comforting, or showing concern for others. By acknowledging these acts of kindness and empathy, parents

reinforce the importance of empathy and motivate children to continue demonstrating empathy in their future interactions. Additionally, parents can engage in meaningful discussions with their children about empathy, its role in building strong and caring relationships, and the positive impact it can have on others and the community as a whole.

In summary, parents play a vital role in cultivating empathy in their children. By modeling empathetic behavior, teaching perspective-taking, and encouraging empathetic actions, parents lay the foundation for their children to develop into caring, compassionate, and understanding individuals. These skills not only benefit their personal relationships but also contribute to building a more empathetic and supportive society.

The Impact of Parental Manipulation on Children

Parental manipulation can have adverse effects on children's emotional development and well-being. In this section, we examine the potential consequences of manipulative parenting.

- Emotional Trauma: Manipulative parenting can have profound and long-lasting effects on a child's emotional well-being, leading to emotional trauma. Emotional trauma occurs when a child experiences distressing and harmful emotional experiences that overwhelm their ability to cope effectively. Manipulative parenting tactics, such as gaslighting, emotional abuse, or neglect, can create a hostile and unpredictable environment for the child, causing them to feel anxious, fearful, and insecure. The child may develop a distorted sense of self-worth, struggle with emotional regulation, and experience difficulties in forming healthy relationships.

- Erosion of Trust: Trust is a fundamental aspect of healthy parent-child relationships. Manipulative parenting erodes trust as it involves intentional deception, dishonesty, or betrayal by the parent. When children experience manipulative behaviors from their parents, they may become wary and hesitant to trust others, including future caregivers, friends, or romantic partners. The erosion of trust can hinder open communication and emotional connection between the parent and child, leading to emotional distance and strained relationships.

- Hindrance to Empathy Development: Empathy is the ability to understand and share the feelings of others, and it plays a crucial role in building meaningful and compassionate relationships. Manipulative parenting, which may involve emotional exploitation or lack of emotional attunement, can hinder the development of empathy in children. When a child's emotional needs are consistently dismissed or invalidated, they may struggle to recognize and respond to the emotions of others. This hindrance to empathy development can have long-term consequences, as empathy is a vital skill in maintaining healthy social connections and fostering emotional intelligence.

In-depth Explanation:

- Emotional Trauma: Manipulative parenting can create an emotionally toxic environment for a child, leaving them vulnerable to emotional trauma. Emotional trauma occurs when a child experiences overwhelming and distressing emotions that exceed their capacity to cope effectively. Manipulative parenting tactics, such as gaslighting (where the parent distorts the child's perception of reality), emotional abuse (such as verbal insults and humiliation), or neglect (emotional or physical), can all contribute to emotional trauma. These experiences can lead to the child feeling anxious, fearful, or unloved, which can have long-lasting impacts on their self-esteem and overall emotional well-being. Emotional trauma from manipulative parenting may manifest in adulthood as difficulties in forming healthy relationships, anxiety, depression, or other mental health issues.
- Erosion of Trust: Trust is a cornerstone of secure parent-child relationships. Manipulative parenting erodes trust by undermining the child's belief in the parent's honesty, reliability, and care. When a child experiences manipulative behaviors from their parent, such as broken promises, emotional manipulation, or intentional deception, their trust in the parent is damaged. This erosion of trust can have far-reaching consequences on the parent-child relationship, as trust is the foundation of emotional safety and open communication. Children may become guarded, hesitant to share their feelings, or reluctant to seek support from their parents. In the long run, this lack of trust can impact the child's ability to form secure attachments and may affect their ability to trust others in future relationships.
- Hindrance to Empathy Development: Empathy is a fundamental social and emotional skill that allows individuals to understand and relate to the emotions of others. Children learn empathy through emotional attunement and responsive caregiving from their parents. Manipulative parenting can hinder empathy development in several ways. For example, if a parent consistently dismisses or ignores a child's emotions, the child may struggle to recognize and understand their own emotions, let alone those of others. Emotional

exploitation or manipulation from a parent can also lead to confusion and ambivalence about emotions, making it difficult for the child to empathize with others. Additionally, if a parent uses emotional manipulation to control the child's emotions, the child may become emotionally guarded, inhibiting their ability to connect with and understand others. In the absence of empathetic modeling and emotional validation from a manipulative parent, a child's empathy development may be hindered, affecting their capacity for emotional intelligence and fostering meaningful relationships.

In summary, manipulative parenting can have significant negative impacts on children's emotional well-being and overall development. It can lead to emotional trauma, erode trust in parent-child relationships, and hinder the development of empathy. Recognizing the effects of manipulative parenting is crucial for promoting healthy parent-child interactions and fostering emotionally secure and empathetic individuals. Supportive and nurturing parenting practices, such as validation, emotional attunement, and open communication, are essential in building strong parent-child relationships and promoting positive emotional development in children.

Raising Emotionally Intelligent and Resilient Kids

Empathetic parenting nurtures emotionally intelligent and resilient children. In this section, we explore strategies for raising emotionally intelligent and resilient kids.

- Emotional Regulation: Emotional regulation is a crucial skill that involves recognizing and managing one's emotions in a constructive manner. Teaching children emotional regulation skills helps them understand and cope with their feelings effectively. By learning how to identify and express emotions in healthy ways, children can avoid impulsive or destructive reactions to challenging situations. Emotional regulation empowers children to navigate their emotions, leading to improved self-control, reduced stress, and better interpersonal relationships. When children can manage their emotions, they are better equipped to handle conflicts, setbacks, and other emotional challenges in a balanced and composed manner.
- Communication and Active Listening: Open communication and active listening are essential in nurturing emotionally healthy relationships with children. Encouraging open communication means creating an environment where children feel safe to express their thoughts and emotions without judgment. By actively listening to children, adults demonstrate empathy and

validate their feelings, promoting emotional understanding and connection. Effective communication enhances emotional bonding, as children feel heard and understood, which leads to greater trust and emotional security. Moreover, active listening helps adults gain valuable insights into children's experiences and emotions, enabling them to provide appropriate support and guidance.

- Encouraging Independence: Fostering independence in children is pivotal for their emotional and psychological development. Allowing children to take age-appropriate responsibilities empowers them to develop resilience and self-confidence. As children handle tasks and make decisions independently, they learn to navigate challenges, problem-solve, and take ownership of their actions. This sense of autonomy and competence contributes to a positive self-image and builds emotional resilience. Encouraging independence also helps children develop a growth mindset, where they see mistakes and failures as opportunities for learning and growth. Additionally, promoting independence nurtures a sense of self-reliance, allowing children to face the world with greater self-assurance and emotional stability.

In-depth Explanation:

- Emotional Regulation: Emotional regulation refers to the ability to understand and manage emotions effectively. Children are constantly exposed to various emotional experiences, and emotional regulation skills enable them to navigate these emotions in a healthy manner. When children can identify their feelings and express them constructively, they are less likely to resort to impulsive or destructive behaviors in response to emotional challenges. Emotional regulation fosters emotional well-being by reducing stress and promoting a positive outlook on life. As children develop emotional regulation skills, they become better equipped to handle conflicts, frustrations, and disappointments with resilience and composure.
- Communication and Active Listening: Communication is the foundation of any healthy relationship, including the parent-child relationship. Encouraging open communication means creating an environment where children feel safe and comfortable expressing themselves. When children feel heard and understood, they are more likely to share their thoughts, feelings, and concerns openly. Active listening is a vital aspect of communication, where adults focus their attention on the child, listen without interrupting, and show genuine empathy. Active listening communicates care and support, strengthening the emotional bond between adults and children. Moreover,

active listening provides valuable insights into children's emotions, helping adults offer appropriate emotional support and guidance when needed.

- Encouraging Independence: Nurturing independence in children is essential for their growth and development. Allowing children to take on age-appropriate responsibilities helps build their sense of competence and self-confidence. As children engage in tasks independently, they learn problem-solving skills, resilience, and self-reliance. These qualities contribute to positive self-esteem and emotional well-being. Encouraging independence also fosters a growth mindset, where children embrace challenges and view setbacks as opportunities for learning and improvement. By promoting independence, adults help children develop the belief in their abilities, which can serve as a foundation for emotional resilience and success in various areas of life.

In summary, teaching emotional regulation skills, promoting open communication and active listening, and encouraging independence are vital components of supporting children's emotional well-being and overall development. These practices empower children to manage their emotions effectively, build trusting relationships, and develop a positive self-image. By equipping children with these essential skills, adults provide them with the tools to navigate life's emotional challenges and foster emotional resilience.

Conclusion

Empathetic parenting serves as the cornerstone for raising emotionally intelligent and resilient children. By nurturing empathy in children, recognizing the potential impact of parental manipulation, and employing strategies for fostering emotional intelligence and resilience, we lay the groundwork for a generation of compassionate and empathetic individuals. Together, we foster a community that values empathetic parenting, emotional intelligence, and resilience, creating a society where children are equipped with the tools to navigate the complexities of human emotions and build meaningful and supportive relationships. As we cultivate empathetic parenting and childhood development, we contribute to a world where empathy becomes the bedrock of social interactions, and compassionate understanding becomes the bridge that unites humanity in a shared journey towards a brighter and more empathetic future.

CHAPTER 40

THE GRAY AREA: ETHICS AND THE LINE OF MANIPULATION

Navigating the Ethical Labyrinth: The Intersection of Ethics and Manipulation

Introduction

The intricate realm of ethics and manipulation is where the line between acceptable persuasion and manipulation can be ambiguous. This chapter explores the ethical dilemmas in psychology and manipulation research, the challenges of defining the boundaries of ethical persuasion, and the complexities that arise when examining the ethics of manipulation.

Ethical Dilemmas in Psychology and Manipulation Research

Psychology and manipulation research raise significant ethical considerations. In this section, we explore the dilemmas researchers face when studying manipulation and its potential impacts.

- Informed Consent: In research studies, informed consent is a critical ethical requirement that involves obtaining explicit permission from participants before their involvement. This process ensures that participants are fully aware of the study's purpose, procedures, potential risks, and benefits. In studies involving manipulation, obtaining informed consent becomes particularly challenging, as researchers must strike a delicate balance between informing participants about the study's objectives without revealing the manipulation itself, which could compromise the study's validity. Researchers must provide clear and comprehensive information to potential participants, enabling them to make autonomous and well-informed decisions about participating. Upholding informed consent safeguards participants' autonomy, respect for their rights, and protects them from potential harm.
- Potential Harm: Manipulation research holds the potential to cause harm to both individual participants and society at large. The deliberate use of manipulation techniques can lead to psychological distress, emotional

discomfort, or adverse reactions in participants. In certain cases, individuals may unknowingly experience negative effects, such as altered perceptions or attitudes due to the manipulative interventions. Moreover, when manipulation research findings are disseminated without proper ethical considerations, they might be misused by individuals or organizations for malicious purposes, further exacerbating potential harm. Researchers must carefully evaluate the potential risks and benefits of manipulation studies, taking measures to minimize harm and prioritize participant well-being.

- Research Transparency: Research transparency refers to openly sharing the study's methods, procedures, data, and results to ensure accountability and enhance the study's validity. In the context of manipulation research, transparency becomes crucial for maintaining the integrity of the study and allowing other researchers to replicate the findings. Transparent reporting of methodologies helps readers understand how manipulation was conducted ethically and provides insights into the study's validity and reliability. Moreover, transparency builds trust between researchers and the public, fostering confidence in the research community's ethical standards. By adhering to transparent reporting, researchers contribute to the scientific knowledge base while respecting the principles of honesty and accountability.

In-depth Explanation:

- Informed Consent: Informed consent is a foundational principle in research ethics that aims to protect participants' rights and autonomy. When conducting studies involving manipulation, researchers face a unique challenge in obtaining informed consent. Manipulation studies often require the participants to be unaware of the specific experimental conditions to ensure unbiased results. However, researchers must still provide comprehensive information about the study's general objectives, potential risks, and benefits. Striking this balance is crucial to ensure that participants fully understand what their involvement entails without compromising the study's integrity. Researchers should employ clear and accessible language when explaining the study, and participants should be given the option to withdraw their consent at any point during the research process.
- Potential Harm: Manipulation research involves deliberately altering variables to observe their effects on participants' thoughts, behaviors, or emotions. While this can provide valuable insights into human behavior, it also carries the risk of causing emotional distress or harm to participants.

Researchers must carefully assess the potential risks and benefits of manipulation studies before conducting them. Ethical considerations should prioritize the well-being of participants, and any potential harm must be minimized through debriefing and follow-up procedures. Additionally, researchers should consider the broader societal impact of manipulation studies, ensuring that the findings are used responsibly and ethically.

- Research Transparency: Transparency in research is essential for maintaining the credibility and integrity of scientific inquiry. When conducting manipulation studies, researchers should clearly outline their methodologies, including the specific manipulations used and their rationale. Transparent reporting allows other researchers to evaluate the study's methods and replicate the findings, enhancing the study's reliability and validity. Moreover, transparency fosters accountability and builds public trust in the scientific community. Transparent research practices help ensure that manipulation studies are conducted ethically and that the results are accurately reported, contributing to the advancement of knowledge while upholding ethical standards.

In summary, informed consent, potential harm assessment, and research transparency are crucial ethical considerations in manipulation research. Researchers must be mindful of the ethical implications of their studies, prioritize participant well-being, and ensure transparent reporting of their methodologies and findings. By upholding these ethical principles, researchers can conduct manipulation studies responsibly and contribute valuable insights to the scientific community while safeguarding the rights and welfare of participants.

Defining the Boundaries of Ethical Persuasion

Ethical persuasion seeks to influence others while respecting their autonomy and well-being. In this section, we examine the principles that guide the boundaries of ethical persuasion.

- Respect for Autonomy: Respect for autonomy is a fundamental principle in ethics that emphasizes the significance of allowing individuals to make decisions for themselves based on informed consent, free from external coercion or influence. In ethical persuasion, respecting autonomy means giving people the space and information they need to make choices that align with their values and preferences. This involves providing clear and comprehensive information about the persuasive message, being transparent about intentions, and ensuring that individuals have the freedom to accept or reject the message without facing undue pressure. Respecting autonomy recognizes each person's right to self-determination and fosters a sense of empowerment and agency in decision-making.

- Beneficence and Non-Maleficence: Beneficence and non-maleficence are ethical principles that guide practitioners to promote the well-being of others while minimizing potential harm. In ethical persuasion, striking a balance between the benefits and potential harm of persuasive techniques is crucial to avoid exploiting vulnerable individuals or manipulating them into making decisions that are not in their best interest. Ethical persuaders prioritize the positive impact of their messages, ensuring that the intended outcomes align with the well-being and interests of the individuals they are persuading. They also take precautions to avoid using coercive tactics or deceptive practices that could cause harm to the recipients of the persuasive message.
- Transparency and Honesty: Transparency and honesty are essential aspects of ethical persuasion that contribute to building trust and credibility. Being transparent involves being open and forthcoming about the persuasive intentions, methods, and potential consequences of the message. Ethical persuaders do not hide relevant information or use manipulative tactics to achieve their goals. Instead, they provide accurate and truthful information, giving the audience the necessary context to make informed decisions. By emphasizing transparency and honesty, ethical persuaders ensure that individuals are not misled or deceived, which is crucial in maintaining respectful and mutually beneficial communication.

In-depth Explanation:

- Respect for Autonomy: Respect for autonomy acknowledges the inherent value and dignity of each individual, recognizing their capacity to make decisions that align with their values and preferences. In the context of persuasion, this principle emphasizes that individuals should be free from coercion or manipulation when receiving persuasive messages. Ethical persuaders seek to empower their audience by providing relevant information, allowing them to make decisions that best serve their interests and needs. Respecting autonomy involves active listening and understanding the concerns and perspectives of the audience. It also requires avoiding tactics that exploit vulnerabilities or manipulate emotions to gain compliance. Ultimately, honoring autonomy fosters respectful and meaningful communication, promoting trust between persuaders and their audience.

- Beneficence and Non-Maleficence: Beneficence refers to the ethical obligation to promote the well-being of others and act in their best interest. Non-maleficence, on the other hand, requires avoiding actions that cause harm or negative consequences. In ethical persuasion, these principles guide persuaders to carefully consider the potential impact of their messages on the recipients. Ethical persuaders prioritize the positive outcomes of their persuasive efforts, aiming to enhance the well-being and interests of those they communicate with. This may involve providing valuable information, offering solutions to problems, or promoting beneficial behaviors. At the same time, persuaders are cautious not to engage in manipulative tactics that could cause harm or lead individuals to make decisions that go against their best interests. By balancing beneficence and non-maleficence, ethical persuaders demonstrate a genuine concern for the welfare of their audience, ensuring that their persuasive efforts contribute to positive and meaningful outcomes.
- Transparency and Honesty: Transparency and honesty form the bedrock of ethical persuasion. They involve being open and forthright about the intentions, methods, and potential consequences of the persuasive message. Ethical persuaders are candid about the reasons behind their message and the desired outcomes. They avoid using deceptive tactics or withholding information that could mislead or manipulate the audience. Instead, they provide accurate and relevant information, enabling individuals to make well-informed decisions. Transparency builds trust between persuaders and their audience, as it demonstrates a commitment to genuine communication and mutual respect. When individuals feel that the persuader is transparent and honest, they are more likely to engage in a receptive and open manner, fostering a positive and productive exchange of ideas and information.

In summary, ethical persuasion centers on respecting autonomy, balancing beneficence and non-maleficence, and upholding transparency and honesty. By adhering to these principles, persuaders can foster respectful and empowering communication while promoting the well-being and interests of their audience. Ethical persuasion builds trust, encourages informed decision-making, and ultimately contributes to meaningful and positive interactions between persuaders and their audience.

Exploring the Complexities of Manipulation Ethics

The realm of manipulation ethics is fraught with complexities, as intentions and outcomes may intertwine. In this section, we navigate the intricacies of ethical considerations in manipulation.

- Intentions versus Outcomes: When discussing manipulation, it is important to recognize that the intentions of manipulators may not always align with the actual outcomes of their actions. Manipulators may employ persuasive tactics with the intention of achieving a specific goal, such as gaining control or advancing their interests. However, the consequences of their actions can be far-reaching and unintended. For example, manipulative tactics can lead to emotional distress, strained relationships, or a loss of trust. This discrepancy between the intentions and outcomes of manipulation highlights the complexity of human behavior and the potential for unintended harm in persuasive efforts.
- Context Matters: Understanding the ethical implications of manipulation requires considering the context and motivations behind it. While some forms of persuasion may be well-intentioned and aimed at promoting positive change or encouraging beneficial behaviors, others may exploit vulnerabilities or deceive individuals for selfish gains. For instance, in marketing, persuasive tactics can be used to inform consumers about products and services genuinely, but they can also be employed deceptively to manipulate consumer choices. Analyzing the context allows us to discern between ethical persuasion, where transparency and respect for autonomy are prioritized, and manipulation, where deception and coercion may be present. This recognition of context helps us distinguish between ethical and unethical uses of persuasive techniques.
- Balancing Competing Values: One of the challenges in persuasive efforts is striking a balance between promoting positive change and avoiding manipulation. Persuasion can be a powerful tool for motivating individuals to adopt beneficial behaviors or support meaningful causes. However, it also carries the risk of manipulating emotions, exploiting vulnerabilities, and eroding trust. Balancing these competing values requires thoughtful consideration of the ethical principles involved, such as respect for autonomy, honesty, and empathy. Ethical persuaders aim to achieve their goals while ensuring that individuals are informed, empowered, and not coerced into decisions against their best interests. This delicate balance entails using persuasion responsibly and avoiding manipulation that could harm others or undermine their autonomy.

In-depth Explanation:

- Intentions versus Outcomes: Manipulative behavior is often driven by specific intentions, such as gaining power, control, or personal advantage. The manipulator may employ various tactics, including emotional manipulation, deception, or coercion, to achieve their desired outcomes. However, despite their intentions, the actual consequences of their actions may not align with what they had intended. For example, a manipulator may seek to gain control over someone's decisions, but this can lead to damaged relationships, mistrust, and emotional harm. The discrepancy between intentions and outcomes underscores the complexity of human interactions and the potential for unintended negative repercussions in manipulative situations. It also highlights the importance of considering the broader impact of persuasive efforts beyond the immediate objectives.

- Context Matters: The ethical implications of manipulation are contingent upon the context in which it occurs. Persuasion can be a legitimate and beneficial means of motivating individuals towards positive behavior change or advocating for important causes. In such cases, persuasion aligns with ethical principles, as it respects autonomy, provides accurate information, and empowers individuals to make informed decisions. On the other hand, manipulative tactics that exploit vulnerabilities, use deceptive techniques, or override individuals' autonomy can lead to harmful outcomes. For example, in interpersonal relationships, emotional manipulation can create a sense of dependency and undermine a person's sense of self-worth. Understanding the context allows us to differentiate between ethical persuasion, which respects the rights and well-being of individuals, and manipulation, which seeks to exert control or influence without genuine regard for their autonomy.
- Balancing Competing Values: Persuasion and manipulation are not always clear-cut, and finding a balance between these competing values can be challenging. Ethical persuasion aims to influence positively and inspire individuals to make choices that benefit their well-being or align with shared values. In this approach, persuaders uphold principles of transparency, honesty, and respect for autonomy. However, the temptation to use manipulative tactics may arise when persuaders seek quick results or when facing resistance to change. Balancing these competing values requires an awareness of the potential for manipulation and a commitment to ethical conduct. Ethical persuaders avoid manipulative tactics that undermine individual agency and prioritize building trust and rapport with their audience. They recognize that even well-intentioned efforts can inadvertently veer into manipulation, so they continuously examine their methods to ensure that their persuasive efforts remain ethical and constructive.

In summary, understanding the complexities of manipulation involves examining the intentions versus outcomes of manipulative actions, considering the context and motivations behind persuasive efforts, and striving to strike a balance between positive influence and ethical conduct. By doing so, individuals can promote ethical persuasion that respects autonomy, fosters meaningful change, and avoids manipulative tactics that could cause harm or undermine trust.

Conclusion

The intersection of ethics and manipulation unveils a labyrinth of complexities, where the boundaries between ethical persuasion and manipulation can be blurred. By exploring the ethical dilemmas in psychology and manipulation research, defining the principles that guide ethical persuasion, and navigating the complexities of manipulation ethics, we strive to find our way through this gray area responsibly. Together, we foster a community that values ethical practices, transparency, and empathy, creating a society where the line between ethical persuasion and manipulation becomes clearer, and our interactions are guided by respect for autonomy and the well-being of others. As we navigate the ethical labyrinth with mindfulness and compassion, we contribute to a world where persuasive efforts become a force for positive change, where manipulation finds no place, and where integrity and empathy guide our interactions toward a brighter and more ethically conscious future.

PART VIII: LOOKING BEYOND OURSELVES

CHAPTER 41

SOCIAL RESPONSIBILITY AND EMPOWERMENT

Empowering Humanity: Taking Social Responsibility in a Manipulative World

Introduction

The concept of social responsibility and empowerment is where individuals rise above the challenges of a manipulative world to create positive change. This chapter highlights the importance of individual responsibility, using knowledge for constructive purposes, and contributing to a more empathetic society.

Individual Responsibility in a Manipulative World

In a manipulative world, individuals possess the power to make choices that impact their lives and those around them. In this section, we delve into the significance of personal responsibility.

- Self-Reflection: Self-reflection is a process that encourages individuals to introspect and examine their thoughts, beliefs, and behaviors to gain insight into their biases and vulnerabilities to manipulation. It involves taking a step back to assess one's own motivations and reactions to various stimuli, including persuasive messages. By engaging in self-reflection, individuals can become more conscious of their emotional triggers, cognitive biases, and areas where they might be susceptible to manipulation. This heightened awareness allows them to develop a more critical and discerning approach to information and influences, reducing the likelihood of falling victim to manipulative tactics.

- Conscious Choices: Emphasizing the value of making conscious choices entails encouraging individuals to be deliberate and thoughtful in their decision-making processes. It involves considering the potential consequences of their actions, both on a personal level and in their interactions with others. Making conscious choices means being mindful of the underlying motives behind decisions and evaluating whether they align with personal values, ethical principles, and the greater good. By making decisions consciously, individuals become less susceptible to manipulative influences that might exploit impulsive or emotional responses. Instead, they adopt a more rational and ethical approach to navigating complex situations, making it harder for manipulators to exploit their vulnerabilities.

- Ethical Decision-Making: Advocating for ethical decision-making emphasizes the importance of aligning choices with personal values and societal well-being. Ethical decision-making involves considering the impact of decisions on oneself and others and making choices that uphold principles such as fairness, honesty, and respect for autonomy. When individuals prioritize ethical decision-making, they become more resistant to manipulative tactics that seek to undermine their moral compass or lead them astray. Ethical decision-making involves weighing the potential benefits and harms of actions, understanding the potential implications of one's choices, and taking responsibility for the consequences. By promoting ethical decision-making, individuals can guard against manipulation and contribute to a more trustworthy and compassionate society.

In-depth Explanation:

- Self-Reflection: Self-reflection is an introspective process that involves taking a close and honest look at oneself, including beliefs, attitudes, biases, and vulnerabilities. It is a valuable tool for developing self-awareness and understanding one's thought patterns and emotional responses. By engaging in self-reflection, individuals can identify their own susceptibilities to manipulation and the factors that may influence their decision-making. For instance, recognizing emotional triggers or cognitive biases can help individuals become more vigilant when faced with persuasive messages designed to exploit these vulnerabilities. Self-reflection empowers individuals to develop a deeper understanding of themselves and their decision-making processes, allowing them to make more informed choices and resist manipulative tactics.

- Conscious Choices: Making conscious choices involves deliberate decision-making that considers both immediate and long-term consequences. It requires individuals to be aware of their options, the values and principles they uphold, and the potential effects of their actions on themselves and others. By being mindful of the consequences of their choices, individuals can avoid impulsive reactions and carefully weigh the ethical implications of their decisions. This mindfulness allows them to navigate situations with greater clarity and avoid being swayed by manipulative strategies that aim to trigger emotional or automatic responses. By making conscious choices, individuals become more proactive in their decision-making, reducing their vulnerability to manipulation and maintaining a sense of control over their lives.

- Ethical Decision-Making: Ethical decision-making involves evaluating choices based on moral principles, societal values, and the well-being of oneself and others. It requires individuals to consider the potential impact of their actions on the broader community and to prioritize fairness, honesty, and integrity in their choices. Ethical decision-making is crucial in safeguarding against manipulation because it serves as a moral compass, guiding individuals away from actions that may exploit or harm others. By adhering to ethical principles, individuals become less susceptible to manipulative tactics that seek to lead them astray from their values or promote unethical behavior. Ethical decision-making fosters a culture of trust, respect, and empathy, contributing to healthier relationships and communities.

In summary, promoting self-reflection, conscious choices, and ethical decision-making empowers individuals to develop greater resilience against manipulation. Self-reflection helps individuals recognize their own vulnerabilities, conscious choices lead to deliberate and thoughtful decision-making, and ethical decision-making aligns choices with personal values and societal well-being. By adopting these practices, individuals can become more discerning and resistant to manipulative influences, ultimately contributing to a more ethical and compassionate society.

Using Knowledge for Positive Change

Knowledge is a powerful tool that can be wielded for positive transformation. In this section, we explore the role of knowledge in creating constructive change.

- Awareness and Education: Promoting awareness and education on manipulation involves raising public consciousness about manipulative tactics and their potential consequences. By increasing awareness, individuals can become more vigilant and recognize when they might be targeted by manipulators. Education plays a crucial role in empowering people with the knowledge and skills needed to identify and resist manipulative techniques. Understanding the psychology behind manipulation, cognitive biases, and emotional triggers enables individuals to develop a more critical and discerning mindset. Education also equips individuals with the tools to protect themselves and others from falling victim to manipulation in various domains, including politics, media, and interpersonal relationships. By fostering an informed society, awareness and education become a powerful defense against manipulation.

- Advocacy and Activism: Encouraging individuals to use their knowledge to advocate for positive causes and engage in activism enhances the impact of awareness and education efforts. When people recognize the prevalence and harmful effects of manipulation, they are more motivated to take action. Advocacy involves promoting awareness on a larger scale, such as organizing awareness campaigns, sharing information through social media, or participating in public discussions. Activism takes the next step by actively working towards creating meaningful change in the areas affected by manipulation. This may involve supporting organizations that combat manipulation, standing up against misinformation, or lobbying for policy changes that protect individuals from manipulative practices. By channeling their awareness into advocacy and activism, individuals become agents of change and contribute to the collective effort of countering manipulation.
- Responsible Use of Information: Highlighting the importance of responsibly sharing information and combating misinformation addresses the role of individuals in perpetuating or mitigating manipulation. In today's digital age, the rapid spread of information, both true and false, has significant consequences. Individuals must be aware of the potential impact of their actions when sharing information. Responsible use of information involves fact-checking before sharing, verifying the credibility of sources, and being mindful of the potential harm caused by spreading misinformation. By being responsible in their information-sharing practices, individuals contribute to building a more trustworthy and reliable information environment. Moreover, they actively combat manipulation by refusing to participate in the dissemination of deceptive or harmful content. Responsible information sharing is not only a personal responsibility but also a collective effort to create a healthier information ecosystem that resists manipulation.

In-depth Explanation:

- Awareness and Education: Promoting awareness and education on manipulation is essential to equip individuals with the knowledge and tools to recognize and counter manipulative tactics effectively. Awareness involves shedding light on the various forms of manipulation, such as emotional manipulation, gaslighting, and misinformation campaigns. By understanding how manipulation operates, individuals can develop a heightened sense of vigilance and skepticism towards persuasive messages. Education, on the other hand, goes beyond awareness and delves into the psychology and mechanisms of manipulation. Through education, individuals learn about cognitive biases, emotional triggers, and psychological vulnerabilities that manipulators exploit. This knowledge empowers them to become more discerning consumers of information, less susceptible to manipulation, and better equipped to protect themselves and others.

- Advocacy and Activism: Encouraging individuals to engage in advocacy and activism amplifies the impact of awareness and education efforts. Once individuals understand the implications of manipulation, they often feel compelled to take action to address the issue. Advocacy involves actively promoting awareness at a broader level, and raising public consciousness through various channels like social media, public events, or community outreach programs. Advocates strive to bring the issue of manipulation to the forefront of public discussions and ensure it receives the attention it deserves. Activism takes the commitment further by actively working towards bringing about change in the areas affected by manipulation. This may include supporting organizations that combat manipulation, participating in protests against deceptive practices, or advocating for legislation that protects individuals from manipulative tactics. By engaging in advocacy and activism, individuals become proactive agents of change, contributing to a collective effort to resist and counter manipulation.
- Responsible Use of Information: Responsible use of information addresses the role that individuals play in the dissemination of information, both online and offline. In the digital age, information spreads rapidly, making it crucial for individuals to exercise caution before sharing content. Responsible information sharing involves verifying the accuracy of information before disseminating it and being mindful of the potential impact of sharing false or misleading content. This responsibility extends to social media platforms, where individuals should be vigilant about the sources and credibility of information they encounter and share. By practicing responsible information sharing, individuals contribute to the cultivation of a trustworthy and reliable information ecosystem. Moreover, they actively combat manipulation by refusing to participate in the dissemination of deceptive or harmful content, thereby reducing the reach and impact of manipulative tactics.

In summary, awareness and education on manipulation empower individuals to recognize and resist manipulative tactics effectively. Advocacy and activism take awareness to the next level, as individuals actively work towards positive change. Responsible use of information ensures that individuals play a responsible role in combating misinformation and manipulation. By combining these efforts, individuals become active agents in building a more informed, resilient, and ethical society that guards against manipulation.

Contributing to a More Empathetic Society

The collective efforts of individuals can shape a more empathetic society. In this section, we examine strategies to foster empathy and compassion on a broader scale.

- Supporting Empathetic Initiatives: Participating in and supporting initiatives that promote empathy, understanding, and compassion involves actively engaging in projects, programs, or organizations that aim to foster a more empathetic and compassionate society. These initiatives may include community outreach programs, educational workshops, or advocacy campaigns that raise awareness about the importance of empathy and emotional intelligence. By actively participating in these initiatives or supporting them, individuals contribute to the creation of a more empathetic culture, where people are more attuned to each other's emotions and experiences.
- Encouraging Dialogue: Advocating for open dialogue and respectful communication is essential in fostering empathy and understanding. Open dialogue allows individuals to express their thoughts and emotions without fear of judgment or condemnation. It creates a safe space for people to share their perspectives and experiences, leading to a deeper understanding of each other. When individuals engage in respectful communication, they are more likely to listen actively and empathize with others' viewpoints, even if they disagree. Encouraging dialogue also helps bridge divides, reduce misunderstandings, and build stronger connections among people from different backgrounds and beliefs.
- Empowering Others: Empowering others to navigate the challenges of a manipulative world involves sharing knowledge, insights, and tools to help individuals protect themselves from manipulation and make informed decisions. This can be achieved through mentoring, coaching, or simply offering emotional support and encouragement. Empowering others with

the understanding of manipulation tactics, emotional self-awareness, and critical thinking skills can significantly enhance their ability to recognize and resist manipulative attempts. By empowering others, individuals contribute to building a community that is better equipped to deal with manipulative influences and create a more empathetic and supportive environment for everyone.

In-depth Explanation:

- Supporting Empathetic Initiatives: Participating in and supporting initiatives that promote empathy, understanding, and compassion are essential steps towards building a more empathetic society. Empathy is a powerful force that fosters human connection and strengthens relationships. By participating in empathy-driven initiatives, individuals actively contribute to the cultivation of a more caring and compassionate community. These initiatives may take various forms, such as volunteering for organizations that assist vulnerable populations, supporting mental health awareness campaigns, or advocating for inclusive policies that prioritize empathy and understanding.
- Encouraging Dialogue: Open and respectful dialogue plays a pivotal role in nurturing empathy and understanding. When people engage in meaningful conversations, they have the opportunity to listen actively, share their perspectives, and gain insights into others' experiences. Through dialogue, individuals can discover common ground, find shared values, and recognize the similarities that bind us as humans. Encouraging dialogue also helps bridge divides and promote unity, as it allows for the exploration of diverse viewpoints and the dismantling of stereotypes or misconceptions. By advocating for open and respectful communication, individuals foster an environment that values empathy and collaboration, creating the conditions for deeper understanding and stronger bonds among individuals and communities.
- Empowering Others: Empowering others to navigate the challenges of a manipulative world is a form of support and solidarity that can lead to positive change. The ability to recognize and resist manipulation is a vital skill in today's complex and interconnected world. By sharing knowledge about manipulation tactics and providing tools for emotional self-awareness and critical thinking, individuals empower others to protect themselves from deceptive practices. Empowering others also involves providing emotional support and encouragement, especially in times of vulnerability or uncertainty. When individuals feel supported and informed, they gain

confidence in their ability to navigate a manipulative world, making them less susceptible to exploitation. Ultimately, by empowering others, individuals contribute to the development of a resilient and empathetic community where everyone can thrive and build meaningful connections.

Conclusion

In a manipulative world, social responsibility and empowerment offer a path to positive change and a more empathetic society. By recognizing individual responsibility, harnessing knowledge for constructive purposes, and contributing to a society built on empathy and compassion, we elevate humanity beyond the shadows of manipulation. Together, we foster a community that values conscious choices, ethical decision-making, and the responsible use of information, creating a world where individuals are empowered to navigate a manipulative landscape with wisdom and empathy. As we unite in our efforts to build a more empathetic society, we contribute to a world where empathy becomes the bridge that connects humanity, and our collective actions inspire transformative change for a brighter and more compassionate future.

CHAPTER 42

EDUCATION AND MEDIA LITERACY

Illuminating Minds: The Transformative Role of Education and Media Literacy

Introduction

Education and media literacy play a crucial role in combatting manipulation and empowering individuals with the tools to navigate a complex world. This chapter highlights the significance of teaching critical thinking and media literacy to foster a generation capable of discerning truth from manipulation and safeguarding their autonomy.

The Role of Education in Combatting Manipulation

Education serves as a powerful weapon against manipulation, empowering individuals with knowledge and critical skills. In this section, we explore the transformative role of education in combatting manipulation.

- Empowering Critical Minds: Nurturing critical thinking skills involves encouraging individuals to develop the ability to question, analyze, and evaluate information critically. Critical thinking is a cognitive process that goes beyond accepting information at face value. It encourages individuals to actively engage with the material, consider different perspectives, and assess the evidence and reasoning behind various claims. By empowering critical minds, people become better equipped to discern reliable sources of information, identify logical fallacies, and spot manipulative tactics used to sway opinions or beliefs. This skill is crucial in a world inundated with information, where misinformation and deceptive messaging can easily influence decision-making and behaviors.
- Promoting Empathy and Emotional Intelligence: Cultivating empathy and emotional intelligence is key to fostering understanding and resilience against manipulation. Empathy is the ability to understand and share the feelings of others, while emotional intelligence involves recognizing and managing one's own emotions and understanding their impact on oneself

and others. By promoting empathy, individuals become more attuned to the emotions and experiences of those around them, which can help build stronger connections and prevent manipulation attempts that prey on emotions. Emotional intelligence, on the other hand, empowers individuals to regulate their emotions and respond thoughtfully to challenging situations, reducing vulnerability to emotional manipulation.

- Encouraging Ethical Values: Instilling ethical values that guide decision-making is fundamental to promoting responsible and compassionate behavior. Ethical values are principles that shape how individuals interact with others and the world around them. By encouraging ethical values such as honesty, respect, fairness, and empathy, individuals develop a strong moral compass that guides their actions. Ethical values also act as a shield against manipulative tactics that may conflict with one's principles. When individuals make decisions based on ethical values, they are less likely to be swayed by deceptive appeals that go against their sense of integrity and social responsibility.

  In-depth Explanation:

- Empowering Critical Minds: Nurturing critical thinking skills is crucial in a world where information is abundant, but not all of it is accurate or reliable. Critical thinking encourages individuals to go beyond passively accepting information and to engage in active and thoughtful analysis. It involves questioning the source of information, evaluating the evidence and reasoning presented, and considering alternative viewpoints. By empowering critical minds, individuals become more discerning consumers of information, less prone to falling for manipulative techniques that rely on exploiting cognitive biases or presenting false information. Critical thinkers are better equipped to make informed decisions, navigate complex issues, and resist attempts to sway their opinions or beliefs through deceptive tactics.

- Promoting Empathy and Emotional Intelligence: Empathy and emotional intelligence are essential qualities that enable individuals to connect with others on a deeper level and understand their emotions and experiences. By promoting empathy, individuals can better comprehend the feelings and perspectives of others, fostering a sense of understanding and compassion in relationships. Empathy acts as a powerful buffer against manipulation, as it allows individuals to recognize and respond to emotional manipulation attempts. Emotional intelligence complements empathy by enabling individuals to manage their own emotions and respond rationally to emotional triggers. By cultivating empathy and emotional intelligence, individuals become more resilient to emotional manipulation and are better equipped to build supportive and authentic relationships.

- Encouraging Ethical Values: Ethical values are guiding principles that inform our behaviors and decisions, reflecting our moral compass. Encouraging ethical values in individuals helps shape a society built on honesty, integrity, and fairness. By instilling ethical values such as honesty, respect, and compassion, individuals are more likely to act responsibly and treat others with kindness and consideration. Ethical values also provide a framework for making decisions that align with personal beliefs and societal well-being. When individuals uphold ethical values, they are less susceptible to manipulation attempts that go against their principles. Ethical values act as a protective shield, helping individuals resist coercive tactics that may conflict with their sense of right and wrong, and guiding them towards choices that contribute positively to themselves and the community.

Teaching Critical Thinking and Media Literacy

Critical thinking and media literacy form the cornerstone of informed decision-making in a digital age. In this section, we emphasize the importance of teaching these skills to future generations.

- Recognizing Bias and Manipulative Techniques: In an era of vast information and media consumption, teaching students to identify biases and manipulative techniques in media content is vital. Bias refers to the predisposition of presenting information from a particular perspective, influencing how events and issues are portrayed. Manipulative techniques in media can include emotional appeals, selective storytelling, or false equivalency to sway opinions and beliefs. By developing critical thinking skills, students can discern when information is being presented with a biased lens or when manipulative tactics are used to manipulate public sentiment. Recognizing bias and manipulative techniques empowers students to become more discerning consumers of information, making informed decisions based on a deeper understanding of the content they encounter.
- Fact-Checking and Verification: In the age of rapid information dissemination through various channels, equipping students with tools to fact-check and verify information is paramount. Fact-checking involves verifying the accuracy of claims and ensuring the information comes from

credible sources. By teaching students fact-checking methodologies, they can independently assess the reliability of information and discern between credible sources and misinformation. Encouraging verification before accepting information as truth fosters intellectual honesty and prevents the spread of false or misleading content. Fact-checking empowers students to be responsible and reliable sources of information, contributing to a well-informed and intellectually honest society.

- Engaging with Diverse Perspectives: Encouraging students to engage with diverse perspectives is essential for developing a comprehensive understanding of complex issues. Exposure to diverse viewpoints, experiences, and cultures broadens students' horizons and nurtures empathy and open-mindedness. Engaging with diverse perspectives allows students to challenge their preconceived notions and biases, fostering critical thinking and analytical skills. It also nurtures a respectful and inclusive environment where individuals value and appreciate the richness of diversity. By exploring diverse perspectives, students gain a more nuanced and well-rounded understanding of the world, enabling them to make informed decisions and contribute positively to society.

Empowering Future Generations Against Manipulation

By empowering future generations with education and media literacy, we create a generation better equipped to navigate manipulation and shape a compassionate and just society. In this section, we explore strategies to empower the youth against manipulation.

- Fostering Media Literacy Programs: In today's digital age, integrating media literacy programs into educational curriculums is crucial to developing informed and discerning media consumers. Media literacy empowers students with the skills to analyze, evaluate, and interpret media content critically. Through these programs, students learn to identify biases, manipulative techniques, and misinformation prevalent in various media forms such as news articles, videos, and social media posts. By cultivating media literacy, students become more aware of the persuasive intent behind media messages, making them less susceptible to manipulation and misinformation. Media literacy programs equip students with the tools to be active and informed participants in the media landscape, contributing to a more media-literate society.

- Encouraging Critical Media Consumption: Inspiring students to be critical consumers of media goes hand in hand with media literacy education. Critical media consumption entails engaging with media content thoughtfully and analytically, seeking reliable sources, and cross-referencing information. Rather than passively accepting information at face value, critical media consumers question the authenticity, credibility, and objectivity of the content they encounter. This practice not only enhances students' ability to recognize manipulative tactics and biases but also encourages them to seek out diverse viewpoints and well-researched information. Encouraging critical media consumption nurtures independent thinkers who can make informed decisions and actively participate in shaping public discourse.
- Cultivating Digital Citizenship: With the increasing role of the internet and social media in our lives, promoting responsible digital citizenship is paramount. Digital citizenship encompasses ethical and responsible behavior while engaging with digital platforms. In the context of media consumption, it involves sharing and forwarding information responsibly, fact-checking before spreading information, and respecting others' opinions online. Cultivating digital citizenship also emphasizes the importance of empathetic and respectful communication in online interactions. By promoting digital citizenship, educators empower students to navigate the online world with integrity and empathy, fostering a positive and inclusive digital community. Ultimately, cultivating digital citizenship contributes to a safer and more constructive online environment, where individuals contribute responsibly and critically to digital discussions.

Conclusion

Education and media literacy hold the key to emancipating minds from manipulation's grip, fostering a generation capable of critical thinking, empathy, and discernment. By recognizing the role of education in combating manipulation, teaching critical thinking and media literacy, and empowering future generations against manipulation, we pave the way for a more enlightened society. Together, we foster a community that values education, critical thinking, and media literacy, creating a world where individuals navigate the digital landscape with wisdom, compassion, and resilience. As we invest in the education of future generations, we contribute to a world where manipulation finds little fertile ground, and the light of knowledge shines brightly, guiding humanity toward a brighter and more conscious future.

CHAPTER 43

PSYCHOLOGICAL WELL-BEING AT A GLOBAL SCALE

Healing the World: Promoting Mental Health Awareness and Support

Introduction

Psychological well-being holds vital importance on a global scale. This chapter emphasizes the significance of mental health awareness, combating mental health stigma, and establishing accessible mental health support systems to uplift humanity's emotional and mental health.

Mental Health Awareness and Global Well-being

Mental health awareness is the foundation of a thriving and compassionate society. In this section, we explore the profound impact of mental health on global well-being.

- Recognizing the Global Mental Health Burden: The first step in addressing mental health challenges on a global scale is to understand the prevalence and impact of these issues worldwide. Mental health problems affect millions of people across all age groups, ethnicities, and socioeconomic backgrounds. From depression and anxiety to more severe conditions like schizophrenia, the burden of mental health issues can be immense. By recognizing the global scope of this problem, policymakers, healthcare providers, and communities can work together to develop effective strategies and allocate resources to support those in need.
- The Socioeconomic Impact: Mental health is not just an individual concern; it also has significant implications for societies and economies. People dealing with mental health challenges often face difficulties in maintaining employment, leading to decreased productivity and increased absenteeism in the workforce. Additionally, untreated mental health conditions can contribute to higher healthcare costs and strain on healthcare systems. Beyond the economic aspect, mental health issues can impact the overall well-being and harmony of societies, affecting relationships, families, and communities. Addressing mental health on a global scale requires

an understanding of these broader socioeconomic consequences and a commitment to developing comprehensive solutions.

- Integrating Mental Health into Public Health Agendas: To effectively address the global mental health burden, it is crucial to integrate mental health initiatives into public health priorities at both national and international levels. This means recognizing mental health as a fundamental aspect of overall health and well-being. By integrating mental health into public health agendas, governments and health organizations can allocate resources, develop policies, and implement programs that promote mental health, prevent mental health issues, and provide accessible and effective treatment and support for those in need. This approach acknowledges the interconnectedness of physical and mental health and works towards creating a more holistic and inclusive healthcare system.

In summary, recognizing the global mental health burden involves understanding the widespread prevalence and impact of mental health challenges, including their socioeconomic implications. By integrating mental health into public health agendas, societies can address mental health issues more effectively, promote overall well-being, and create a more supportive and empathetic environment for those struggling with mental health conditions.

Addressing Mental Health Stigma

The stigma surrounding mental health creates barriers to seeking help and support. In this section, we explore strategies to combat mental health stigma on a global scale.

- Raising Awareness: Promoting mental health awareness campaigns is essential to challenge misconceptions and stereotypes surrounding mental health. Many people still hold stigmatizing beliefs about mental health conditions, which can lead to discrimination and hinder individuals from seeking help. By raising awareness through targeted campaigns, educational programs, and media initiatives, societies can work towards breaking down these barriers. This involves providing accurate information about mental health, highlighting the prevalence of mental health challenges, and emphasizing that seeking support is a sign of strength, not weakness.
- Open Conversations: Encouraging open conversations about mental health is a powerful way to create a supportive and empathetic environment. When people feel comfortable discussing mental health openly, it reduces the

sense of isolation and shame that can accompany mental health struggles. Open conversations also allow individuals to share their concerns, fears, and experiences, leading to increased understanding and empathy among friends, family members, colleagues, and communities. It is crucial to foster a culture that welcomes and respects discussions about mental health, where individuals can seek support without fear of judgment or discrimination.

- Sharing Personal Stories: Sharing personal experiences is a powerful tool to humanize mental health struggles and encourage empathy. When individuals with lived experiences share their stories, it helps break down barriers and reduces the sense of shame and stigma associated with mental health challenges. Personal narratives can inspire others to seek help, offer hope, and foster a sense of community among those facing similar issues. Storytelling allows people to connect on a deeper level, and it shows that mental health issues can affect anyone, regardless of age, gender, or background. By sharing personal stories, individuals not only raise awareness but also become advocates for mental health, paving the way for greater understanding and support.

In summary, promoting mental health awareness through campaigns, encouraging open conversations, and sharing personal stories are vital steps towards creating a more empathetic and understanding society. These actions help challenge stigmas, break down barriers, and create an environment where individuals can seek help and support without fear of judgment. By collectively working towards building a more compassionate and inclusive community, we can better support those facing mental health challenges and foster a sense of solidarity and resilience.

Creating Accessible Mental Health Support Systems

Access to mental health support is a fundamental right for all individuals. In this section, we discuss the importance of creating accessible mental health support systems globally.

- Integrating Mental Health Services: Integrating mental health services into existing healthcare systems is a crucial step in reducing barriers to access for individuals seeking mental health support. Historically, mental health has been treated separately from physical health, leading to fragmented care and limited resources for those in need. By integrating mental health services into primary care settings and other healthcare facilities, individuals can receive comprehensive care that addresses both their physical and mental well-being. This integration ensures that mental health concerns are not overlooked or stigmatized, and it allows for early detection and intervention for those at risk of developing mental health issues.

- Telehealth and Digital Support: Utilizing technology, such as telehealth and digital support platforms, is a powerful way to provide remote mental health services, particularly in underserved regions or during times of crisis. Telehealth allows individuals to access mental health professionals and resources from the comfort of their homes, eliminating geographical barriers and increasing convenience. Additionally, digital support platforms, such as mental health apps and online support groups, provide accessible and affordable resources for self-help, psychoeducation, and connecting with others who share similar experiences. These technologies have proven to be effective in improving mental health outcomes and reducing the stigma associated with seeking help.
- Community-Based Support: Establishing community-based mental health programs is vital in fostering a sense of belonging and support for individuals facing mental health challenges. Community-based initiatives engage local resources, such as schools, religious organizations, and community centers, to create a network of care and support. These programs may include mental health workshops, support groups, and outreach services tailored to the unique needs of the community. By incorporating cultural and social contexts into mental health interventions, community-based support can be more effective in engaging individuals and encouraging them to seek help. Furthermore, these initiatives reduce the sense of isolation often experienced by individuals with mental health concerns, promoting a more inclusive and understanding community.

In summary, integrating mental health services into existing healthcare systems, utilizing telehealth and digital support, and establishing community-based mental health programs are all essential steps in promoting mental health and well-being. These approaches help reduce barriers to access, improve the reach of mental health services, and create a more supportive and inclusive environment for individuals seeking help. By combining different strategies, we can work towards building a comprehensive and compassionate mental health care system that addresses the diverse needs of individuals and communities.

Conclusion

Promoting psychological well-being at a global scale requires collective efforts to raise awareness, address stigma, and establish accessible mental health support systems. By recognizing mental health as an integral component of global well-being, combating mental health stigma, and providing accessible mental health services, we embark on a journey of healing for humanity. Together, we foster a community that values mental health, compassion, and empathy, creating a world where mental health support is readily available and stigma becomes a relic of the past. As we invest in the psychological well-being of the global population, we contribute to a world where individuals are supported in their journey towards emotional health, and where collective efforts create a global tapestry of resilience, understanding, and compassion for a brighter and emotionally healthier future.

CHAPTER 44

A GLOBAL PURSUIT OF MENTAL HEALTH

Nurturing Minds, Healing the World: A Global Pursuit of Mental Health

Introduction

Delving into the paramount importance of psychological well-being on a global scale this chapter highlights the significance of promoting mental health awareness, combating the pervasive mental health stigma, and establishing accessible mental health support systems to uplift humanity's emotional and mental well-being worldwide.

Mental Health Awareness and Global Well-being

Mental health awareness is the bedrock upon which a thriving global society is built. In this section, we delve into the profound impact of mental health on global well-being.

- A Global Mental Health Crisis: The recognition of a global mental health crisis stems from the understanding of the widespread prevalence and scale of mental health challenges affecting diverse populations worldwide. Mental health issues, ranging from depression and anxiety to more severe conditions like schizophrenia, impact individuals of all ages, backgrounds, and socioeconomic statuses. This crisis transcends borders and cultures, affecting people in both developed and developing countries. It highlights the urgency of addressing mental health as a significant public health concern that requires collective efforts from governments, healthcare systems, communities, and individuals.
- Fostering Emotional Resilience: Emotional resilience plays a crucial role in building communities that can effectively overcome adversities and cope with life's challenges. Psychological well-being and emotional resilience are interconnected concepts. When individuals possess emotional resilience, they are better equipped to adapt to stress, bounce back from setbacks, and maintain a stable mental state even during difficult times. By fostering emotional resilience in individuals and communities, societies can create a buffer against

the negative impacts of the global mental health crisis. This involves promoting positive coping strategies, providing access to mental health resources, and creating supportive environments that prioritize mental well-being.

- Investing in Global Mental Health Initiatives: To effectively address the global mental health crisis, there is an urgent need to increase investment in mental health initiatives at the global level. This includes allocating resources to mental health research, prevention, treatment, and awareness campaigns. Investing in mental health initiatives not only benefits individuals but also has positive ripple effects on communities and economies. When mental health is prioritized, individuals can lead more fulfilling and productive lives, contributing to stronger and more resilient societies overall. Global mental health initiatives should aim to reduce stigma, increase access to mental health services, and promote mental health literacy among populations.

In summary, recognizing the magnitude of the global mental health crisis is the first step towards finding effective solutions. Fostering emotional resilience is essential for building communities that can weather challenges and emerge stronger. Additionally, investing in global mental health initiatives is vital to address the diverse needs of populations and promote mental well-being on a global scale. By prioritizing mental health, we can collectively work towards a more compassionate, resilient, and healthier world for all individuals and communities.

Addressing Mental Health Stigma

The stigma surrounding mental health issues hinders progress and denies individuals the support they need. In this section, we explore strategies to address and dismantle mental health stigma on a global level.

- Challenging Misconceptions: One of the primary objectives of mental health awareness campaigns is to challenge and dispel misconceptions surrounding mental health. Misconceptions and stigmas often prevent individuals from seeking help or understanding the true nature of mental health challenges. Through targeted awareness efforts, these campaigns aim to educate the public about mental health conditions, their prevalence, and the fact that they can affect anyone. By providing accurate information, campaigns help combat the fear and ignorance associated with mental health issues, ultimately leading to a more informed and empathetic society.
- Humanizing Mental Health Struggles: Personal stories and experiences play a powerful role in humanizing mental health struggles. When individuals share their journeys with mental health challenges, they provide a face to

an often misunderstood and stigmatized issue. These narratives help others see the real impact of mental health on individuals and their families, breaking down barriers and fostering empathy. Humanizing mental health struggles not only reduces the stigma but also encourages others to seek help and support, knowing that they are not alone in their experiences. Such storytelling can also inspire hope and resilience, showing that recovery and growth are possible with the right resources and support.

- Encouraging Open Conversations: Open conversations about mental health create safe and accepting spaces where people can share their thoughts, feelings, and experiences without fear of judgment. These conversations are vital in breaking the silence and shame often associated with mental health challenges. When individuals feel comfortable discussing their mental health, they are more likely to seek help and support when needed. Additionally, open conversations promote understanding and reduce stigma within communities and workplaces. By encouraging open dialogue, society can collectively work towards creating a culture of acceptance and compassion, supporting those with mental health challenges and fostering an environment of emotional well-being.

In summary, challenging misconceptions, humanizing mental health struggles, and encouraging open conversations are all essential components of comprehensive mental health awareness efforts. By promoting awareness campaigns that provide accurate information and dispel stigmas, society can become more empathetic and understanding towards mental health issues. Humanizing mental health challenges through personal stories helps break down barriers and encourages others to seek support. Open conversations create safe spaces where people can share and connect, fostering a culture of acceptance and emotional well-being for all.

Creating Accessible Mental Health Support Systems

Universal access to mental health support is essential for a compassionate and equitable world. In this section, we discuss the importance of establishing accessible mental health support systems globally.

- Integrated Healthcare: Integrated healthcare refers to the merging of mental health services with primary healthcare systems, ensuring that individuals receive comprehensive and holistic support for their overall well-being. Traditionally, mental health has been treated separately from physical health, leading to fragmented care. By integrating mental health services into primary healthcare, individuals can access mental health support in conjunction with their physical health needs. This approach recognizes the interconnectedness of mental and physical health and promotes a more coordinated and efficient healthcare system.

- Telehealth and Digital Solutions: Telehealth and digital solutions have revolutionized the delivery of mental health services by leveraging technology to provide remote support. Through telehealth platforms, mental health professionals can offer virtual consultations, therapy sessions, and interventions to individuals in even the most remote and underserved regions. This approach breaks down geographical barriers, enabling people with limited access to mental health services to receive support from qualified professionals. Telehealth also offers convenience and flexibility, allowing individuals to engage in therapy or counseling from the comfort of their homes, reducing stigma and increasing accessibility.
- Community-Based Interventions: Community-based mental health programs are initiatives designed to offer localized and culturally sensitive support to individuals within their communities. These programs recognize the significance of social and cultural factors in mental health and aim to tailor interventions to specific community needs. By involving local organizations, community leaders, and grassroots efforts, these interventions build trust and familiarity, making individuals more likely to seek help when needed. Community-based programs can include support groups, counseling services, outreach programs, and educational initiatives. They promote a sense of belonging and solidarity, fostering an environment where mental health is destigmatized and actively addressed.

In summary, integrated healthcare, telehealth, and community-based interventions represent crucial advancements in mental health support. Integrating mental health into primary healthcare systems ensures that individuals receive comprehensive care for both their mental and physical well-being. Telehealth and digital solutions enhance accessibility by providing remote services, bridging gaps in mental health access. Community-based interventions offer localized and culturally sensitive support, breaking down barriers and stigma associated with mental health. Together, these approaches contribute to a more inclusive and compassionate mental healthcare landscape, supporting individuals in their journeys towards well-being and resilience.

Conclusion

Promoting psychological well-being at a global scale is an endeavor that demands collective effort and unwavering commitment. By recognizing mental health as a fundamental pillar of global well-being, confronting mental health stigma, and establishing accessible mental health support systems, we embark on a transformative journey to heal minds and hearts worldwide. Together, we foster a global community that values mental health, compassion, and empathy, creating a world where mental health support is a universal right, and stigma becomes a relic of the past. As we prioritize the psychological well-being of all individuals, we contribute to a world where emotional health is cherished and celebrated, and where our collective efforts form a tapestry of resilience, understanding, and compassion for a brighter and emotionally healthier future for all humanity.

CHAPTER 45

ETHICAL LEADERSHIP AND SOCIETAL IMPACT

Guiding Lights: The Transformative Power of Ethical Leadership

Introduction

The critical role of ethical leadership lies in shaping societal values and fostering a positive impact on the world. This chapter highlights the significance of ethical leadership principles, the importance of fostering trust and integrity in leadership, and the transformative potential of leaders who prioritize ethical decision-making.

The Role of Leaders in Shaping Society's Values

Leaders play a pivotal role in influencing the values and direction of society. In this section, we delve into the profound impact of leaders on shaping societal values.

- Leading by Example: Leading by example refers to the practice of leaders demonstrating the behaviors and actions they expect from their followers. When leaders exhibit the values and principles they promote, they create a powerful influence on the attitudes and behaviors of their teams or the broader community. This concept is rooted in the idea that actions speak louder than words, and when leaders embody the qualities they advocate, they build trust and credibility with their followers. By displaying integrity, empathy, and accountability, leaders foster a culture of authenticity and encourage others to emulate these traits.
- Setting the Tone: Leaders play a significant role in setting the tone for the organization or society they lead. Their messages, actions, and values create a guiding framework that shapes the culture and behavior of their followers. By communicating a clear and compelling vision, leaders inspire a sense of purpose and direction, motivating their teams or communities to work towards common goals. When leaders prioritize ethical values and foster a culture of inclusivity and respect, they create an environment that encourages cooperation, creativity, and productivity.

- Inspiring Change: Ethical leaders are instrumental in inspiring positive change and promoting social responsibility. Through their vision and commitment to ethical principles, they influence their followers to adopt a proactive and empathetic approach to addressing societal challenges. Ethical leaders lead with empathy, seeking to understand the needs and perspectives of others, and they use their influence to drive initiatives that create positive impacts on individuals and communities. By demonstrating courage and resilience in the face of adversity, ethical leaders encourage others to embrace change and work towards a more just and compassionate world.

In summary, leading by example, setting the tone, and inspiring change are essential components of ethical leadership. When leaders embody the values they espouse, they create a strong and positive influence on their followers. By setting a clear vision and prioritizing ethical values, leaders shape the culture and behavior of their organizations or societies. Ethical leaders inspire positive change by driving initiatives that promote social responsibility and address societal challenges. Their leadership serves as a catalyst for positive transformations, creating a more ethical, compassionate, and inclusive environment for all.

Ethical Leadership Principles

Ethical leadership is grounded in a set of principles that guide decision-making and actions. In this section, we explore key ethical leadership principles.

- Integrity: Integrity is a fundamental quality in ethical leadership, emphasizing the importance of honesty, transparency, and moral soundness in leaders' actions. Leaders with integrity consistently adhere to ethical principles and values, demonstrating consistency between their words and deeds. They are truthful and transparent in their communications, which builds trust and credibility with their followers. When leaders act with integrity, they inspire others to do the same, creating a culture where ethical behavior is valued and expected. Integrity is not only about adhering to ethical standards but also about demonstrating moral courage to make difficult decisions that align with the greater good, even when faced with challenges or temptations.
- Accountability: Accountability is the concept of holding leaders responsible for their decisions and actions. Ethical leaders take ownership of their mistakes and shortcomings and are willing to face the consequences of their choices. By being accountable, leaders foster a culture of responsibility

and create an environment where others feel empowered to take ownership of their actions as well. When leaders are accountable, they set a positive example for their followers, reinforcing the importance of ethical conduct and demonstrating that no one is above the rules or exempt from consequences.

- Empathy: Empathy is a crucial quality in ethical leadership, involving the ability to understand and share the feelings and perspectives of others. Ethical leaders cultivate empathy by actively listening to their team members or constituents, valuing their input, and showing genuine concern for their well-being. Through empathy, leaders build strong relationships based on trust and mutual respect. They consider the impact of their decisions on others and seek to make choices that promote the welfare and interests of all stakeholders. Empathy in leadership also involves promoting diversity and inclusion, ensuring that everyone's voice is heard and valued, and fostering an environment of understanding and compassion.

In summary, integrity, accountability, and empathy are essential pillars of ethical leadership. Leaders with integrity prioritize honesty and transparency in their actions, setting an example for their followers to follow ethical principles. Accountability reinforces responsibility and ensures that leaders are held responsible for their decisions and actions, contributing to a culture of ethical conduct. Empathy allows leaders to understand and connect with others, creating a supportive and inclusive environment. Together, these qualities form the foundation of ethical leadership, inspiring trust, respect, and positive change within organizations and society.

Fostering Trust and Integrity in Leadership

Trust is the cornerstone of effective leadership. In this section, we examine the significance of fostering trust and integrity in leadership.

- Building Trustworthy Relationships: Trust is a vital element in any relationship, be it personal or professional. Trust is earned through consistent actions, reliability, and genuine concern for others' well-being. When individuals consistently demonstrate honesty, and reliability, and show genuine care and empathy towards others, they lay the foundation for building trustworthy relationships. Trust is not developed overnight; it requires time, effort, and consistent behavior to establish and maintain. Trustworthy leaders prioritize transparency and open communication to foster an environment where people feel comfortable expressing themselves and sharing their concerns.

- Transparency and Communication: Transparency is a key factor in building trust and promoting shared values within a relationship. It involves being honest, forthcoming, and open about intentions, decisions, and challenges. By being transparent, leaders demonstrate their commitment to ethical conduct and build credibility with their followers. Transparency goes hand-in-hand with effective communication, which allows leaders to convey their vision, goals, and values clearly. Open communication ensures that all stakeholders are well-informed and have a clear understanding of the organization's direction. It also encourages open feedback and constructive dialogue, creating an environment of trust and collaboration.
- Ethical Decision-Making: Ethical decision-making is an integral part of building trustworthiness in relationships. Ethical leaders consistently prioritize moral principles and values in their decision-making processes. They consider the impact of their choices on all stakeholders, seeking to do what is fair and just for everyone involved. Even in challenging situations, ethical leaders remain committed to upholding their ethical standards, demonstrating their integrity and commitment to doing what is right. By consistently making ethical decisions, leaders build trust and credibility with their followers, fostering a culture of ethical behavior and responsibility.

In summary, building trustworthy relationships requires a combination of consistent actions, transparency, open communication, and ethical decision-making. Trust is earned over time through genuine concern for others, reliability, and a commitment to shared values. Transparent and open communication fosters an environment of trust and collaboration, where all stakeholders feel valued and informed. Ethical decision-making demonstrates a leader's integrity and commitment to doing what is right, regardless of the challenges faced. Together, these elements create a strong foundation for building trustworthy relationships, leading to stronger bonds and positive outcomes in personal and professional settings.

Conclusion

Ethical leadership stands as a guiding light, capable of transforming society for the better. By recognizing the profound role of leaders in shaping societal values, adhering to ethical leadership principles, and fostering trust and integrity, we pave the way for a more compassionate, just, and empathetic world. Together, we foster a community that values ethical leadership, integrity, and accountability, creating a world where leaders inspire positive change and set a moral compass for others to follow. As we prioritize ethical leadership and its societal impact, we contribute to a world where leadership is a force for good, and where collective efforts drive us towards a brighter and more ethically conscious future for all.

CHAPTER 46

THE PATH FORWARD: EMBRACING LIGHT AND SHADOW

Uniting Opposites: Empowering Humanity to Embrace Both Light and Shadow

Introduction

Explore the complexities of dark psychology and the lessons learned. This chapter emphasizes the significance of balancing the light and dark aspects of human nature, empowering ourselves and others to resist manipulation, and embracing the full spectrum of our humanity.

Reflection on the Journey Through Dark Psychology

Our journey through dark psychology has been enlightening and challenging. In this section, we reflect on the insights gained and the lessons learned from delving into the realm of manipulation and human behavior.

- Self-Discovery: Self-discovery is the process of exploring and understanding our own beliefs, values, emotions, and vulnerabilities. It involves introspection and self-awareness, which allows us to identify aspects of ourselves that may be susceptible to manipulation. By recognizing our own vulnerabilities and blind spots, we become more conscious of potential areas where others could exploit or manipulate us. Self-discovery also helps us understand our triggers and emotional responses, enabling us to respond to manipulation attempts more effectively and rationally.
- Empathy and Compassion: Empathy and compassion are essential qualities that enable us to understand and connect with others on a deeper level. By cultivating empathy, we can better recognize the vulnerabilities and emotional struggles of individuals who may fall victim to manipulative tactics. Understanding the human nature of vulnerability and the universal need for emotional connection, we become less judgmental and more compassionate towards those who have been manipulated. Empathy allows us to build stronger connections with others, fostering a supportive and caring community that can protect each other from manipulative influences.

- Knowledge as Armor: Knowledge is a powerful tool that acts as a shield against manipulation. By continuously seeking to expand our knowledge and understanding of various topics, we become more informed consumers of information. Being well-informed enables us to discern between factual information and manipulation attempts, making us less susceptible to being deceived or influenced by false narratives. Knowledge empowers us to critically evaluate information, ask probing questions, and make well-informed decisions based on evidence and reason. It enables us to resist manipulation and make conscious choices that align with our values and beliefs.

In summary, self-discovery, empathy, compassion, and knowledge work together to protect us from manipulation. Self-discovery helps us identify and address our vulnerabilities, making us more resilient to manipulation attempts. Empathy and compassion foster a caring and supportive community that looks out for one another, reducing the chances of falling prey to manipulative tactics. Knowledge acts as a shield, allowing us to critically analyze information and make conscious decisions. By embracing these qualities, we can navigate through a manipulative world with greater self-awareness, empathy, and resilience, promoting a more conscious and empowered society.

Balancing the Light and Dark Aspects of Human Nature

The human psyche is a tapestry of light and shadow, and embracing both aspects is essential for a holistic understanding of ourselves and others. In this section, we explore the significance of finding balance within ourselves.

- Self-acceptance: Self-acceptance is the process of fully embracing ourselves, including our imperfections, vulnerabilities, and darker aspects, without judgment or self-criticism. It involves developing self-compassion, which means treating ourselves with the same kindness and understanding that we would offer to a friend. When we practice self-acceptance, we let go of unrealistic expectations and perfectionism, allowing us to embrace our authentic selves. By accepting our flaws and imperfections, we create a foundation for personal growth and development, as we become more open to learning from our mistakes and experiences.
- Harnessing Positive Traits: Recognizing and harnessing our positive qualities and strengths empowers us to build resilience against manipulative influences. When we focus on our strengths, we develop a stronger sense of self-worth and confidence. By nurturing our positive traits, we become less

susceptible to manipulation attempts that aim to exploit our insecurities and weaknesses. Furthermore, embracing and developing our positive qualities enables us to contribute positively to our relationships and communities, fostering a more supportive and caring environment.

- Integrating the Shadow: The shadow aspect of our psyche represents the hidden and less desirable parts of ourselves that we often suppress or deny. These aspects may include unresolved traumas, fears, and negative emotions. Integrating the shadow involves acknowledging and understanding these elements without judgment, denial, or repression. By facing and accepting our shadow, we prevent it from controlling our behaviors and choices unconsciously. Integrating the shadow allows us to gain a deeper understanding of ourselves and develop a more balanced and authentic sense of self.

In summary, self-acceptance, harnessing positive traits, and integrating the shadow are interconnected processes that support our emotional well-being and resilience against manipulation. Self-acceptance enables us to embrace our imperfections with compassion and fosters personal growth. By harnessing our positive qualities, we build inner strength and reduce our vulnerability to manipulative influences. Integrating the shadow allows us to face and understand our hidden aspects, preventing them from influencing us unconsciously. Embracing these practices empowers us to lead more authentic and emotionally resilient lives, navigating through challenges and manipulative influences with greater self-awareness and self-compassion.

Empowering Ourselves and Others to Resist Manipulation

Armed with knowledge and self-awareness, we can empower ourselves and those around us to resist manipulation. In this section, we discuss strategies to build resilience against manipulative tactics.

- Promoting Critical Thinking: Promoting critical thinking involves encouraging individuals to develop and apply their analytical skills to question and evaluate information critically. This process goes beyond accepting information at face value and involves examining evidence, sources, and underlying assumptions. By cultivating critical thinking, people become more discerning consumers of information, less susceptible to manipulation, and better equipped to make well-informed decisions. Critical thinking also fosters a deeper understanding of complex issues, enabling individuals to engage in constructive and evidence-based discussions.

- Strengthening Emotional Intelligence: Emotional intelligence refers to the ability to recognize, understand, and manage one's own emotions and the emotions of others. Cultivating emotional intelligence empowers individuals to navigate their emotions in a healthy and constructive manner. By being in tune with their feelings, people can better recognize manipulative tactics that aim to exploit their emotions. Moreover, emotional intelligence helps individuals develop empathy, which enables them to understand others' perspectives and motivations, fostering healthier relationships and reducing the likelihood of falling victim to emotional manipulation.
- Creating Supportive Networks: Establishing supportive communities is crucial for fostering open dialogue, empathy, and mutual empowerment. In such environments, individuals feel safe to express their thoughts and emotions without fear of judgment or manipulation. Supportive networks provide a space for sharing experiences, offering advice, and gaining insights from others. By being part of a caring and understanding community, people can reinforce their emotional well-being, strengthen their resilience against manipulative influences, and collectively work towards positive change and growth.

In summary, promoting critical thinking encourages individuals to think independently, question information, and make informed judgments. Strengthening emotional intelligence empowers individuals to navigate their emotions and recognize manipulative tactics, fostering healthier relationships. Creating supportive networks builds a sense of belonging and empowerment, providing a safe space for open dialogue and mutual support. Together, these three elements contribute to individuals' overall well-being and equip them with the tools to navigate a world where manipulation and deception may be present.

Conclusion

The path forward lies in embracing both light and shadow, and understanding that the human experience is a mosaic of complexities. By reflecting on our journey through dark psychology, finding balance within ourselves, and empowering ourselves and others to resist manipulation, we transcend the shadows and embrace the light. Together, we foster a community that values self-awareness, empathy, and knowledge, creating a world where individuals navigate the manipulative landscape with resilience, understanding, and compassion. As we unite the opposites within ourselves, we contribute to a world where humanity stands strong against manipulation, where the light of awareness and empathy shines brightly, guiding us towards a brighter and more empowered future for all.

PART IX: GLOBAL CONFLICT RESOLUTION

CHAPTER 47

EMPATHY IN GLOBAL CONFLICT RESOLUTION

Bridging Divides: Harnessing Empathy for Global Peace

Introduction

The transformative power of empathy resides in resolving conflicts on a global scale. This chapter highlights the pivotal role of empathy in promoting understanding and peace, emphasizing the significance of empathetic diplomacy and negotiation in fostering harmonious relations among nations and peoples.

The Role of Empathy in Resolving Conflicts

Empathy stands as a potent force in conflict resolution, bridging the gap between opposing parties and fostering a deeper understanding of each other's perspectives. In this section, we delve into the profound impact of empathy in resolving conflicts.

- Humanizing the Other: Humanizing the Other involves acknowledging the shared humanity in individuals who may be perceived as adversaries or from different backgrounds. It requires looking beyond surface differences and recognizing that all humans have their own unique experiences, emotions, and motivations. By practicing humanization, we cultivate compassion and empathy for others, regardless of our differences or disagreements. This approach enables us to see the multifaceted nature of individuals and opens the door to understanding their perspectives more deeply. Humanizing the Other is a critical step in reducing hostility and polarization, as it fosters a sense of connection and commonality among diverse groups.

- Facilitating Dialogue: Facilitating dialogue refers to creating an environment conducive to open and empathetic communication. In such settings, individuals are encouraged to express their thoughts, feelings, and concerns without fear of judgment or reprisal. Through active listening and respectful exchange, participants can explore common ground and shared values, even amidst differing opinions. Dialogue helps to bridge divides, build bridges of understanding, and promote a sense of unity within communities or between opposing parties. By engaging in open dialogue, we can address conflicts constructively and seek collective solutions that benefit everyone involved.

- Building Trust: Building trust is essential for fostering meaningful connections and fostering constructive communication. Empathetic engagement plays a crucial role in nurturing trust between individuals and groups. When we approach others with genuine empathy and compassion, we signal our willingness to listen and understand their perspectives without judgment. This empathetic approach helps to break down barriers that may exist due to past conflicts or misunderstandings. As trust grows, individuals become more open to collaborating, sharing ideas, and finding common ground, leading to more effective problem-solving and cooperation.

In summary, humanizing the Other involves recognizing the shared humanity in those who may seem different or opposing to us, fostering empathy and compassion. Facilitating dialogue creates an environment where open and empathetic communication can occur, encouraging the exploration of common ground and shared values. Building trust through empathetic engagement is vital for breaking barriers and facilitating constructive communication, leading to greater understanding and collaboration among individuals and groups. By practicing these principles, we can contribute to a more inclusive and harmonious society, where differences are embraced, and constructive dialogue leads to positive change.

Promoting Understanding and Peace on a Global Scale

Empathy serves as a compass guiding us towards global peace and understanding. In this section, we explore strategies to promote empathy and peace on a global level.

- Cross-Cultural Empathy: Cross-cultural empathy entails developing an understanding and appreciation for individuals from diverse cultural backgrounds. It goes beyond tolerating cultural differences and aims to transcend cultural divides, fostering a genuine connection and respect for people with varied traditions, beliefs, and experiences. By encouraging cross-cultural empathy, we can break down stereotypes, prejudices, and biases, which are often barriers to meaningful relationships and collaboration. Embracing diversity through empathy allows us to learn from one another and enrich our perspectives, contributing to a more inclusive and harmonious global community.

- Empathetic Media and Storytelling: Empathetic media and storytelling involve presenting narratives that humanize all parties involved in conflicts or contentious issues. Instead of portraying one side as inherently good or bad, this approach seeks to provide a nuanced perspective that acknowledges the complexities of human experiences. Empathetic storytelling encourages audiences to see beyond surface differences and understand the motivations, struggles, and emotions of all individuals involved. By highlighting the shared humanity and vulnerabilities of diverse characters, empathetic media fosters empathy among viewers, promoting understanding and compassion for others' struggles.
- Empathy Education: Empathy education refers to integrating empathy-based learning into school curriculums, emphasizing the value of understanding and compassion in interpersonal interactions. By teaching empathy, students develop the ability to recognize and respond to the feelings and perspectives of others, enhancing their emotional intelligence. Empathy education nurtures a generation that values kindness, tolerance, and open-mindedness, creating a more empathetic and supportive society. Students who learn empathy are more likely to be respectful, considerate, and accepting of diversity, which contributes to the establishment of healthier relationships and a more harmonious community.

In summary, cross-cultural empathy encourages understanding and appreciation for individuals from diverse cultural backgrounds, leading to a more inclusive global community. Empathetic media and storytelling humanize all parties involved in conflicts, fostering empathy among audiences and promoting understanding. Empathy education integrated into school curriculums instills values of compassion and kindness, creating a generation that values empathy and embraces diversity. These three aspects work together to create a society that values empathy, respects diversity, and builds connections based on understanding and compassion.

Empathetic Diplomacy and Negotiation

Empathetic diplomacy and negotiation offer an alternative path to resolving conflicts. In this section, we examine the significance of empathy in diplomatic efforts.

- Active Listening: Active listening is a communication technique that involves fully concentrating, understanding, responding, and remembering the information conveyed by the speaker. In conflicts or challenging situations, active listening plays a crucial role in fostering empathy and understanding. When we actively listen, we not only hear the words spoken but also pay attention to non-verbal cues, emotions, and underlying needs or concerns. This level of engagement allows us to genuinely understand the perspectives and feelings of all parties involved, creating a foundation for more effective communication and conflict resolution.

- Finding Common Ground: Finding common ground involves seeking areas of agreement and shared interests among parties with differing views or conflicting interests. By identifying common ground, individuals can establish a starting point for collaboration and problem-solving. This process helps bridge divides, reduces tension, and creates opportunities for building positive relationships. When parties recognize that they have shared goals or values, it becomes easier to work together towards solutions that benefit everyone involved.
- Constructive Compromise: Constructive compromise entails arriving at solutions that acknowledge the concerns and needs of all stakeholders, even if it requires giving up some individual preferences. It is a collaborative approach that takes into account the perspectives of all parties and aims to find a balanced and equitable resolution. Empathetic compromise is not about winners and losers but about finding a middle ground that respects the interests and emotions of all involved. By embracing this approach, individuals can build trust, strengthen relationships, and foster a cooperative and empathetic environment.

In summary, active listening is a fundamental communication skill that enables individuals to genuinely understand the concerns and needs of others. Finding common ground helps identify shared interests and common objectives, creating a basis for collaboration and understanding. Constructive compromise embraces empathetic solutions that consider the well-being of all stakeholders, fostering a cooperative and empathetic environment for conflict resolution and relationship-building. Together, these three practices contribute to more effective communication, greater empathy, and the establishment of mutually beneficial outcomes.

Conclusion

Empathy serves as a powerful bridge that connects humanity across divides, fostering understanding, peace, and reconciliation. By recognizing the role of empathy in resolving conflicts, promoting global understanding and peace, and embracing empathetic diplomacy and negotiation, we pave the way for a world where conflicts find resolution through compassion and understanding. Together, we foster a community that values empathy, active listening, and constructive communication, creating a world where nations and peoples engage in dialogue rather than confrontation, and empathy becomes the foundation of peaceful relations. As we harness the power of empathy for global peace, we contribute to a world where understanding prevails over animosity, and our collective efforts build a tapestry of harmony, compassion, and unity for a brighter and more peaceful future for all.

CHAPTER 48

MEDIA LITERACY FOR A MANIPULATION-FREE SOCIETY

Empowering Minds, Liberating Society: Nurturing Media Literacy

Introduction

The instrumental role of media literacy in fostering a manipulation-free society is increasingly required. This chapter emphasizes the significance of empowering individuals through media literacy, recognizing and countering media manipulation, and the importance of media literacy education and initiatives.

Empowering Individuals through Media Literacy

Media literacy stands as a powerful tool that equips individuals with the skills to navigate the vast landscape of media content. In this section, we delve into the transformative potential of media literacy.

- Developing Critical Thinkers: Fostering critical thinking skills involves empowering individuals to question, analyze, and evaluate media messages critically. In an age of information overload, it is crucial to equip people with the ability to discern between credible information and misleading content. Critical thinkers are open-minded, curious, and willing to challenge assumptions. They apply logical reasoning and evidence-based analysis to assess the credibility and validity of information presented to them. By encouraging critical thinking, we empower individuals to be active participants in their own learning and decision-making processes, reducing susceptibility to manipulation and misinformation.

- Empowering Informed Consumers: Educating individuals to become informed consumers means equipping them with the tools to seek reliable sources and verify information. In today's digital era, misinformation and fake news can spread rapidly, leading to confusion and divisiveness. Informed consumers actively fact-check information, consult reputable sources, and look for evidence to support claims. By promoting media literacy and encouraging a fact-checking mindset, we create a society that values accuracy and evidence-based knowledge, contributing to a more informed and discerning public.

- Nurturing Digital Citizenship: Cultivating responsible digital citizenship involves teaching individuals to navigate the online world with integrity and discernment. As technology continues to shape our daily lives, it is essential to foster a culture of responsible online behavior and digital ethics. Digital citizens are mindful of their online interactions, respectful of others' perspectives, and vigilant against cyber threats. They also protect their personal information and understand the consequences of their online actions. By nurturing digital citizenship, we create a safer and more compassionate online environment, where individuals can engage with one another responsibly and thoughtfully.

In summary, developing critical thinkers involves empowering individuals with the skills to question and evaluate media messages critically. Empowering informed consumers means educating individuals to seek reliable sources and verify information to combat misinformation. Nurturing digital citizenship entails cultivating responsible online behavior and digital ethics to create a more compassionate and secure online community. Together, these three approaches contribute to a more informed, discerning, and responsible society, better equipped to navigate the complexities of the modern information age.

Recognizing and Countering Media Manipulation

Media manipulation is pervasive, and media literacy empowers individuals to discern truth from falsehood. In this section, we explore strategies to recognize and counter media manipulation.

- Understanding Biases: Encouraging individuals to recognize and address their biases is essential to avoid falling prey to manipulation. Biases are cognitive shortcuts and mental predispositions that influence our perceptions and decision-making processes. They can be conscious or unconscious and are shaped by our upbringing, experiences, culture, and beliefs. When we are unaware of our biases, we become more susceptible to manipulation as our judgment may be clouded by preconceived notions. By fostering self-awareness and introspection, we can identify our biases and work towards mitigating their impact on our thoughts and actions. This empowers us to think more objectively and critically, reducing the likelihood of being swayed by manipulative tactics.
- Spotting Misinformation: Teaching individuals how to identify misinformation, disinformation, and propaganda is crucial in the age of information overload. Misinformation refers to false or misleading

information shared without harmful intent, while disinformation involves the deliberate spreading of false information to deceive or manipulate. Propaganda is a systematic effort to manipulate public opinion and influence beliefs. Recognizing these forms of misleading information involves fact-checking, cross-referencing sources, and being critical of sensational or extreme claims. By equipping individuals with the skills to spot misinformation, they can make more informed and rational decisions based on accurate information, thus reducing susceptibility to manipulation.

- Media Fact-Checking: Promoting media fact-checking initiatives is a vital step in holding media outlets accountable for accuracy and truthfulness. In today's digital landscape, information spreads rapidly, and verifying its credibility becomes challenging. Fact-checking involves independent verification of claims made in news articles, reports, and other media content. Fact-checkers use credible sources, evidence, and expert opinions to assess the accuracy of information. By promoting media fact-checking, we encourage media outlets to uphold journalistic integrity and avoid sensationalism or misleading narratives. This, in turn, helps create a media environment where individuals can rely on accurate and trustworthy information, reducing the potential for manipulation.

In summary, encouraging individuals to understand their biases helps them avoid being manipulated by preconceived notions. Teaching people how to spot misinformation, disinformation, and propaganda equips them with the tools to make informed decisions. Promoting media fact-checking initiatives holds media outlets accountable for accurate reporting and fosters a reliable information ecosystem. By addressing biases, spotting misinformation, and supporting media fact-checking, we cultivate a more discerning and informed society, less susceptible to manipulation and misinformation.

Media Literacy Education and Initiatives

Media literacy education is essential in creating an informed and empowered society. In this section, we highlight the importance of media literacy education and initiatives.

- Integrating Media Literacy in Education: Advocating for the integration of media literacy into school curriculums is crucial in nurturing media-savvy generations. Media literacy refers to the ability to access, analyze, evaluate, and critically interpret media messages. In today's digital age, where information is easily accessible and constantly flowing, young learners need the skills to navigate this vast sea of information. By integrating media literacy education into schools, students can learn how to discern reliable sources from misinformation, identify biases in media content, and become more critical consumers of information. It also empowers them to understand the persuasive techniques used in media and how these can influence beliefs and behaviors. Equipping students with media literacy skills not only enhances their ability to make informed decisions but also enables them to become active and responsible participants in society.

- Promoting Media Literacy Campaigns: Supporting media literacy initiatives that raise awareness and provide resources for individuals is essential in a media-driven world. Media literacy campaigns aim to educate the public about the importance of critical media consumption and equip them with tools to navigate the complexities of information dissemination. These campaigns can include public service announcements, workshops, and educational materials that teach individuals how to fact-check, identify misinformation, and be mindful of their media consumption habits. By promoting media literacy campaigns, we empower individuals to take control of their media diet and become more discerning consumers, which ultimately contributes to a more informed and less susceptible society.
- Collaborating with Media Outlets: Encouraging collaboration between educators, policymakers, and media outlets is a powerful way to foster media literacy. Media outlets play a significant role in shaping public opinion and information dissemination. By partnering with educators and policymakers, media outlets can contribute to media literacy initiatives by promoting accurate and ethical reporting, avoiding sensationalism, and providing transparency about their sources and methodologies. Such collaborations can also lead to the development of media literacy programs that cater to specific age groups and address emerging challenges in the media landscape. Building strong partnerships between these stakeholders ensures a collective effort to promote media literacy and ultimately contributes to a more informed, critical, and media-literate society.

In summary, integrating media literacy in education helps cultivate media-savvy generations capable of navigating the information age. Supporting media literacy campaigns raises awareness and equips individuals with tools to discern reliable information. Collaborating with media outlets fosters responsible and ethical media practices. By addressing media literacy through education, campaigns, and collaborations, we empower individuals to be critical consumers of media and reduce susceptibility to manipulation and misinformation.

Conclusion

Media literacy is a transformative force that liberates minds from manipulation and empowers individuals to make informed decisions. By recognizing the power of media literacy in empowering minds, countering manipulation, and promoting media literacy education and initiatives, we pave the way for a manipulation-free society. Together, we foster a community that values critical thinking, media literacy, and digital responsibility, creating a world where individuals navigate the media landscape with discernment and integrity. As we nurture media literacy and empower minds, we contribute to a society that is informed, resilient, and immune to manipulation, and our collective efforts drive us toward a brighter and more media-literate future for all.

CHAPTER 49

EMPOWERING MARGINALIZED VOICES

Amplifying Strength: Empowering Marginalized Communities

Introduction

The vital significance of empowering marginalized voices in our society is now a strategy to accept and grow. This chapter sheds light on the manipulation and power dynamics that affect marginalized communities, emphasizing the importance of amplifying their voices and stories, and creating inclusive and empathetic spaces where their experiences are recognized and valued.

Understanding Manipulation and Power Dynamics in Marginalized Communities

Marginalized communities often face unique challenges when it comes to manipulation and power dynamics. In this section, we delve into the complexities of these issues.

- Systemic Oppression: Systemic oppression refers to the entrenched and institutionalized discrimination and prejudice that perpetuates power imbalances and negatively impacts marginalized groups within society. It is a form of structural inequality that operates through policies, practices, and cultural norms that systematically advantage certain groups while disadvantaging others based on factors like race, ethnicity, gender, sexual orientation, socioeconomic status, and more. The effects of systemic oppression can be far-reaching, impacting access to resources, education, healthcare, employment opportunities, and overall quality of life for marginalized communities.
- Manipulative Narratives: Manipulative narratives are stories or representations constructed by media and societal influences that intentionally manipulate perceptions and reinforce stereotypes about marginalized communities. These narratives can be subtle or explicit, shaping public opinion and attitudes toward these groups. By perpetuating negative stereotypes and biased portrayals, manipulative narratives further marginalize and stigmatize these communities, hindering their progress and

integration into society. Recognizing manipulative narratives is crucial in fostering a more inclusive and empathetic society that seeks to challenge harmful stereotypes and promote genuine understanding.

- Disempowerment and Exploitation: Vulnerable populations, particularly marginalized communities, are often targets of disempowerment and exploitation by those in positions of power or influence. Manipulators may exploit their vulnerabilities to exert control, advance their agendas, or gain economic advantages at the expense of these communities. The disempowerment and exploitation of vulnerable populations further exacerbate the impact of systemic oppression, reinforcing the cycle of marginalization and hindering opportunities for these communities to thrive and advocate for their rights. Recognizing and addressing disempowerment and exploitation is essential in advocating for social justice, equality, and human rights.

In summary, systemic oppression perpetuates power imbalances and adversely affects marginalized communities, leading to disempowerment and exploitation. Manipulative narratives further reinforce stereotypes, exacerbating the marginalization of these groups. Understanding these issues is crucial in creating a more just and equitable society, where individuals actively challenge manipulative narratives, advocate for marginalized communities, and work towards dismantling systemic oppression. It requires fostering empathy, engaging in critical thinking, and actively supporting efforts to empower and uplift vulnerable populations.

Amplifying Marginalized Voices and Stories

Amplifying the voices of marginalized individuals is essential to breaking the cycle of oppression and manipulation. In this section, we explore ways to uplift these voices.

- Diverse Representation: Diverse representation is the call for inclusivity and the fair portrayal of individuals from all walks of life, including those from marginalized communities, in media, storytelling, and various forms of expression. It is the recognition that every individual has a unique story and experience that deserves to be heard and acknowledged. Advocating for diverse representation aims to challenge stereotypes, break down barriers, and promote empathy and understanding among different groups. By featuring a wide range of perspectives, cultures, and identities, diverse representation not only enriches the narratives we consume but also helps build bridges of empathy between different communities.

- Platforms for Expression: Providing platforms and opportunities for marginalized voices means creating spaces where individuals from marginalized communities can express themselves freely and share their stories, struggles, and achievements. It involves actively seeking out and elevating underrepresented voices in various fields, such as media, arts, literature, and public discourse. By offering platforms for expression, society can amplify these voices, bring attention to their unique perspectives, and foster an environment that values diverse storytelling and experiences.
- Active Listening: Active listening involves fully engaging with and genuinely seeking to understand the perspectives and experiences shared by marginalized individuals. It goes beyond passive hearing and involves being present, empathetic, and receptive to the emotions and thoughts conveyed by the speaker. Active listening is an essential part of fostering empathy and breaking down prejudices and misconceptions. By actively listening to the lived experiences of marginalized communities, individuals can gain valuable insights, challenge their own biases, and become advocates for social change and justice.

In summary, diverse representation calls for fair and inclusive portrayal of individuals from all backgrounds, providing opportunities for marginalized voices to be heard and valued. Advocating for diverse representation and providing platforms for expression creates a more inclusive and empathetic society, where everyone's stories are recognized and respected. Active listening further enhances empathy and understanding by engaging with the lived experiences of marginalized individuals and promoting genuine connection and support for their struggles and aspirations. Together, these initiatives foster a more compassionate and equitable world where all voices are heard and appreciated.

Creating Inclusive and Empathetic Spaces

Creating inclusive and empathetic spaces fosters a sense of belonging and validation for marginalized communities. In this section, we discuss strategies to create such environments.

- Cultivating Empathy: Cultivating empathy involves actively promoting and encouraging understanding, compassion, and consideration for the feelings and perspectives of others. It is about creating an environment where individuals can put themselves in the shoes of others, acknowledging their struggles, joys, and experiences. By fostering empathy, society can bridge divides and foster inclusivity by promoting a sense of connection and shared humanity among diverse individuals.

- Challenging Bias and Discrimination: Addressing bias and discrimination is crucial to combatting exclusion and marginalization within society. This involves confronting and challenging preconceived notions and stereotypes that perpetuate unequal treatment and limited opportunities for certain groups. By raising awareness about biases and their negative impacts, society can work towards creating a more just and inclusive environment that respects and values the dignity of all individuals.
- Advocating for Equal Rights: Advocating for equal rights entails actively supporting policies, initiatives, and movements that strive for fairness and equal opportunities for everyone, regardless of their background or identity. It involves standing up against any form of discrimination and working towards dismantling systemic barriers that hinder certain groups from accessing the same rights and privileges as others. By advocating for equal rights, society can move closer to achieving a more equitable and inclusive world where everyone can thrive.

In summary, cultivating empathy promotes understanding and compassion among individuals, fostering inclusivity and connectedness. Addressing bias and discrimination challenges unjust attitudes and practices, leading to a more fair and respectful society. Advocating for equal rights supports policies and actions that strive for a level playing field, ensuring that all individuals have the same opportunities to live fulfilling and meaningful lives. By combining these efforts, society can work towards a more harmonious and equitable future, where empathy, justice, and inclusivity prevail.

Conclusion

Empowering marginalized voices is essential to dismantling the structures of manipulation and oppression that have plagued our society. By understanding manipulation and power dynamics in marginalized communities, amplifying their voices and stories, and creating inclusive and empathetic spaces, we pave the way for a more just and equitable world. Together, we foster a community that values diversity, empathy, and inclusivity, creating a world where marginalized voices are recognized, valued, and uplifted. As we empower marginalized communities, we contribute to a society that stands against manipulation and discrimination, and where collective efforts create a tapestry of strength, unity, and empowerment for a brighter and more inclusive future for all.

CHAPTER 50

MINDFULNESS AND ENVIRONMENTAL CONSCIOUSNESS

Nurturing Harmony: Mindfulness in Environmental Stewardship

Introduction

This chapter explores the profound connection between mindfulness and environmental consciousness. It highlights the importance of incorporating mindfulness in environmental decision-making processes, ensuring that choices are made with full awareness of their ecological impact. By fostering mindfulness, individuals and organizations can avoid falling prey to greenwashing and manipulation, which may mislead the public about the true environmental impact of certain practices or products.

Moreover, the chapter emphasizes the role of empathy for the natural world in promoting sustainable practices. When individuals develop a deep sense of connection and compassion for the environment, they are more likely to take responsible actions to protect and preserve it. This empathy-driven approach encourages a more authentic and meaningful commitment to eco-conscious efforts, moving beyond superficial gestures.

Ultimately, cultivating mindfulness in environmental consciousness leads to more responsible and ethical practices that benefit not only the environment but also society as a whole. By combining mindfulness with empathy, individuals and communities can create a more sustainable and harmonious relationship with the natural world, ensuring a better future for future generations.

Cultivating Mindfulness in Environmental Decision-Making

Mindfulness plays a crucial role in guiding thoughtful and responsible environmental choices. In this section, we explore the transformative potential of mindfulness in environmental decision-making.

- Awareness of Interconnectedness: Awareness of interconnectedness refers to recognizing the intricate and inseparable relationship between human actions and the natural world. It involves understanding that every choice and behavior, whether at an individual or societal level, has consequences that affect the environment. This awareness fosters a sense of responsibility and accountability for the impact of human activities on the planet, emphasizing the need for sustainable and mindful practices.

- Eco-Conscious Consumption: Eco-conscious consumption entails adopting mindful and environmentally responsible behaviors in how we use and consume resources. It involves making informed choices to reduce waste, conserve natural resources, and minimize harm to the environment. This can include practices such as recycling, reducing single-use plastics, choosing sustainable products, and supporting eco-friendly businesses. By embracing eco-conscious consumption, individuals contribute to mitigating environmental degradation and promoting a healthier planet.
- Ethical Considerations: Integrating ethical considerations into decision-making processes involves prioritizing the well-being of the planet and future generations. It means making choices that align with values such as environmental stewardship, social responsibility, and intergenerational equity. Ethical considerations prompt individuals and organizations to evaluate the potential impact of their actions on the environment and the broader global community. This can lead to the adoption of sustainable practices, the support of eco-friendly policies, and the implementation of responsible business practices.

In summary, awareness of interconnectedness highlights the interdependence between human actions and the environment, prompting individuals to take responsibility for their impact on the planet. Eco-conscious consumption encourages mindful and sustainable practices to reduce environmental harm. Integrating ethical considerations into decision-making processes ensures that choices align with values that prioritize the well-being of the planet and future generations. Together, these principles contribute to a more sustainable and responsible approach to living and interacting with the natural world.

Overcoming Greenwashing and Manipulation in Eco-Conscious Efforts

Greenwashing and manipulation can obscure genuine eco-conscious efforts. In this section, we discuss strategies to recognize and overcome manipulation in environmental messaging.

- Educating for Awareness: Educating for awareness involves providing comprehensive education on greenwashing and manipulation tactics to empower individuals to make informed choices. Greenwashing refers to the deceptive marketing practices used by businesses and organizations to present themselves as environmentally friendly when, in reality, their practices may not align with sustainable principles. By raising awareness about greenwashing and manipulation tactics, individuals can develop critical thinking skills to discern between authentic environmental efforts and misleading claims. This knowledge enables consumers to make conscious decisions and support genuinely eco-conscious products and services.

- Authenticity and Transparency: Encouraging businesses and organizations to be authentic and transparent about their environmental efforts is essential in building trust and fostering accountability. When companies openly share their sustainability practices, goals, and progress, consumers can evaluate their commitment to environmental responsibility more accurately. Transparency not only helps in holding companies accountable but also empowers consumers to support businesses that align with their values. By promoting authenticity and transparency, we create a more honest and responsible marketplace that values genuine environmental efforts.
- Valuing Substance over Symbolism: Encouraging the evaluation of genuine environmental impact rather than superficial gestures emphasizes the importance of substance over symbolism. Some companies engage in tokenistic actions, such as green packaging or marketing slogans, without implementing substantial sustainability practices. By valuing substance over symbolism, individuals and organizations prioritize actions that have a tangible and positive impact on the environment. This approach drives businesses to implement meaningful changes, leading to real progress in sustainability and environmental protection.

In summary, educating for awareness equips individuals with the knowledge to recognize greenwashing and manipulation tactics, empowering them to make informed choices. Encouraging authenticity and transparency fosters trust and accountability between businesses and consumers. Valuing substance over symbolism ensures that environmental efforts are genuinely impactful and contribute to a more sustainable future. Together, these principles promote responsible consumerism and drive businesses to adopt authentic sustainability practices.

Promoting Sustainable Practices through Empathy

Empathy for the natural world is the foundation of sustainable practices. In this section, we explore the significance of empathy in promoting a harmonious relationship with the environment.

- Connecting with Nature: Cultivating a deep connection with nature involves developing a sense of care and responsibility for the environment by fostering a profound bond with the natural world. When individuals spend time in nature, observe its beauty, and witness its intricate ecosystems, they are more likely to appreciate its significance and recognize the need to protect it. This connection with nature can evoke feelings of awe, wonder, and gratitude, motivating people to take action to preserve and conserve the environment.
- Valuing Biodiversity: Recognizing the value of biodiversity emphasizes the importance of preserving the immense variety of life forms on Earth and the ecosystems they inhabit. Biodiversity plays a crucial role in maintaining ecological balance, resilience, and stability. Each species, no matter how small, contributes to the intricate web of life, and their disappearance can have far-reaching consequences. By understanding and valuing biodiversity, individuals are more likely to support conservation efforts and take measures to protect endangered species and their habitats.
- Long-Term Thinking: Adopting a long-term perspective in environmental decision-making involves considering the impacts of actions not only in the present but also on future generations and the overall health of the planet. Often, environmental issues require solutions that address complex and interconnected challenges, which may take time to yield results. By prioritizing long-term thinking, individuals and policymakers focus on strategies that promote sustainable practices, minimize environmental degradation, and secure a livable planet for future generations.

In summary, connecting with nature nurtures a sense of care and responsibility for the environment, motivating individuals to protect it. Valuing biodiversity acknowledges the importance of preserving the rich variety of life forms and their habitats. Adopting a long-term perspective ensures that environmental decisions prioritize the well-being of the planet and future generations. Embracing these principles collectively contributes to a more sustainable and ecologically conscious approach to protecting our natural world.

Conclusion

Mindfulness in environmental stewardship serves as a powerful catalyst for sustainable and ethical choices. By cultivating mindfulness in environmental decision-making, overcoming greenwashing and manipulation, and promoting sustainable practices through empathy, we pave the way for a more harmonious and respectful relationship with the natural world. Together, we foster a community that values mindfulness, transparency, and empathy, creating a world where individuals and organizations prioritize the preservation and restoration of our planet. As we nurture mindfulness and environmental consciousness, we contribute to a society that stands as a guardian of the Earth, where collective efforts create a tapestry of ecological harmony, compassion, and sustainability for a brighter and greener future for all.

CHAPTER 51

CULTIVATING EMPATHY IN THE DIGITAL AGE

The Digital Compassion: Empathy in a Connected World

Introduction

In the digital age, technology has significantly impacted empathy and social interactions. This chapter delves into the importance of maintaining authentic connections amidst the prevalence of digital communication. It highlights the need to cultivate empathy and understanding even in virtual spaces to foster meaningful relationships.

While technology can sometimes be blamed for reducing face-to-face interactions, the chapter also acknowledges its potential for positive change. It explores how technology can be harnessed as a tool to build empathy and create connections across diverse cultures and geographical boundaries.

The focus of this chapter is on striking a balance between the benefits and drawbacks of technology. It encourages individuals to be mindful of how they use technology to nurture empathy and genuine connections, while also being aware of potential pitfalls that might hinder empathetic interactions.

The chapter underscores the importance of using technology responsibly and thoughtfully to maintain and enhance empathy in the digital age. By doing so, individuals can harness the power of technology for positive change and create a more empathetic and connected world.

The Impact of Technology on Empathy and Social Interactions

Technology has revolutionized how we connect and interact with others, but it also brings challenges to empathy and social relationships. In this section, we delve into the impact of technology on empathy.

- Digital Disconnect: The digital disconnect refers to the potential negative impact of technology on our ability to form genuine emotional connections and experience empathy in our interactions. In a digitally connected world, where much of our communication happens through screens and devices, there is a risk of losing the depth and authenticity of face-to-face interactions. Virtual communication can create emotional distance, making it challenging to fully understand and empathize with others' feelings and experiences.

- Empathy Deficit: The empathy deficit highlights concerns about a decline in empathy observed in society, partly attributed to the increasing reliance on digital communication. With the rise of social media and online interactions, people may become more disconnected from the emotional cues present in in-person conversations, leading to a reduced capacity to empathize with others' emotions and experiences. This deficit can result in misunderstandings, misinterpretations, and a lack of emotional connection, impacting our ability to relate to others on a deeper level.
- Fostering Empathy Online: Fostering empathy in digital spaces is essential to maintaining authentic and meaningful connections. Several strategies can be employed to promote empathy in online interactions. First, individuals can practice active listening and give their full attention to others during virtual conversations. This includes acknowledging emotions and responding with empathy and understanding. Second, users can use emojis, gifs, and other visual cues to express emotions and convey tone, bridging the gap left by the absence of nonverbal cues in digital communication.
- Furthermore, promoting open and respectful dialogue in online communities can create an environment conducive to empathy. Encouraging users to share personal stories and experiences allows others to understand different perspectives and challenges, fostering empathy and compassion. Digital platforms can also implement features that encourage positive interactions, discourage cyberbullying, and support users in reporting harmful content.
- Educating individuals about the potential limitations of digital communication in conveying emotions and fostering empathy is vital. By raising awareness of the digital disconnect and empathy deficit, people can make conscious efforts to bridge the gap through intentional communication and genuine understanding.

In summary, recognizing the digital disconnect and empathy deficit is crucial for promoting empathetic interactions in a digitally connected world. By fostering empathy online, individuals can build more authentic and meaningful connections, creating a compassionate and supportive digital community. Through awareness, education, and empathetic practices, we can enhance our ability to connect emotionally in the digital realm and maintain genuine relationships with others.

Nurturing Genuine Connections in a Digital World

Amidst the digital landscape, fostering genuine connections is essential for preserving empathy. In this section, we explore strategies to nurture meaningful relationships in the digital age.

- Mindful Presence: Mindful presence refers to the practice of being fully present and attentive during digital interactions, consciously engaging with others and their emotions. In a digital world filled with distractions, practicing mindfulness helps individuals to focus on the present moment and be aware of the emotional cues and needs of others during online conversations. By being mindful, individuals can better understand and empathize with others' feelings and experiences, leading to more meaningful and supportive interactions.
- Empathetic Communication: Empathetic communication involves actively listening to others, seeking to understand their perspectives, and acknowledging their emotions with compassion and validation. In online interactions, where nonverbal cues may be limited, empathetic communication becomes even more crucial. By expressing empathy, individuals can create a safe and supportive space for others to share their thoughts and feelings, fostering a sense of connection and understanding.
- Virtual Community Building: Virtual community building focuses on creating online spaces that promote empathy, belonging, and support among members. In the digital realm, where physical distances can separate individuals, virtual communities serve as platforms where people with shared interests and experiences can come together. These communities play a vital role in nurturing a sense of belonging and connection, enabling individuals to find support, empathy, and understanding from others who may be facing similar challenges or experiences.
- In virtual communities, empathetic communication and mindful presence are essential components. Members actively listen to one another, validate each other's emotions, and offer support when needed. The sense of belonging and camaraderie within these communities encourages individuals to share their thoughts and feelings openly, knowing they will be met with empathy and understanding.
- Furthermore, virtual community leaders can play a significant role in fostering empathy by setting a positive example through their own empathetic communication and actions. By emphasizing the importance of respectful and compassionate interactions, leaders create a culture of empathy within the community, encouraging others to follow suit.

In summary, promoting mindful presence, empathetic communication, and virtual community building are crucial steps toward creating a more empathetic and supportive digital world. By being fully present in online interactions, actively listening, and validating others' experiences, individuals can cultivate genuine connections and understanding. Virtual communities that prioritize empathy and support provide valuable spaces for individuals to share their thoughts and emotions, fostering a sense of belonging and connection in an otherwise digitally disconnected world.

Using Technology for Positive Change and Empathy-Building

Technology can be harnessed as a powerful tool for fostering empathy and positive change. In this section, we discuss how to leverage technology for empathy-building.

- Digital Empathy Initiatives: Digital empathy initiatives refer to various efforts and campaigns aimed at fostering understanding, compassion, and empathy in the online world. These initiatives recognize the importance of empathy in building meaningful connections and supporting one another in the digital realm.
- Supporting and participating in digital empathy initiatives involves actively contributing to and promoting efforts that promote empathy, compassion, and emotional support in digital spaces. These initiatives can take various forms, such as online workshops, webinars, or campaigns that educate individuals about the importance of empathy and how to practice it effectively in their online interactions. By supporting these initiatives, individuals become part of a collective effort to create a more empathetic and caring digital community.
- Social Media for Good: Utilizing social media platforms for good means leveraging these powerful digital tools to raise awareness about important causes and issues that need public attention. Social media provides an accessible and far-reaching platform to share information, stories, and experiences that can evoke empathy and understanding. By sharing content that humanizes global issues, such as poverty, inequality, or environmental challenges, individuals can help others relate to these issues on a personal level and develop empathy for those affected by them.
- Moreover, social media can be used to promote positive actions and initiatives that support vulnerable communities. By amplifying the voices of those working towards positive change and sharing information about volunteer opportunities or donation drives, individuals can inspire others to take empathetic actions and contribute to meaningful causes.

- Digital Activism: Digital activism, also known as online activism or internet activism, involves using digital tools and platforms to advocate for social and political change. Engaging in digital activism can be a powerful way to foster empathy for marginalized communities and promote awareness about their struggles and challenges. Digital activists often create and share content, such as infographics, videos, and articles, that shed light on social injustices and advocate for human rights.
- Through digital activism, individuals can collaborate with like-minded people from around the world, forming a global network of empathy and support. Digital activists may organize online petitions, participate in social media campaigns, or join virtual rallies to draw attention to pressing issues and encourage empathy among a broader audience. By using their online presence to create positive change, digital activists inspire empathy and compassion, motivating others to become more involved and invested in creating a better world.

In summary, digital empathy initiatives, utilizing social media for good, and engaging in digital activism are valuable approaches to fostering empathy and understanding in the digital landscape. By supporting and participating in these initiatives, individuals can contribute to a more compassionate online community, create awareness about global issues, and advocate for positive change. These efforts collectively encourage a culture of empathy and compassion in the digital world, promoting understanding and support for one another, regardless of physical distances or cultural backgrounds.

Conclusion

In the digital age, cultivating empathy remains crucial for maintaining genuine connections and promoting positive change. By understanding the impact of technology on empathy and social interactions, nurturing authentic connections in a digital world, and harnessing technology for empathy-building, we pave the way for a more compassionate and connected society. Together, we foster a community that values mindful presence, empathetic communication, and digital empathy initiatives, creating a world where technology becomes a vehicle for understanding, compassion, and positive change. As we embrace empathy in the digital age, we contribute to a society that bridges digital divides, where collective efforts create a tapestry of empathy, kindness, and connection for a brighter and more empathetic future for all.

PART X: EMBRACING ETHICAL LEADERSHIP

CHAPTER 52

ETHICAL LEADERSHIP AND ORGANIZATIONAL CULTURE

Cultivating Ethical Roots: Nurturing a Culture of Integrity

Introduction

Ethical leadership has a transformative impact on organizational culture. This chapter highlights the crucial role that ethical leaders play in influencing workplace dynamics, fostering a culture of empathy and integrity, and cultivating resilient and ethical teams.

The chapter delves into how ethical leaders serve as role models for their teams, demonstrating honesty, transparency, and moral soundness in their actions. By leading with integrity and setting high ethical standards, they inspire employees to follow suit and contribute to a positive and ethical work environment.

Ethical leaders prioritize the well-being of their team members and consider their perspectives and needs when making decisions. They encourage open communication and active listening, creating a supportive and inclusive atmosphere where employees feel valued and heard.

Additionally, the chapter explores how ethical leadership builds trust among team members and with stakeholders. By upholding honesty and accountability, ethical leaders earn the trust and respect of their workforce, fostering a sense of loyalty and commitment.

Furthermore, the chapter highlights how ethical leadership contributes to the development of resilient teams. When employees feel supported by their leaders and work in an environment of trust and empathy, they are more likely to navigate challenges and setbacks with resilience.

The chapter emphasizes that ethical leadership is not only essential for maintaining ethical standards but also for creating a positive and cohesive organizational culture. Through ethical leadership, organizations can foster empathy, integrity, and resilience, leading to the overall success and well-being of their teams.

The Influence of Ethical Leadership on Organizational Culture

Ethical leadership serves as the cornerstone of a healthy and ethical organizational culture. In this section, we delve into the profound influence of ethical leadership on workplace dynamics.

- Setting the Tone: Ethical leaders play a crucial role in setting the tone and ethical standards for the entire organization. They lead by example and demonstrate through their actions and decisions that ethical behavior is a non-negotiable aspect of the organizational culture. When leaders prioritize integrity, honesty, and fairness, it creates a ripple effect throughout the organization, inspiring employees to follow suit and embrace ethical values in their own conduct. By fostering a culture of ethics from the top down, ethical leaders create an environment where ethical behavior is not only expected but celebrated and rewarded.
- Trust and Transparency: Building trust is a cornerstone of ethical leadership, and it goes hand in hand with transparency in communication and decision-making. Ethical leaders ensure that information is shared openly and honestly with employees, stakeholders, and the public when appropriate. This transparency helps to build credibility and fosters a sense of trust among all stakeholders. When people trust their leaders, they are more likely to feel secure and committed to the organization's mission, knowing that they are being treated fairly and with respect. Ethical leaders understand that trust is a valuable asset that requires consistent effort to build and maintain.
- Empowerment and Accountability: Ethical leaders empower their employees by giving them the autonomy and authority to make ethical choices within their roles. They encourage a culture of open dialogue and encourage employees to speak up if they encounter ethical dilemmas or concerns. By fostering an environment where ethical decision-making is supported and encouraged, ethical leaders empower their team members to act with integrity and take responsibility for their actions. At the same time, ethical leaders also hold everyone accountable for adhering to ethical standards. They ensure that unethical behavior is not tolerated and take appropriate action when necessary to address any violations of ethical principles. This combination of empowerment and accountability helps to create a culture of ethics where individuals feel responsible for their actions and are motivated to act in a principled manner.

In summary, ethical leadership encompasses setting the tone, building trust and transparency, and promoting empowerment and accountability. Ethical leaders act as role models, demonstrating through their actions the ethical behavior they expect from others. They prioritize honesty, integrity, and fairness, creating a culture of ethics that permeates the organization. By fostering trust and transparency, ethical leaders establish credibility and build strong relationships with employees and stakeholders. They also empower their team members to make ethical decisions and hold everyone accountable for adhering to ethical standards. Ethical leadership creates an environment where individuals are motivated to act with integrity, contributing to the overall success and reputation of the organization.

Encouraging Empathy and Integrity in the Workplace

Empathy and integrity are pillars of an ethical workplace culture. In this section, we discuss strategies to encourage these qualities within the organization.

- Empathetic Leadership: Empathetic leadership is a leadership style that places a strong emphasis on understanding and valuing the well-being of employees. It involves actively seeking to understand the perspectives, emotions, and needs of team members and taking those into consideration when making decisions. Empathetic leaders demonstrate genuine care and concern for their employees, creating a supportive and compassionate work environment. By showing empathy, leaders can build trust and strong relationships with their team, which can lead to increased job satisfaction, higher levels of engagement, and improved overall performance.
- Embracing Diverse Perspectives: A key aspect of empathetic leadership is fostering a culture that embraces and values diverse perspectives. This means creating an inclusive environment where individuals from different backgrounds, experiences, and identities feel welcomed and appreciated. Empathetic leaders recognize that diversity of thought leads to more innovative solutions and better decision-making. They encourage open dialogue and active listening to ensure that all voices are heard and respected. By embracing diverse perspectives, leaders can tap into the collective wisdom of their team and promote a culture of respect and understanding.
- Ethical Decision-Making Training: Ethical decision-making training is an essential component of empathetic leadership. It provides employees with the knowledge, tools, and resources to navigate ethical dilemmas and make principled choices. This training helps individuals develop their moral reasoning skills and understand the potential impact of their decisions on

others and the organization. Ethical decision-making training also helps employees recognize and address conflicts of interest, biases, and other factors that may influence their judgment. By providing such training, empathetic leaders empower their team to make ethical choices in their daily work and contribute to a culture of integrity and trust.

In summary, empathetic leadership involves promoting the well-being of employees, valuing diverse perspectives, and providing ethical decision-making training. Empathetic leaders demonstrate genuine care and concern for their team members, fostering a supportive and compassionate work environment. They also encourage open dialogue and actively embrace diverse perspectives, recognizing the value of different viewpoints in driving innovation and success. Additionally, ethical decision-making training equips employees with the skills and knowledge to navigate ethical dilemmas and make principled choices, contributing to a culture of integrity and trust. Together, these elements of empathetic leadership create a positive and inclusive workplace that benefits both individuals and the organization as a whole.

Building Resilient and Ethical Teams

Resilient and ethical teams are the bedrock of a thriving organization. In this section, we explore ways to build such teams.

- Collaborative Approach: A collaborative approach in leadership emphasizes the importance of teamwork, cooperation, and shared decision-making among team members. It fosters a sense of unity and collective responsibility, where individuals work together towards common goals. Encouraging collaboration allows team members to pool their diverse skills, knowledge, and perspectives, leading to more innovative solutions and improved problem-solving. This approach promotes a positive team culture where every member's contributions are valued, and individuals feel empowered to share their ideas and opinions. Collaborative leadership enables teams to work cohesively, achieve higher levels of productivity, and adapt more effectively to changing circumstances.
- Learning from Mistakes: An essential aspect of a supportive and growth-oriented leadership style is creating an environment where mistakes are viewed as opportunities for learning and growth, rather than sources of blame or punishment. Leaders who promote learning from mistakes encourage their team members to take risks, experiment with new ideas, and explore creative solutions without fear of failure. When mistakes happen, they are seen as

valuable learning experiences that help individuals and teams improve and develop resilience. By embracing a learning-oriented approach, leaders can foster a culture of continuous improvement and innovation, where employees are motivated to seek out challenges and take on new responsibilities.

- Ethical Conflict Resolution: Ethical conflict resolution involves providing resources and support for addressing conflicts and disagreements in a constructive and principled manner. Leaders who prioritize ethical conflict resolution encourage open communication, active listening, and mutual respect among team members. They create a safe and non-judgmental space for discussing differences and resolving conflicts based on shared values and ethical standards. Ethical conflict resolution involves seeking win-win solutions that consider the interests and needs of all parties involved. It avoids manipulative tactics or coercive approaches, ensuring that the resolution process is fair, respectful, and aligned with the organization's values.

In summary, a collaborative approach in leadership emphasizes teamwork and cooperation among team members, fostering a sense of unity and collective responsibility. It promotes a positive team culture where individuals are encouraged to share their ideas and learn from one another. Learning from mistakes is a crucial aspect of a growth-oriented leadership style, as it creates an environment where mistakes are viewed as opportunities for learning and development. Ethical conflict resolution involves providing resources and support for resolving conflicts constructively, based on shared values and principles. Together, these elements contribute to a positive and supportive team environment, where individuals can thrive, learn, and contribute their best efforts to achieving common goals.

Conclusion

Ethical leadership creates a ripple effect that shapes the very essence of an organization's culture. By understanding the influence of ethical leadership on organizational culture, encouraging empathy and integrity in the workplace, and building resilient and ethical teams, we pave the way for a culture that values ethical conduct, fosters empathy, and upholds integrity. Together, we foster a community that values ethical leadership, trust, and accountability, creating a workplace where employees feel respected, supported, and empowered to make ethical decisions. As we embrace ethical leadership, we contribute to a society that prioritizes ethical conduct, where collective efforts create a tapestry of integrity, empathy, and resilience for a brighter and more ethical future for all.

CHAPTER 53

THE ETHICAL RESPONSIBILITY OF TECH COMPANIES

Beyond Innovation: Navigating the Ethical Frontier in Tech

Introduction

In the digital age, tech companies hold an ethical responsibility that this chapter explores in detail. The focus is on addressing manipulation and ethical concerns prevalent in tech industry practices, while also striking a balance between profit-seeking and social responsibility.

The chapter emphasizes the significance of recognizing the potential for manipulation and exploitative tactics employed by some tech companies to influence user behavior and maximize profits. It sheds light on the need for transparency and ethical guidelines to safeguard user data and privacy, ensuring that users' trust is not compromised.

Furthermore, the chapter discusses the importance of striking a balance between pursuing profit and fulfilling social responsibilities. Tech companies are encouraged to consider the wider societal impact of their products and services, taking into account factors such as accessibility, inclusivity, and environmental impact.

Ethical tech practices also entail promoting diversity and inclusion within the industry, ensuring fair and equal treatment of employees, and mitigating algorithmic bias that could perpetuate discrimination.

Moreover, the chapter explores the role of tech companies in shaping a more ethical tech landscape. It advocates for collaboration between tech companies, policymakers, and stakeholders to develop industry-wide ethical standards and guidelines.

Ultimately, this chapter aims to raise awareness about the ethical responsibilities that tech companies carry in the digital age. By addressing manipulation and ethical concerns, striking a balance between profit and social responsibility, and actively shaping an ethical tech landscape, tech companies can contribute positively to society and foster trust among users and stakeholders.

Addressing Manipulation and Ethical Concerns in Tech Industry Practices

The rapid advancement of technology has brought about ethical challenges and concerns. In this section, we explore the need for addressing manipulation and ethical issues in tech practices.

- User Data and Privacy: In today's digital age, user data and privacy have become paramount concerns. Recognizing the importance of safeguarding user data means taking measures to protect personal information collected by tech products and services. Companies should implement robust security measures to prevent unauthorized access to user data and be transparent about how they collect, store, and use this information. Providing clear and accessible privacy policies can help users make informed decisions about sharing their data and maintaining control over their personal information.
- Algorithmic Bias: As technology becomes more prevalent in our lives, algorithms play an increasingly significant role in decision-making processes, ranging from recommendation systems to hiring practices. Addressing algorithmic bias is crucial to ensure fairness and inclusivity in tech products and services. Bias can inadvertently be introduced into algorithms due to biased data or flawed design, leading to unequal treatment of different user groups. To mitigate bias, companies need to test their algorithms rigorously, consider diverse perspectives during development, and regularly audit them to identify and rectify any discriminatory outcomes.
- Digital Addiction and Mental Health: The widespread use of tech products and services has raised concerns about their potential impact on mental health. Acknowledging the potential for digital addiction means recognizing the addictive nature of certain apps, platforms, or games that can lead to excessive screen time and neglect of other important activities. Companies should take steps to promote healthy digital habits and provide tools that allow users to monitor and manage their screen time. Additionally, raising awareness about the potential negative effects of excessive tech use on mental health can help individuals make informed choices about their digital consumption.

In summary, user data and privacy are essential aspects of responsible technology use. Transparency in data collection and usage builds trust between users and tech companies. Addressing algorithmic bias ensures that tech products and services treat all users fairly and inclusively. Recognizing the potential impact of tech products on mental health allows individuals to make mindful choices about their digital consumption and promotes the development of healthier tech environments. By considering these factors, tech companies can contribute to a more responsible and user-friendly digital landscape.

Balancing Profit with Social Responsibility

Tech companies have a unique opportunity to balance profit motives with social responsibility. In this section, we discuss strategies for ethical decision-making in the pursuit of profits.

- Corporate Social Responsibility (CSR): Corporate Social Responsibility is a business approach that emphasizes the responsibility of tech companies towards society and the environment. It involves integrating social and environmental concerns into business operations and decision-making processes. Tech companies are increasingly recognizing the significance of CSR in building a positive reputation, attracting socially conscious consumers, and contributing to sustainable development.
- Ethical Product Development: Ethical product development involves prioritizing ethical considerations throughout the entire product development lifecycle. This includes conducting ethical impact assessments to identify and mitigate potential negative consequences, such as privacy violations, algorithmic bias, or environmental harm. Companies need to ensure that their products align with ethical standards, protect user rights, and do not compromise individuals' well-being or societal values.
- Stakeholder Engagement: Effective stakeholder engagement is essential for tech companies to understand and address the concerns and interests of various stakeholders, including customers, employees, communities, investors, and regulators. Engaging with stakeholders fosters transparency, accountability, and inclusivity in decision-making processes. It allows companies to gain valuable insights, build trust, and co-create solutions that benefit both the company and its stakeholders.
- By embracing corporate social responsibility, tech companies can demonstrate a commitment to making a positive impact on society and the environment. Ethical product development ensures that the technologies created serve the greater good while avoiding harm. Engaging with stakeholders ensures that the company's actions align with the expectations and needs of its diverse stakeholders. Collectively, these practices contribute to a more responsible, sustainable, and socially conscious tech industry.

Shaping a More Ethical Tech Landscape

Collective efforts are needed to shape a more ethical tech landscape. In this section, we explore ways to create a culture of ethical innovation within the tech industry.

- Ethical Guidelines and Standards: Advocating for the establishment of industry-wide ethical guidelines and standards is crucial to ensure a consistent and principled approach to technology development and implementation. These guidelines provide a framework for tech companies to navigate ethical dilemmas, make responsible decisions, and uphold the well-being of users and society. By defining clear ethical standards, the tech industry can create a shared understanding of what is acceptable and what is not, promoting trust and accountability.
- Ethical Leadership: Ethical leadership is essential for shaping the culture and values of tech companies. Leaders who prioritize ethical decision-making set a positive example for employees and stakeholders, guiding them to act with integrity. Ethical leaders consider the broader impact of their decisions on all stakeholders, including customers, employees, and society. They foster an environment where employees feel empowered to raise ethical concerns and challenge unethical practices. Ethical leadership is instrumental in driving responsible innovation and ensuring that the company's mission aligns with ethical principles.
- Collaboration and Knowledge Sharing: Encouraging collaboration among tech companies and sharing best practices for ethical innovation benefits the entire industry. By collaborating, companies can pool their resources, expertise, and insights to tackle complex ethical challenges collectively. Knowledge sharing allows tech companies to learn from one another's experiences, successes, and failures in navigating ethical dilemmas. It fosters a culture of continuous improvement, where companies can evolve and adapt their ethical approaches based on shared knowledge and emerging best practices.
- Overall, these three aspects play a pivotal role in promoting ethics and responsibility within the tech industry. Ethical guidelines and standards set a common ethical framework, providing a compass for decision-making. Ethical leadership ensures that these values are upheld throughout the organization and drive responsible behavior. Collaboration and knowledge sharing enables companies to collectively enhance their ethical practices and contribute to a more ethical and socially responsible tech sector.

Conclusion

Tech companies hold immense power in shaping the future of our digital world. By addressing manipulation and ethical concerns in tech industry practices, balancing profit with social responsibility, and shaping a more ethical tech landscape, we pave the way for a tech industry that values ethics, transparency, and social impact. Together, we foster a community that values data privacy, fairness, and ethical innovation, creating a tech landscape where user well-being and societal benefit are paramount. As we embrace the ethical responsibility of tech companies, we contribute to a society where technology serves as a force for good, and our collective efforts create a tapestry of ethical tech advancements for a brighter and more responsible future for all.

CHAPTER 54

MEDIA ETHICS AND RESPONSIBLE JOURNALISM

Truth and Integrity: Upholding Ethical Journalism

Introduction

In the realm of journalism, the chapter emphasizes the vital importance of media ethics and responsible journalism. It sheds light on the ethical considerations that journalists and media outlets must navigate in their pursuit of truth and accuracy.

The chapter explores the delicate balance between sensationalism and truth in media reporting. It highlights the ethical responsibility of journalists to present information in a fair, balanced, and objective manner, avoiding sensationalism that can distort facts and mislead audiences.

Furthermore, the chapter emphasizes the significance of fostering media outlets that prioritize ethical reporting. This includes transparency in disclosing sources, fact-checking information before publication, and providing proper context to avoid misinterpretations.

Additionally, the chapter delves into the impact of responsible journalism on public trust. By upholding media ethics, journalists and media outlets can build credibility and foster a sense of trustworthiness among their audiences.

The chapter also addresses the ethical dilemmas that journalists may encounter, such as reporting on sensitive and private matters. It advocates for exercising sensitivity and respect for individuals' privacy while fulfilling the role of informing the public on matters of importance.

Moreover, the chapter emphasizes the need for journalists to be accountable for their actions and to acknowledge and correct errors promptly if they occur. This helps maintain integrity and credibility in media reporting.

The chapter underscores the critical role of media ethics and responsible journalism in providing accurate, unbiased, and trustworthy information to the public. By adhering to ethical principles and prioritizing truthful reporting, journalists and media outlets can contribute to a well-informed society and uphold the essential values of journalism in a responsible manner.

Ethical Considerations in Journalism and Media Reporting

Journalists play a crucial role in informing the public and shaping public opinion. In this section, we delve into the ethical considerations that guide responsible journalism.

- Truth and Accuracy: Upholding the principles of truthfulness and accuracy in reporting is fundamental to the credibility and trustworthiness of journalism. Journalists have a responsibility to provide accurate and reliable information to their audiences. This requires thorough fact-checking, corroborating information from multiple sources, and verifying the authenticity of data and quotes. Adhering to truth and accuracy standards helps prevent the spread of misinformation and ensures that the public is well-informed.
- Independence and Impartiality: Maintaining journalistic independence and impartiality is essential for presenting news stories without bias or undue influence. Journalists must avoid conflicts of interest and refrain from promoting personal or organizational agendas. An impartial approach to reporting helps readers, viewers, and listeners make their own informed judgments without being influenced by a particular viewpoint. Independence and impartiality safeguard the integrity of journalism and protect it from being used as a tool for propaganda or manipulation.
- Privacy and Sensitivity: Respecting individuals' privacy and exercising sensitivity in reporting on personal and sensitive matters is crucial for ethical journalism. Journalists should exercise caution when reporting on sensitive topics such as tragedies, personal crises, or health issues. They should obtain informed consent from individuals before publishing personal information, especially when it pertains to vulnerable or traumatized individuals. Respecting privacy and sensitivity ensures that journalism does not cause unnecessary harm to individuals or invade their personal lives.

In summary, truth and accuracy, independence and impartiality, and privacy and sensitivity are fundamental principles of ethical journalism. Upholding these principles helps maintain the integrity and credibility of journalism as a profession, and it fosters a sense of trust and respect between journalists and their audiences. Adhering to these principles is essential for promoting a well-informed and democratic society.

Navigating the Fine Line Between Sensationalism and Truth

Sensationalism can compromise the integrity of media reporting. In this section, we discuss the challenges of balancing engaging storytelling with factual reporting.

- Responsible Use of Clickbait: Clickbait refers to headlines or content designed to attract attention and entice users to click on a link, often using sensationalism or misleading information. Responsible use of clickbait involves refraining from using deceptive or exaggerated headlines that may mislead or disappoint readers. Instead, journalists should aim to create honest, engaging headlines that accurately reflect the content of the article. By using clickbait responsibly, media outlets can build trust with their audiences and avoid undermining the credibility of their reporting.
- Fact-Checking and Verification: Fact-checking and verification are essential steps in the journalistic process. Before publishing any information, journalists should thoroughly investigate and verify the accuracy of the facts presented in their articles. This includes cross-referencing information from multiple credible sources, confirming the authenticity of quotes and data, and checking for any potential biases or errors. Fact-checking helps prevent the dissemination of false or misleading information, protecting the public from misinformation and preserving the integrity of journalism.
- Elevating Impactful Reporting: In today's fast-paced media landscape, there can be a temptation to prioritize sensational or viral stories over substantive and impactful reporting. However, responsible journalists understand the importance of elevating stories that have a meaningful and lasting impact on their audiences. These stories may delve into complex social issues, shed light on underrepresented communities, or uncover systemic problems that require attention. By focusing on impactful reporting, journalists can engage their readers in critical issues, promote awareness and understanding, and contribute to positive social change.

In summary, responsible journalism involves avoiding deceptive clickbait, prioritizing fact-checking and verification, and focusing on impactful reporting. By adhering to these principles, media outlets can uphold their commitment to truth, accuracy, and public service, fostering trust with their audiences and contributing to a well-informed and democratic society.

Fostering Media Outlets that Prioritize Ethical Reporting

Media outlets play a significant role in shaping journalistic practices. In this section, we explore strategies to promote ethical reporting in media organizations.

- Editorial Standards and Guidelines: Establishing clear editorial standards and guidelines is a crucial aspect of responsible journalism. These standards serve as a foundation for newsrooms and media organizations, outlining the principles and values that govern their reporting practices. Editorial guidelines prioritize accuracy, integrity, and fairness in news coverage. They often include guidelines on fact-checking, source verification, handling conflicts of interest, avoiding plagiarism, and respecting individuals' privacy and dignity. By adhering to these standards, journalists ensure that their reporting is credible, reliable, and trustworthy, fostering public confidence in the media.
- Ethical Training and Support: Ethical training and support are essential for journalists to navigate the ethical challenges and complexities they may encounter in their reporting. Media organizations should provide ongoing training that equips journalists with the knowledge and tools to make ethical decisions. This training may involve case studies, workshops, and discussions on ethical dilemmas. Additionally, newsrooms should create a supportive environment where journalists feel comfortable seeking guidance from editors and colleagues when faced with ethical dilemmas. Ethical training and support empower journalists to uphold high ethical standards and make informed choices in their reporting.
- Public Accountability: Transparency and accountability are fundamental principles of responsible journalism. Media outlets have a responsibility to be open about their reporting processes and to be accountable for their actions. This includes disclosing potential conflicts of interest, acknowledging and correcting errors promptly, and providing a platform for public feedback and criticism. Public accountability not only helps maintain the credibility of media organizations but also fosters a healthy relationship with the audience. When media outlets demonstrate transparency and accountability, they build trust with their readers, viewers, and listeners, which is essential for a thriving democracy.

In summary, responsible journalism involves establishing clear editorial standards and guidelines, providing ethical training and support for journalists, and being transparent and accountable to the public. By prioritizing accuracy, integrity, and transparency, media organizations can uphold the principles of journalism and serve as reliable sources of information in society.

Conclusion

Ethical journalism forms the bedrock of a well-informed society. By embracing ethical considerations in journalism and media reporting, navigating the fine line between sensationalism and truth, and fostering media outlets that prioritize ethical reporting, we pave the way for responsible journalism that upholds the values of truth and integrity. Together, we foster a community that values factual reporting, independence, and ethical storytelling, creating a media landscape where the public can trust the information they receive. As we uphold media ethics and responsible journalism, we contribute to a society where journalism serves as a pillar of democracy, and our collective efforts create a tapestry of credible, responsible, and trustworthy media for a brighter and more informed future for all.

CHAPTER 55

GOVERNMENTAL RESPONSIBILITY AND PUBLIC TRUST

Trustworthy Governance: Upholding Ethical Leadership

Introduction

The chapter explores the critical relationship between governmental responsibility and public trust. It underscores the paramount importance of rebuilding public trust through ethical governance, particularly in the face of growing skepticism and disillusionment among citizens.

To foster public trust, the chapter highlights the need for government institutions to prioritize transparency and accountability. By being open and forthcoming about their actions, decisions, and policies, governments can demonstrate a commitment to serving the best interests of the public.

Moreover, the chapter emphasizes the role of ethical leadership in government. Ethical leaders who prioritize the well-being of the citizens they serve and adhere to moral principles can inspire confidence and trust among the population.

The chapter also delves into the threat of manipulation in the political realm and its potential consequences for democracy. By addressing and countering manipulative tactics, governments can safeguard the democratic process and protect citizens from being misled or deceived.

Furthermore, the chapter advocates for engaging citizens in the decision-making process and involving them in shaping policies that affect their lives. By promoting citizen participation and incorporating diverse perspectives, governments can ensure that their actions align with the needs and aspirations of the people.

The chapter underscores the significance of governmental responsibility in rebuilding public trust and promoting a healthy democratic society. Through ethical governance, transparency, accountability, and genuine engagement with citizens, governments can strengthen the bond of trust with the public and secure the foundation of a resilient and democratic nation.

Rebuilding Public Trust through Ethical Governance

Public trust in government is essential for a healthy democracy. In this section, we discuss the steps needed to rebuild public trust through ethical governance.

- Integrity and Honesty: Integrity and honesty are foundational principles in effective and responsible governance. Demonstrating integrity means adhering to moral and ethical principles, being truthful, and acting in the best interests of the public. Honesty involves being transparent about government actions and decisions, ensuring that information is conveyed accurately and without manipulation. When government officials prioritize integrity and honesty, they build trust with the public and foster a positive relationship that is essential for a functioning democracy.
- Addressing Corruption: Corruption poses a significant threat to the stability and credibility of a government. It involves the abuse of power for personal gain and undermines public trust in institutions. Addressing corruption requires strong measures such as implementing robust anti-corruption laws, establishing independent oversight bodies, and promoting a culture of accountability and transparency within government institutions. By actively combatting corruption, governments can uphold the rule of law, protect public resources, and ensure that policies and decisions are made in the public's best interest.
- Engaging with the Public: Effective governance involves actively engaging with the public to understand their concerns, needs, and aspirations. This can be achieved through open dialogues, town hall meetings, public consultations, and other forms of direct engagement. By listening to the voices of citizens, government officials can gain valuable insights into the issues affecting their communities and make more informed decisions. Public engagement also fosters a sense of ownership and accountability, as citizens become active participants in the governance process.

In summary, effective and responsible governance entails demonstrating integrity and honesty in government actions, addressing corruption through robust measures, and actively engaging with the public to understand their concerns. By upholding these principles, governments can build trust, maintain legitimacy, and work towards creating a more inclusive and responsive society.

Transparency and Accountability in Government Institutions

Transparency and accountability are the pillars of good governance. In this section, we explore strategies to promote transparency and accountability within government institutions.

- Open Government Initiatives: Open government initiatives aim to enhance transparency, accountability, and citizen engagement by providing easy access to government information and data. By making government data and information readily available to the public, these initiatives promote transparency in decision-making processes and allow citizens to better understand how their government operates. Open data portals, public records, and government websites are examples of tools used in open government initiatives. The availability of this information empowers citizens to hold their government accountable and participate in the democratic process with a more informed perspective.
- Independent Oversight: To ensure checks and balances within the government, independent oversight bodies are established. These bodies operate separately from the government and are tasked with monitoring government actions, investigating potential misconduct, and holding government officials accountable for their actions. Examples of independent oversight bodies include ombudsman offices, inspector general offices, and commissions for audit and investigation. The presence of independent oversight helps prevent abuse of power, corruption, and other unethical practices by ensuring that government actions are subject to scrutiny and external review.
- Whistleblower Protection: Whistleblower protection is essential for encouraging individuals within government institutions to come forward and expose wrongdoing without fear of retaliation. Whistleblowers play a critical role in uncovering corruption, fraud, and other misconduct that may be concealed from the public. By providing legal protection and safeguards to whistleblowers, governments create a conducive environment for exposing malpractices and fostering a culture of accountability. These protections may include anonymity, confidentiality, and legal safeguards against workplace retaliation.

In summary, open government initiatives promote transparency and citizen engagement by providing easy access to government information and data. Independent oversight bodies serve as watchdogs to monitor government actions and ensure accountability. Whistleblower protection encourages individuals within government institutions to report wrongdoing without fear of reprisal, contributing to a culture of integrity and ethical conduct in government. Together, these measures enhance trust in government, improve public governance, and reinforce democratic principles.

Safeguarding Democracy from Manipulation

Democracy can be vulnerable to manipulation and misinformation. In this section, we discuss ways to safeguard democracy from external influences.

- Media Literacy Education: Promoting media literacy education to empower citizens to critically evaluate information and recognize manipulation.
- Election Integrity: Ensuring the integrity of elections through secure voting systems and safeguards against interference.
- Strengthening Democratic Institutions: Strengthening the independence and effectiveness of democratic institutions to resist manipulation.

Conclusion

Governmental responsibility and public trust are intertwined in a functioning democracy. By rebuilding public trust through ethical governance, promoting transparency and accountability in government institutions, and safeguarding democracy from manipulation, we pave the way for a trustworthy and resilient democratic system. Together, we foster a community that values ethical leadership, transparency, and citizen engagement, creating a government that serves the interests of the public with integrity and dedication. As we embrace governmental responsibility and public trust, we contribute to a society where democracy thrives, and our collective efforts create a tapestry of ethical governance, democratic resilience, and public confidence for a brighter and more participatory future for all.

CHAPTER 56

LEADERS AS AGENTS OF EMPATHY AND POSITIVE CHANGE

Empathetic Leadership: Igniting a Tapestry of Positive Transformation

Introduction

The chapter explores the profound impact of leaders as agents of empathy and positive change. It emphasizes the transformative power of leading with empathy and compassion, inspiring a culture of understanding and support within organizations and society as a whole.

Ethical leadership is highlighted as a pivotal aspect of driving positive change. Leaders who uphold moral values and prioritize the well-being of others can influence societal values and set a strong ethical foundation for their organizations and communities.

The chapter also emphasizes the importance of empowering others to become empathetic leaders. By encouraging and supporting individuals to cultivate their empathetic skills, leaders can create a ripple effect of compassion and empathy throughout various spheres of influence.

Through empathetic leadership, leaders can foster a sense of belonging and emotional safety among their team members and stakeholders. This creates an environment where individuals feel valued, heard, and appreciated, ultimately leading to higher levels of engagement and productivity.

Additionally, empathetic leaders are better equipped to address conflicts and challenges with understanding and fairness, building trust and strengthening relationships within their teams and communities.

Overall, the chapter highlights how leaders who embody empathy and positive values can have a profound impact on the world. By leading with empathy, promoting ethical principles, and empowering others to follow in their footsteps, these leaders can shape a more compassionate and socially responsible society.

Leading with Empathy and Compassion

Empathy and compassion are powerful attributes that can transform leadership. In this section, we discuss the importance of leading with empathy and compassion.

- Emotional Intelligence: Emotional intelligence refers to the ability to recognize, understand, and manage both our own emotions and the emotions of others. It involves being aware of our feelings and those of others, effectively expressing emotions, and using emotional information to guide our thinking and behavior. Cultivating emotional intelligence is crucial in building strong interpersonal relationships, promoting effective communication, and fostering empathy. By understanding and connecting with the emotions and needs of others, individuals can create a more supportive and compassionate work environment, leading to increased collaboration and improved team dynamics.
- Supportive Leadership: Supportive leadership involves providing guidance, encouragement, and assistance to team members to help them reach their full potential. A supportive leader empowers their team, fosters a sense of belonging, and actively listens to their concerns and ideas. Such leadership style creates a positive work environment where team members feel valued, respected, and motivated. Supportive leaders also recognize and appreciate the unique contributions of each team member, leading to increased job satisfaction and productivity.
- Empathetic Decision-Making: Empathetic decision-making entails considering the feelings, perspectives, and needs of individuals and communities that may be affected by a particular decision. By incorporating empathy into the decision-making process, leaders can gain a deeper understanding of the potential impact of their choices on others. This approach ensures that decisions are not solely driven by data and metrics but also consider the human aspect of the outcomes. Empathetic decision-making can lead to more ethical and socially responsible choices that align with the organization's values and positively impact stakeholders.

In summary, emotional intelligence plays a vital role in creating a supportive and inclusive work environment by helping individuals understand and connect with others' emotions. Supportive leadership empowers and motivates team members, fostering a positive and collaborative workplace culture. Empathetic decision-making takes into account the feelings and needs of individuals and communities, leading to more ethical and socially responsible choices. Together, these elements contribute to a healthier and more compassionate work environment that promotes overall well-being and success for both individuals and the organization as a whole.

Influencing Societal Values through Ethical Leadership

Leaders have the capacity to shape societal values and norms. In this section, we explore how ethical leadership can influence positive change in society.

- Leading by Example: Leading by example means demonstrating ethical behavior and values in one's actions and decisions, which inspires and motivates others to do the same. Ethical leaders are authentic and consistent in their actions, and they hold themselves to high moral standards. When leaders model integrity, honesty, and respect, it creates a culture of trust and accountability within the organization. Employees are more likely to respect and emulate leaders who exhibit ethical behavior, which can positively influence the overall ethical climate of the workplace.
- Advocating for Social Justice: Ethical leaders use their position and influence to advocate for social justice and equality. They recognize the importance of addressing social issues and promoting fairness and inclusivity in society. By speaking out against discrimination, inequality, and systemic injustices, ethical leaders can inspire others to become socially responsible and engage in advocacy efforts. Advocating for social justice goes beyond merely acknowledging issues; it involves actively supporting policies, initiatives, and organizations that work towards creating a more equitable society.
- Prioritizing Social and Environmental Responsibility: Ethical leadership extends beyond profit-making to consider the impact of an organization's actions on society and the environment. Ethical leaders prioritize social and environmental responsibility by incorporating sustainable practices into their business strategies. They take into account the well-being of employees, customers, and the community, as well as the environmental impact of their operations. By integrating social and environmental responsibility into organizational practices, ethical leaders demonstrate a commitment to the greater good and long-term sustainability.

In summary, ethical leadership involves leading by example by demonstrating ethical behavior and values. Ethical leaders use their influence to advocate for social justice and equality, inspiring others to become socially responsible. They also prioritize social and environmental responsibility by incorporating sustainable practices into their organizations. By embodying these principles, ethical leaders foster a culture of trust, fairness, and accountability, promoting positive change both within their organizations and in the broader community.

Empowering Others to Become Empathetic Leaders

Empathy is a quality that can be nurtured in others. In this section, we discuss strategies to empower and develop empathetic leaders.

- Mentorship and Coaching: Mentorship and coaching play a crucial role in developing empathetic leadership skills in emerging leaders. Through mentorship, experienced leaders guide and support their mentees, sharing their knowledge, experiences, and insights. This guidance allows mentees to learn from the mentor's empathetic leadership approach, understand the importance of empathy in decision-making, and develop their own empathetic leadership style. Coaching, on the other hand, involves providing specific feedback and skill-building opportunities to enhance empathy and emotional intelligence. By having access to mentorship and coaching, emerging leaders can gain valuable perspectives and develop the capacity to lead with empathy.
- Emotional Resilience Training: Emotional resilience training equips leaders with the skills to effectively manage and navigate challenging situations while maintaining empathy towards others. Leadership often involves facing difficult decisions, conflicts, and uncertainties, which can lead to emotional strain and stress. Emotional resilience training teaches leaders how to identify and manage their emotions, cope with adversity, and regulate their responses in high-pressure situations. By being emotionally resilient, leaders can better empathize with the emotions and needs of their team members, maintain a compassionate approach, and foster a supportive work environment.
- Creating a Culture of Empathy: Fostering a culture that values empathy is essential for promoting empathetic leadership development throughout an organization. Leaders can create such a culture by prioritizing empathy in decision-making, communication, and interactions with team members. When leaders actively practice and demonstrate empathy, they set a powerful example for others to follow. Additionally, leaders can encourage open dialogue about empathy, sharing stories of its positive impact, and recognizing empathetic acts within the organization. By instilling empathy as a core value, leaders can cultivate an environment where empathy is valued and celebrated, encouraging everyone to embrace empathetic leadership.

In summary, developing empathetic leadership involves providing mentorship and coaching to emerging leaders, equipping them with emotional resilience skills to navigate challenges with empathy, and fostering a culture that values and supports empathetic leadership. These practices not only enhance the individual capabilities of leaders but also create a ripple effect that positively impacts the entire organization, leading to more compassionate, understanding, and supportive work environments.

Conclusion

Leaders as agents of empathy and positive change hold immense potential to create a better world. By leading with empathy and compassion, influencing societal values through ethical leadership, and empowering others to become empathetic leaders, we pave the way for a tapestry of positive transformation. Together, we foster a community that values empathetic leadership, social responsibility, and compassion, creating a world where leadership is defined by ethical values and the well-being of others. As we embrace leaders as agents of empathy and positive change, we contribute to a society where empathy and compassion flourish, and our collective efforts create a tapestry of inclusive leadership, societal progress, and positive transformation for a brighter and more empathetic future for all.

PART XI: CULTIVATING COLLECTIVE EMPATHY

CHAPTER 57

SOCIAL INITIATIVES FOR EMPATHY AND MENTAL HEALTH

Compassionate Communities: Fostering Empathy and Mental Well-being

Introduction

The chapter delves into the significance of cultivating collective empathy for mental health. It emphasizes the critical role of empathy-based mental health programs and initiatives, which prioritize understanding and compassion towards individuals facing mental health challenges.

One key focus is on reducing the stigma surrounding mental health. By fostering empathy and educating the public about mental health conditions, the chapter aims to break down barriers that prevent open discussions and seeking help.

Moreover, the chapter underlines the importance of increasing mental health awareness within communities. Through empathy-based education, individuals can gain a deeper understanding of mental health issues, recognize the signs of distress in others, and provide support and resources when needed.

Creating a supportive and empathetic community for mental well-being is another central theme. By fostering a culture of empathy, individuals experiencing mental health challenges are more likely to seek help and receive understanding and validation from those around them.

The chapter emphasizes that by cultivating collective empathy for mental health, society can better address the needs of individuals with mental health conditions and promote a more caring and inclusive environment for all.

Empathy-Based Mental Health Programs and Initiatives

Empathy plays a crucial role in promoting mental well-being. In this section, we explore the impact of empathy-based mental health programs and initiatives.

- Empathetic Counseling and Therapy: Empathetic counseling and therapy are essential components of mental health care that focus on providing compassionate and understanding support to individuals seeking help. In these approaches, counselors and therapists strive to create a safe and non-judgmental environment where clients can openly express their thoughts and feelings. Empathetic practitioners actively listen to their clients, validate their experiences, and seek to understand their emotions and perspectives. By demonstrating empathy, counselors and therapists build trust with their clients, which is crucial for facilitating healing and personal growth. Empathetic counseling and therapy help individuals feel heard, understood, and supported, which can lead to positive outcomes in managing mental health challenges.

- Peer Support Programs: Peer support programs create a supportive network where individuals with similar mental health experiences can come together to share their stories, struggles, and coping strategies. These programs often operate on the principle of "peer support" or "mutual aid," where participants provide each other with understanding, empathy, and encouragement. Peers in these groups can relate to one another's experiences, as they may have faced similar challenges in their mental health journeys. By sharing their experiences, peers provide emotional validation, offer hope, and foster a sense of belonging. Peer support programs play a valuable role in combating isolation and stigma, promoting recovery, and empowering individuals to take an active role in managing their mental health.
- Trauma-Informed Care: Trauma-informed care is an approach to providing support and services that takes into account the impact of trauma on individuals' lives. It emphasizes safety, trustworthiness, choice, collaboration, and empowerment. Trauma-informed care practitioners recognize the prevalence of trauma in individuals seeking help and acknowledge the potential triggers and re-traumatization that traditional care settings might inadvertently cause. By approaching care with empathy and sensitivity, trauma-informed practitioners aim to create an environment that promotes healing and growth, rather than exacerbating trauma-related distress. Understanding the role of trauma in individuals' lives allows mental health professionals to offer compassionate and respectful care, helping clients build resilience and move toward recovery.

In summary, empathetic counseling and therapy prioritize compassionate understanding, peer support programs create a network of empathy and mutual aid, and trauma-informed care provides sensitive and supportive services to individuals who have experienced trauma. All three approaches contribute to fostering a supportive and caring environment for those seeking mental health support, helping individuals feel valued, understood, and empowered on their journey to mental well-being.

Reducing Stigma and Increasing Mental Health Awareness

The stigma surrounding mental health can be a barrier to seeking help. In this section, we discuss strategies to reduce stigma and increase mental health awareness.

- Mental Health Education: Comprehensive mental health education is a crucial aspect of promoting understanding and empathy for individuals facing mental health challenges. By integrating mental health education into school curriculums and community programs, we can increase awareness and reduce the stigma surrounding mental health. This education equips individuals with the knowledge and tools to recognize signs of mental health struggles in themselves and others, fostering a supportive and empathetic environment. Students learn about different mental health conditions, coping mechanisms, and resources available for seeking help. By teaching empathy and compassion for those facing mental health issues, we cultivate a generation that values mental well-being and is equipped to offer support and understanding.
- Media Representation: The media plays a powerful role in shaping societal perceptions and attitudes towards mental health. Encouraging accurate and empathetic media portrayals of mental health issues is crucial in challenging harmful stereotypes and promoting empathy. Misrepresentations and stigmatizing portrayals can perpetuate negative attitudes and hinder help-seeking behavior. By depicting mental health issues with sensitivity and accuracy, media can contribute to reducing stigma and increasing understanding. Empathetic media representation includes showcasing diverse experiences and providing realistic portrayals of recovery and resilience. Responsible media representation fosters a more informed and compassionate society, where individuals facing mental health challenges are met with understanding rather than judgment.
- Public Awareness Campaigns: Public awareness campaigns have the power to initiate open conversations about mental health on a broader scale. These campaigns aim to bring mental health issues to the forefront of public discourse, breaking down barriers and encouraging individuals to share their experiences and seek help when needed. By raising awareness through various media channels, community events, and online platforms, public awareness campaigns address the significance of mental health in our lives and advocate for collective support and understanding. Such campaigns can also provide information about available resources and emphasize the

importance of empathy and active listening when supporting those with mental health struggles. By promoting empathy and understanding through public awareness, we build a more compassionate society that values mental health as an integral part of overall well-being.

In summary, mental health education empowers individuals with knowledge and empathy to support those with mental health challenges. Media representation can influence attitudes and perceptions, making accurate and empathetic portrayals critical. Public awareness campaigns initiate conversations and foster a more compassionate society that values mental well-being. Together, these efforts contribute to reducing stigma and creating an environment where individuals feel supported and understood in their mental health journeys.

Community Support for Mental Well-being

Communities play a crucial role in supporting mental well-being. In this section, we explore the importance of community-based initiatives for mental health.

- Community Mental Health Centers: Community mental health centers are vital resources that provide accessible and comprehensive support services to individuals facing mental health challenges. These centers are often located within local communities, making it easier for individuals to access mental health care and support without significant barriers such as transportation or financial constraints. Community mental health centers offer a wide range of services, including counseling, therapy, psychiatric treatment, and support groups. By being situated within the community, these centers can better understand the unique needs and challenges of the local population, providing personalized and culturally sensitive care. They play a crucial role in reducing the stigma associated with seeking mental health support and act as essential hubs for mental health awareness and education.
- Workplace Mental Health Programs: Workplace mental health programs are initiatives implemented by employers to prioritize the well-being of their employees and create a supportive and mentally healthy work environment. These programs recognize that employees' mental health significantly impacts their overall well-being, job performance, and productivity. They may include mental health awareness training for employees and managers, stress management workshops, access to employee assistance programs (EAPs), and flexible work arrangements to accommodate mental health needs. By fostering

a workplace culture that values mental health, employees are more likely to feel supported, understood, and encouraged to seek help when needed. Workplace mental health programs not only benefit individual employees but also contribute to a more productive and engaged workforce.

- Social Integration: Social integration is the process of fostering a sense of belonging and connection among individuals within a community. For those facing mental health challenges, social integration is essential in reducing feelings of isolation and loneliness. It involves creating inclusive spaces and opportunities for individuals to engage with others, build meaningful relationships, and participate in social activities. Social integration helps combat the stigma associated with mental health by fostering empathy and understanding among community members. It also provides a support network that can offer encouragement and assistance during difficult times. By promoting social integration, communities can create a more compassionate and supportive environment for all individuals, including those with mental health struggles.

In summary, establishing accessible community mental health centers provides crucial resources and support services for individuals in need. Workplace mental health programs prioritize employee well-being and contribute to a more mentally healthy workforce. Social integration fosters a sense of belonging and reduces isolation, promoting empathy and support within the community. Together, these initiatives play a vital role in addressing mental health challenges, reducing stigma, and fostering a more empathetic and compassionate society.

Conclusion

Collective empathy is a powerful force in supporting mental well-being. By implementing empathy-based mental health programs and initiatives, reducing stigma, increasing mental health awareness, and fostering community support for mental well-being, we pave the way for compassionate communities that prioritize mental health care and support. Together, we foster a community that values empathy, mental health awareness, and social support, creating a world where mental well-being is recognized as a collective responsibility. As we cultivate collective empathy for mental health, we contribute to a society that empowers individuals to seek help without stigma, and our collective efforts create a tapestry of understanding, compassion, and support for a brighter and mentally healthier future for all.

CHAPTER 58

EDUCATION FOR EMPATHY AND EMOTIONAL INTELLIGENCE

Empathy in Education: Nurturing Compassionate Hearts and Minds

Introduction

The focus is on the importance of integrating empathy education and emotional intelligence into school curricula. The chapter emphasizes the significant impact of fostering empathy and emotional intelligence in students, preparing them for a more compassionate and understanding society.

One key aspect of this chapter is recognizing the crucial role of educators as empathetic role models. Teachers who demonstrate empathy in their interactions with students can inspire and instill these values in their pupils. By modeling empathetic behaviors, educators create a positive learning environment that encourages empathy and emotional intelligence.

The chapter also highlights the value of empathy education in promoting social and emotional skills among students. Through empathy education, young learners develop the ability to recognize and understand others' feelings and perspectives, fostering a sense of connection and community.

Moreover, integrating emotional intelligence in school curricula is essential for equipping students with the tools to manage their emotions effectively. By learning to regulate their emotions, students can navigate challenging situations with resilience and empathy.

The chapter underscores the importance of integrating empathy education and emotional intelligence into school curricula. By doing so, educators can help shape a generation of empathetic and emotionally intelligent individuals, fostering a more compassionate and harmonious society.

Integrating Empathy Education in School Curricula

Empathy is a fundamental skill that can be taught and cultivated. In this section, we discuss the value of integrating empathy education into school curricula.

- Empathy Curriculum: An empathy curriculum is a structured and comprehensive educational program that aims to cultivate empathy among students. It goes beyond traditional academic subjects and places a strong emphasis on understanding and respecting others' perspectives and emotions. The curriculum is designed to teach students how to recognize and validate the feelings of others, develop active listening skills, and understand the impact of their actions on others. Through various activities, discussions, and role-playing exercises, students are encouraged to step into the shoes of others, fostering a deeper understanding of different experiences and promoting compassion. By integrating empathy into the curriculum, schools can play a vital role in nurturing a more empathetic and inclusive generation.
- Social and Emotional Learning (SEL): Social and Emotional Learning (SEL) programs are educational initiatives that focus on developing essential social and emotional skills in students. These skills encompass empathy, emotional regulation, self-awareness, conflict resolution, and responsible decision-making. By incorporating SEL programs into the curriculum, schools aim to equip students with the tools they need to manage their emotions effectively, build positive relationships, and navigate social situations with empathy and understanding. SEL programs often involve interactive activities, group discussions, and mindfulness exercises that encourage self-reflection and empathy development. By promoting emotional intelligence and empathy, SEL programs contribute to the creation of a supportive and emotionally healthy learning environment.
- Culturally Diverse Perspectives: Integrating culturally diverse perspectives into the curriculum is essential for fostering empathy and cross-cultural understanding among students. By including diverse stories, histories, and experiences from different cultures and communities, students gain exposure to a variety of worldviews and realities. This exposure broadens their understanding of the world and helps them develop empathy for people from different backgrounds. It also challenges stereotypes and biases, encouraging students to question their assumptions and recognize the shared humanity that connects us all. Culturally diverse perspectives in the curriculum create opportunities for meaningful conversations and interactions, promoting a more inclusive and empathetic learning environment.

In summary, an empathy curriculum emphasizes the importance of understanding and respecting others' perspectives and feelings, nurturing empathy among students. Social and Emotional Learning (SEL) programs equip students with essential emotional intelligence and empathy skills. Integrating culturally diverse perspectives into the curriculum fosters cross-cultural understanding and challenges biases. Together, these initiatives in education play a pivotal role in shaping a more empathetic and compassionate society.

Fostering Emotional Intelligence and Empathy in Students

Emotional intelligence is key to developing empathy and forming meaningful connections. In this section, we explore strategies to foster emotional intelligence and empathy in students.

- Self-awareness: Self-awareness is a fundamental aspect of emotional intelligence that involves understanding one's own emotions, thoughts, and behaviors. Encouraging students to develop self-awareness allows them to recognize their emotions in various situations and understand how those emotions influence their actions and interactions with others. Through self-awareness, students can identify their strengths and weaknesses, understand their triggers, and gain insight into how they can regulate their emotions effectively. This skill helps students become more mindful and intentional in their responses, fostering empathy by enabling them to consider how their actions impact others' emotions and experiences.
- Empathetic Listening: Empathetic listening is a vital communication skill that involves fully engaging with others' emotions and experiences when they speak. By teaching students active listening techniques, they can learn to give their full attention to others, suspend judgment, and validate the feelings and perspectives of those they are listening to. Empathetic listening helps students develop a deeper understanding of others' needs, concerns, and experiences, which, in turn, strengthens their capacity for empathy. When individuals feel heard and understood, it creates an environment of trust and openness, facilitating meaningful connections and empathetic interactions.
- Empathy Through Art and Literature: Art, literature, and storytelling offer unique ways to promote empathy by allowing students to explore and connect with different characters' emotions and experiences. When students engage with diverse narratives and stories, they gain insights into the complexities of human emotions and the diversity of human experiences. Reading literature

or viewing art that depicts characters facing various challenges and emotions encourages students to empathize with these fictional personas, translating this empathy into their real-life interactions. By experiencing and understanding the emotions of others through artistic expression, students can broaden their perspectives and develop a deeper sense of empathy and compassion.

In summary, fostering empathy in students involves promoting self-awareness to understand their emotions and their impact on others, teaching empathetic listening to validate and understand others' experiences, and using art and literature to connect with diverse emotions and experiences. By cultivating these skills and experiences in the educational setting, students are more likely to develop empathy, leading to a more empathetic and compassionate society.

Educators as Empathetic Role Models

Educators play a crucial role in modeling empathetic behavior for students. In this section, we discuss the importance of educators as empathetic role models.

- Empathy Training for Educators: Empathy training for educators involves providing professional development and training sessions to enhance their empathetic skills and approaches. Educators learn techniques and strategies to better understand and relate to their students' emotions, perspectives, and experiences. Through this training, educators gain insights into the importance of empathy in the learning process and its positive impact on students' overall well-being and academic performance. They learn to recognize and respond to the diverse emotional needs of their students, creating a more supportive and nurturing learning environment.
- Compassionate Classroom Environment: Creating a compassionate classroom environment is crucial for fostering empathy among students. Educators focus on establishing a positive and inclusive classroom culture where students feel valued and respected. They encourage open communication and active listening, allowing students to express their emotions and experiences without fear of judgment. In a compassionate classroom, students are encouraged to empathize with their peers and engage in acts of kindness and understanding. This environment enables students to develop stronger emotional connections, leading to increased empathy and a sense of belonging within the classroom community.
- Conflict Resolution and Mediation: Conflict resolution and mediation training equips educators with the skills to address conflicts among students empathetically. Educators learn to mediate disputes and disagreements by

actively listening to all parties involved and understanding their perspectives and emotions. Through empathetic conflict resolution, educators can help students find common ground, resolve conflicts peacefully, and foster a sense of empathy and understanding between conflicting parties. By guiding students through respectful dialogue and problem-solving, educators teach valuable lessons in empathy and emotional intelligence, promoting a culture of empathy and cooperation within the classroom.

In summary, promoting empathy in the educational context involves providing empathy training for educators to enhance their understanding and connection with students. Creating a compassionate classroom environment emphasizes fostering a supportive and inclusive atmosphere where students feel safe expressing their emotions and experiences. Equipping educators with conflict resolution and mediation skills allows them to address conflicts empathetically, fostering empathy and cooperation among students. By prioritizing empathy in the educational setting, educators lay the foundation for students to develop strong emotional intelligence and build meaningful connections with others, leading to a more empathetic and compassionate society.

Conclusion

Education for empathy and emotional intelligence is fundamental to nurturing compassionate hearts and minds in students. By integrating empathy education in school curricula, fostering emotional intelligence and empathy in students, and encouraging educators to be empathetic role models, we pave the way for a generation of empathetic and emotionally intelligent individuals. Together, we foster a community that values empathy, emotional intelligence, and understanding, creating a world where compassion and empathy are central to interpersonal relationships and societal well-being. As we embrace education for empathy and emotional intelligence, we contribute to a society where empathy is not just taught but lived, and our collective efforts create a tapestry of empathetic and compassionate young minds for a brighter and more empathetic future for all.

CHAPTER 59

EMPATHY IN LAW AND CRIMINAL JUSTICE

Restoring Humanity: The Transformative Power of Empathy in the Legal System

Introduction

The focus is on the critical role of empathy in law and criminal justice. The chapter emphasizes the significance of incorporating restorative justice and empathy in criminal cases, aiming to humanize the legal system and promote a more compassionate approach to justice.

One key aspect of this chapter is the recognition of how empathy can transform the way justice is administered. By adopting restorative justice practices that prioritize understanding and healing, the criminal justice system can move away from punitive measures and focus on supporting rehabilitation and reintegration of offenders.

The chapter also highlights the importance of empathy in improving interactions between legal professionals, offenders, and victims. By fostering empathy within the criminal justice system, legal practitioners can build more meaningful connections with individuals involved in the justice process, ultimately leading to more holistic and fair outcomes.

Moreover, the chapter underscores the significance of empathy in addressing the root causes of criminal behavior. By understanding and acknowledging the emotions and experiences of offenders, the criminal justice system can better identify ways to support rehabilitation and reduce the likelihood of recidivism.

The chapter highlights the critical role of empathy in law and criminal justice. By integrating empathy and restorative justice principles, the legal system can create a more compassionate and effective approach to justice, benefiting all individuals involved in the process.

Restorative Justice and Empathy in Criminal Cases

Empathy lies at the heart of restorative justice, transforming the approach to criminal cases. In this section, we discuss the significance of restorative justice and empathy in the legal system.

- Victim-Centered Approaches: Victim-centered approaches in the criminal justice process prioritize the needs and emotions of victims to foster healing and closure. Traditionally, criminal justice systems have focused primarily on punishing offenders, often leaving victims feeling unheard and disregarded. However, victim-centered approaches place the victim's well-being at the forefront, acknowledging the trauma they have experienced and the impact of the crime on their lives. By providing support and resources tailored to each victim's unique needs, these approaches aim to empower victims, restore their sense of agency, and help them navigate the often daunting criminal justice process. By recognizing victims as essential stakeholders, the criminal justice system can better address their emotional and practical needs, ultimately contributing to their healing and recovery.
- Offender Accountability: Encouraging offender accountability is a crucial aspect of restorative justice. Instead of solely focusing on punishment, restorative justice seeks to hold offenders accountable for their actions in a way that fosters understanding and repair. Offenders are encouraged to take responsibility for their behavior and its consequences, not only in legal terms but also in terms of understanding the harm they have caused to victims and the community. This approach emphasizes the importance of acknowledging the impact of one's actions on others and working towards making amends and restitution. By promoting offender accountability, restorative justice aims to break the cycle of harmful behaviors, facilitate rehabilitation, and prevent future crimes.
- Dialogue and Understanding: Facilitating communication between victims and offenders is a fundamental aspect of restorative justice practices. Engaging in open and honest dialogue enables both parties to share their perspectives, feelings, and experiences related to the crime. This process creates an opportunity for victims to be heard and acknowledged by the offender, and for the offender to gain insight into the consequences of their actions. The goal is to foster empathy and understanding, leading to greater emotional healing for the victim and increased accountability and remorse from the offender. Through dialogue and understanding, restorative justice seeks to build bridges between victims and offenders, promoting a sense of closure and the potential for transformative change.

In summary, victim-centered approaches in the criminal justice system prioritize the well-being of victims, offering tailored support and resources to aid their healing and recovery. Encouraging offender accountability through restorative justice practices helps offenders take responsibility for their actions and understand the impact of their behavior. Facilitating dialogue and understanding between victims and offenders fosters empathy and facilitates a path to healing, ultimately contributing to a more just and compassionate criminal justice system.

Humanizing the Legal System through Empathy

Empathy humanizes the legal system, acknowledging the humanity of those involved in criminal cases. In this section, we explore strategies to infuse empathy into the legal process.

- Trauma-Informed Practices: Trauma-informed practices in legal proceedings aim to acknowledge and address the emotional and psychological impact of crime on both victims and offenders. Trauma, whether experienced directly or indirectly, can have long-lasting effects on individuals, affecting their ability to cope, trust, and participate in legal processes. By incorporating trauma-informed practices, the legal system seeks to create a more compassionate and supportive environment for those involved in criminal cases. This approach involves recognizing the prevalence of trauma and its potential impact on behavior, providing opportunities for victims and offenders to share their experiences, and tailoring support and resources to address their unique needs. By doing so, trauma-informed practices strive to promote healing, enhance communication, and contribute to more equitable and just outcomes.
- Sensitivity Training for Legal Professionals: Sensitivity training and empathy workshops for judges, lawyers, and other legal professionals are crucial components of creating a more empathetic and understanding legal system. These training programs aim to enhance the professionals' ability to empathize with the emotional aspects of criminal cases and improve their interactions with victims and offenders. By developing a deeper understanding of trauma, mental health issues, and diverse backgrounds, legal professionals can adopt more compassionate and respectful approaches in their work. This, in turn, fosters a sense of trust and safety for individuals involved in legal proceedings, encouraging greater cooperation and participation. By investing in sensitivity training, the legal system reinforces its commitment to fairness, inclusivity, and empathy.

- Supporting Vulnerable Populations: Ensuring equitable treatment and support for vulnerable populations within the legal system is essential to address the unique challenges they may face. Vulnerable populations may include minors, individuals with mental health issues, survivors of domestic violence, human trafficking victims, and marginalized communities disproportionately affected by crime. These groups may be more susceptible to trauma and may require additional support to navigate the legal process effectively. By providing specialized support services, access to mental health resources, and tailored accommodations, the legal system can reduce potential retraumatization and foster a more supportive environment. Upholding the rights and dignity of vulnerable populations is crucial to upholding the principles of justice and fairness within the legal system.

In summary, trauma-informed practices in legal proceedings prioritize recognizing and addressing the emotional impact of crime on victims and offenders. Sensitivity training for legal professionals enhances their understanding and empathy, creating a more compassionate and respectful legal system. Supporting vulnerable populations ensures equitable treatment and access to resources, promoting a fair and inclusive legal process. By incorporating these elements, the legal system can work towards a more empathetic, healing-oriented, and just approach to criminal cases.

Supporting Rehabilitation and Reducing Recidivism

Empathy plays a crucial role in supporting rehabilitation and reducing recidivism rates. In this section, we discuss the importance of empathetic approaches to promote successful reintegration into society.

- Empowerment through Education and Skills Training: Empowering offenders with education and vocational training opportunities is a crucial component of promoting successful reentry into society. By providing access to educational programs, including literacy, GED, and vocational training, offenders can acquire valuable skills that increase their employability and self-sufficiency upon release. Education plays a transformative role in helping individuals break the cycle of criminal behavior by expanding their horizons, boosting their confidence, and instilling a sense of purpose. Skills training equips them with practical abilities and knowledge, preparing them for meaningful employment and offering a chance for a fresh start. Empowerment through education and skills training not only benefits the individual but also contributes to a safer and more productive society.

- Mental Health and Substance Abuse Support: Addressing underlying mental health and substance abuse issues is critical for promoting healing and reducing the risk of reoffending. Many offenders have experienced trauma or struggle with mental health challenges, which can significantly impact their behavior and decision-making. Additionally, substance abuse often co-occurs with criminal behavior, further perpetuating the cycle of crime. Providing mental health counseling, therapy, and substance abuse treatment during incarceration and upon release helps offenders confront and manage these issues effectively. By supporting offenders in their journey towards mental and emotional well-being, the likelihood of successful reintegration into society increases, reducing the risk of recidivism and fostering a path towards a healthier and more stable life.
- Community Reintegration Programs: Collaborating with community organizations to establish reintegration programs is essential for a smooth transition back into society. These programs offer various forms of support, including housing assistance, job placement services, mentorship, and peer support groups. Successful reintegration requires a supportive and nurturing environment that helps individuals overcome the challenges of reentering society after incarceration. Community-based programs also foster a sense of belonging, reducing the isolation and stigma that ex-offenders may face. By providing a safety net of resources and opportunities, these programs contribute to the prevention of recidivism and encourage positive community engagement.

In summary, empowerment through education and skills training equips offenders with the tools they need to rebuild their lives and pursue meaningful opportunities. Addressing mental health and substance abuse issues promotes healing and reduces the likelihood of reoffending. Community reintegration programs offer vital support and resources to facilitate a successful transition back into society. By investing in these comprehensive strategies, the criminal justice system can contribute to positive outcomes for offenders, their families, and the broader community, promoting rehabilitation, and reducing recidivism rates.

Conclusion

Empathy in law and criminal justice has the power to transform the legal system and promote healing and rehabilitation for all involved. By embracing restorative justice and empathy in criminal cases, humanizing the legal system through empathy, and supporting rehabilitation to reduce recidivism, we pave the way for a legal system that prioritizes empathy and recognizes the humanity of those impacted by crime. Together, we foster a community that values empathy, justice, and rehabilitation, creating a world where the legal system serves as a force for healing, transformation, and societal well-being. As we embrace empathy in law and criminal justice, we contribute to a society where justice is not just punitive but restorative, and our collective efforts create a tapestry of compassion, understanding, and second chances for a brighter and more empathetic future for all.

CHAPTER 60

EMPATHY IN HEALTHCARE AND PATIENT CARE

Compassionate Care: The Healing Power of Empathy in Healthcare

Introduction

The focus is on the crucial role of empathy in healthcare and patient care. The chapter emphasizes the significance of incorporating empathetic practices in healthcare settings, recognizing empathy as a powerful tool to enhance patient outcomes and overall satisfaction.

One key aspect of this chapter is the exploration of how empathy can positively impact patient care. When healthcare providers demonstrate empathy, patients feel heard, understood, and supported, which can lead to increased trust and cooperation. Empathy also plays a vital role in reducing patient anxiety and stress, contributing to better treatment adherence and faster recovery.

Moreover, the chapter highlights the importance of caring for the emotional well-being of healthcare providers. The demanding nature of their work can lead to emotional exhaustion and burnout. By prioritizing empathetic practices and creating a supportive work environment, healthcare organizations can better support their providers, leading to improved job satisfaction and overall well-being.

The chapter also discusses the significance of empathy in the doctor-patient relationship. By fostering empathetic communication, healthcare providers can better understand their patients' needs, values, and fears, enabling them to tailor treatment plans to meet individual preferences and circumstances.

The chapter underscores the critical role of empathy in healthcare and patient care. By promoting empathetic practices and prioritizing the emotional well-being of healthcare providers, the healthcare system can create a more compassionate and effective approach to patient care, benefiting both patients and healthcare professionals alike.

Empathetic Practices in Healthcare Settings

Empathy is the cornerstone of patient-centered care. In this section, we discuss the importance of empathetic practices in healthcare settings.

- Active Listening and Communication: Active listening is a crucial skill for healthcare professionals to effectively understand and address patients' concerns and fears. It involves not only hearing the words spoken but also paying attention to the emotions and nonverbal cues conveyed by the patient. By practicing active listening, healthcare providers can demonstrate empathy and build trust with their patients, creating a more meaningful and compassionate patient-provider relationship. Patients who feel heard and understood are more likely to openly share important information about their health, leading to better diagnostic accuracy and treatment outcomes.
- Validating Patient Emotions: Visiting a healthcare facility can be an anxiety-inducing experience for many patients. Validating their emotions means acknowledging their feelings and showing empathy and understanding. Healthcare providers can accomplish this by using compassionate language and acknowledging the challenges the patient may be facing. Validating emotions helps create a safe and supportive environment where patients feel comfortable expressing their concerns and seeking guidance. It also helps reduce emotional distress and fosters a sense of trust, leading to better patient satisfaction and adherence to treatment plans.
- Individualized Care Plans: Each patient is unique, with different medical histories, preferences, and lifestyle factors. Therefore, healthcare providers should create individualized care plans tailored to meet the specific needs and preferences of each patient. By involving patients in the decision-making process and considering their input, providers can ensure that the care plan aligns with the patient's goals and values. Individualized care plans not only enhance patient engagement and satisfaction but also improve treatment adherence and health outcomes.

In summary, active listening and communication skills are essential for healthcare professionals to connect with patients on a deeper level and provide compassionate care. Validating patient emotions fosters a supportive environment that encourages open communication and trust. By creating individualized care plans, healthcare providers can meet each patient's unique needs, preferences, and circumstances, ultimately leading to better patient experiences and improved health outcomes. These practices contribute to patient-centered care, which emphasizes the importance of understanding and addressing the whole person, not just the medical condition.

Enhancing Patient Outcomes through Empathy

Empathy has a profound impact on patient outcomes and healing. In this section, we explore the positive influence of empathy on patient care.

- Improved Patient Satisfaction: When healthcare providers deliver empathetic care, it creates a significant impact on patient satisfaction. Empathy involves understanding and acknowledging patients' emotions and concerns, making them feel heard and valued. Patients who receive empathetic care are more likely to perceive their healthcare experience positively, leading to higher levels of satisfaction with the care they receive. This, in turn, can enhance the overall reputation of the healthcare facility and contribute to increased patient retention and loyalty.
- Better Treatment Adherence: Empathetic care plays a vital role in promoting better treatment adherence among patients. When patients feel genuinely cared for and supported by their healthcare providers, they are more likely to trust the prescribed treatment plans. This trust and emotional connection can lead to increased patient engagement and motivation to follow the recommended course of action, including taking medications, attending follow-up appointments, and adopting lifestyle changes. As a result, treatment adherence improves, leading to better health outcomes and reduced rates of treatment failure or relapse.
- Faster Recovery: The emotional support provided through empathetic care can have a positive impact on the healing and recovery process. Patients experiencing illness or injury often face emotional stress and anxiety. Empathy helps alleviate these emotional burdens by providing a sense of comfort and understanding. This emotional support can reduce stress-related physiological responses, such as increased cortisol levels, which can inhibit the body's natural healing mechanisms. As a result, patients who receive empathetic care may experience faster recovery times and better overall health outcomes.

In summary, the practice of empathy in healthcare offers numerous benefits to both patients and healthcare providers. Improved patient satisfaction not only enhances the patient's healthcare experience but also contributes to a positive reputation for the healthcare facility. Additionally, empathetic care fosters better treatment adherence, leading to more successful patient outcomes. Finally, the emotional support provided through empathy can positively influence the recovery process, promoting faster healing and overall well-being. As such, prioritizing empathy in healthcare is essential for delivering patient-centered care and creating a supportive and compassionate healthcare environment.

Caring for Healthcare Providers' Emotional Well-being

Healthcare providers also require emotional support and care. In this section, we discuss strategies to address the emotional well-being of healthcare professionals.

- Encouraging Peer Support: Creating a culture of support and camaraderie among healthcare professionals is crucial for their well-being and emotional health. Peer support provides a safe space for healthcare providers to share their experiences, concerns, and challenges with others who understand the unique demands of their profession. Through debriefing and open communication, healthcare professionals can process their emotions, reduce feelings of isolation, and receive valuable insights and advice from their peers. This fosters a sense of unity and solidarity among the healthcare team, leading to improved job satisfaction and overall well-being.
- Emotional Resilience Training: Healthcare providers often face high levels of stress and emotionally charged situations while caring for patients. Emotional resilience training equips them with coping mechanisms to manage these stressors effectively. Through such training, healthcare professionals learn to recognize and understand their emotions, regulate their responses, and maintain a positive outlook even in challenging circumstances. This training empowers them to navigate emotional difficulties and maintain their psychological well-being while continuing to provide high-quality care. Emotional resilience not only benefits the healthcare providers but also enhances patient care as professionals can approach their work with a clear and composed mindset.
- Work-Life Balance: Healthcare professionals often work in demanding and time-intensive environments, which can lead to burnout and compromised well-being. Encouraging a healthy work-life balance is essential for preventing burnout and maintaining the physical and mental health of healthcare providers. By promoting reasonable working hours, sufficient time off, and support for personal and family commitments, healthcare organizations demonstrate their commitment to the well-being of their staff. A healthy work-life balance allows healthcare professionals to recharge, spend time with loved ones, and engage in activities outside of work, ultimately contributing to increased job satisfaction, reduced stress, and improved retention rates in the healthcare workforce.

In summary, promoting a supportive and empathetic environment in healthcare settings is crucial for the well-being of healthcare professionals. Encouraging peer support enables healthcare providers to share their experiences and emotions openly, fostering a sense of belonging and unity within the team. Emotional resilience training equips healthcare professionals with the skills to manage stress and challenging situations effectively, leading to improved mental and emotional health. Additionally, prioritizing work-life balance helps prevent burnout and promotes the overall well-being of healthcare providers, leading to greater job satisfaction and retention in the healthcare workforce. By prioritizing the emotional well-being of healthcare professionals, organizations can create a healthier and more sustainable healthcare environment for both staff and patients.

Conclusion

Empathy in healthcare and patient care is a powerful force for healing and well-being. By embracing empathetic practices in healthcare settings, enhancing patient outcomes through empathy, and caring for healthcare providers' emotional well-being, we pave the way for a healthcare system that prioritizes compassion and understanding. Together, we foster a community that values empathy, patient-centered care, and emotional support, creating a world where healthcare is not just a service but an expression of genuine care and compassion. As we embrace empathy in healthcare and patient care, we contribute to a society where healing and well-being are at the heart of medical practice, and our collective efforts create a tapestry of compassion, healing, and patient-centered excellence for a brighter and more empathetic future for all.

CHAPTER 61

THE EMPATHETIC FUTURE: HOPE AND TRANSFORMATION

Embracing Empathy: Illuminating the Path to a Brighter Future

Introduction

Envision a world characterized by empathy and interconnectedness. It highlights the profound and transformative power of empathy, showcasing its potential to foster understanding, compassion, and positive change in society.

The chapter emphasizes that empathy goes beyond individual interactions and has the capacity to bridge divides, promote inclusivity, and create harmonious connections among diverse cultures, communities, and perspectives. It envisions a society where empathy becomes a guiding force in shaping interactions, policies, and institutions.

Furthermore, the chapter empowers individuals to play an active role in cultivating empathy and fostering positive change. It encourages readers to engage in empathetic action, whether on a personal level within their communities or on a larger scale, contributing to a more compassionate and interconnected world.

This chapter serves as an inspirational call to embrace empathy as a driving force for positive transformation. By acknowledging the profound impact of empathy and actively fostering an empathetic approach to the world, individuals can collectively contribute to a more empathetic, interconnected, and harmonious society.

Reflecting on the Journey through Dark Psychology and Empathy

The exploration of dark psychology has revealed the potential for manipulation and harm, but empathy offers a counterbalance of hope and healing. In this section, we reflect on the insights gained from understanding dark psychology and its contrast with empathy.

- Lessons from Darkness: This refers to the acknowledgment of the existence of manipulation and its effects on individuals and society. It suggests that we should confront the darker aspects of human behavior, such as manipulation, deceit, and harm, and learn from these experiences to prevent similar occurrences in the future. By recognizing the presence of manipulation and its consequences, we can better protect ourselves and others from falling victim to such tactics. This awareness also serves as a reminder of the ethical responsibility we have towards one another, promoting a more empathetic and compassionate society.

- The Light of Empathy: This highlights the transformative power of empathy as a positive force for understanding, compassion, and positive change. Empathy involves understanding and sharing the feelings of others, allowing us to connect on a deeper level and cultivate a sense of compassion for those around us. By practicing empathy, we can bridge divides, build meaningful relationships, and create a supportive environment where individuals feel valued and understood. Empathy helps us recognize vulnerabilities in others, making us more attuned to potential manipulation attempts. It also strengthens our ability to discern authentic emotions from manipulative tactics, allowing us to respond with empathy and compassion rather than falling prey to deceit.
- Balancing the Shadows: This concept emphasizes the importance of acknowledging and integrating both the dark and light aspects of human behavior within ourselves and society. It recognizes that every individual possesses a range of emotions, behaviors, and tendencies, some of which may not always align with positive values. By acknowledging the existence of both light and dark aspects, we can strive to understand and address the root causes of manipulation and harmful behaviors. Through self-reflection, education, and empathy, we can work towards cultivating a balanced and ethical approach to our actions and interactions with others.

In summary, the concept of "Lessons from Darkness, The Light of Empathy, and Balancing the Shadows" encourages us to confront and learn from the negative aspects of manipulation and deception. Simultaneously, it reminds us of the transformative power of empathy and compassion in fostering a more understanding and ethical society. By acknowledging both the dark and light aspects of human behavior and promoting empathy, we can create a more compassionate and harmonious world for everyone.

Envisioning a More Empathetic and Interconnected World

Empathy has the potential to shape a future where compassion and understanding prevail. In this section, we envision a world grounded in empathy and interconnectedness.

- Empathy as a Foundation: This concept envisions a society in which empathy serves as the fundamental basis for all interactions, policies, and institutions. When empathy becomes a cornerstone of how individuals and organizations operate, it leads to a deeper understanding of one another's experiences, emotions, and needs. By prioritizing empathy, people can forge stronger connections, build trust, and work collaboratively to create a more inclusive and compassionate society. Empathy becomes the driving force behind decision-making, problem-solving, and conflict resolution, leading to more ethical and considerate actions.
- Bridging Divides: This idea imagines a world in which empathy plays a central role in breaking down barriers between individuals from different cultures, backgrounds, and perspectives. Empathy helps people see beyond their own viewpoints and truly understand the experiences and feelings of others. As a result, it fosters harmony and cooperation among diverse communities, promoting mutual respect and appreciation. When empathy becomes the guiding principle in our interactions, it becomes easier to find common ground, bridge gaps, and collaborate for the greater good. It helps create a shared sense of belonging and unity among people with different identities and backgrounds.
- Global Collaboration: This concept envisions a future where empathy drives collective efforts to address global challenges. When individuals and nations empathize with the struggles and aspirations of others across the world, they become more inclined to collaborate on solutions. Empathy enables people to recognize the interconnectedness of global issues, such as climate change, poverty, and health crises. It encourages individuals and nations to look beyond their own interests and work together for the well-being of humanity as a whole. In a world where empathy is at the forefront, international cooperation becomes more effective, and solutions to global problems become more sustainable and equitable.

In summary, the three concepts—Empathy as a Foundation, Bridging Divides, and Global Collaboration—paint a picture of a future society that prioritizes empathy as a guiding principle. In such a society, empathy becomes the basis for all interactions and decisions, leading to a more compassionate and inclusive world. It breaks down barriers between people, fostering harmony and cooperation among diverse cultures and perspectives. Moreover, empathy drives global collaboration, encouraging collective efforts to address shared challenges and promote the well-being of all individuals, regardless of their background or nationality. These concepts offer a powerful vision for a future marked by empathy, understanding, and unity.

Empowering Individuals to Create Positive Change

The power to create positive change lies within each individual. In this section, we discuss how individuals can be empowered to foster empathy and shape a brighter future.

- Cultivating Empathy: This concept emphasizes the importance of actively fostering empathy in individuals and communities. It starts with encouraging self-reflection, allowing individuals to examine their own emotions, biases, and experiences. Through this process, people gain a deeper understanding of themselves and become more open to understanding the feelings and perspectives of others. By promoting empathy development, society can build stronger interpersonal relationships and foster social cohesion. Empathy is a critical skill that allows people to connect with one another, break down barriers, and build bridges of understanding.
- Empathy in Action: This idea highlights the transformative power of putting empathy into action. Encouraging individuals to go beyond understanding and actually practice empathy in their daily lives can lead to meaningful change. Empathetic action involves actively supporting and helping others, being kind and compassionate, and advocating for the needs of those who are marginalized or in distress. Empathy in action can take various forms, such as volunteering, supporting charitable causes, or simply offering a listening ear to someone in need. By promoting empathetic action, society can create a positive impact on individuals and communities, fostering a sense of responsibility and interconnectedness.
- Ripple Effect of Empathy: This concept acknowledges the far-reaching consequences of even the smallest empathetic acts. When one person shows empathy and compassion to another, it creates a ripple effect that extends beyond the immediate interaction. Acts of kindness and understanding can inspire others to do the same, creating a chain reaction of empathy and positive change. The ripple effect of empathy can spread through families, communities, and even across societies, contributing to a more caring and supportive world. It demonstrates that each empathetic act matters and has the potential to create a significant collective impact.

In summary, the three concepts—Cultivating Empathy, Empathy in Action, and Ripple Effect of Empathy—highlight the transformative potential of empathy in society. Cultivating empathy involves promoting self-reflection and empathy development, leading to stronger connections and social cohesion. Empathy in action encourages individuals to actively practice empathy, translating understanding into meaningful support for others. Finally, the ripple effect of empathy emphasizes the significance of empathetic acts, no matter how small, in creating a cascading effect of positive change. By embracing and promoting empathy, individuals and communities can contribute to a more compassionate and harmonious world.

Conclusion

The empathetic future holds the promise of hope and transformation. By reflecting on the journey through dark psychology and empathy, envisioning a more empathetic and interconnected world, and empowering individuals to create positive change, we pave the way for a brighter future. Together, we foster a community that values empathy, compassion, and social responsibility, creating a world where empathy bridges divides and empowers individuals to become agents of positive change. As we embrace the empathetic future, we contribute to a society where understanding and compassion prevail, and our collective efforts create a tapestry of hope, healing, and transformation for a brighter and more empathetic future for all.

AFTERWORD

Humans use a variety of methods to acquire and implement skills. These methods can be broadly categorized into the following:

1. **Observation and Imitation:** One of the most basic ways humans learn is through observing others who are skilled at a particular task and then imitating their actions and techniques. This is common in activities like learning to cook, play a musical instrument, or play sports.

2. **Practice and Repetition:** Skill acquisition often involves a lot of practice and repetition. The more one practices a skill, the more proficient they become. This is particularly true for skills that require muscle memory, such as playing an instrument or learning to type.

3. **Guided Instruction:** Learning from a knowledgeable teacher or instructor who can provide guidance, feedback, and corrections is a common method for skill development. This is prevalent in formal education settings, sports coaching, and vocational training.

4. **Problem-Solving and Trial-and-Error:** In some cases, individuals learn skills by engaging in problem-solving and experimenting with different approaches. They learn from their mistakes and refine their techniques based on the outcomes of their trials.

5. **Mental Visualization and Simulation:** Mental rehearsal and visualization are techniques where individuals imagine themselves performing the skill successfully in their minds. This can improve performance by strengthening neural pathways associated with the skill.

6. **Chunking and Breaking Down Skills:** Breaking a complex skill into smaller, more manageable parts, and then mastering each part before combining them is an effective method. This approach is common in learning complex dance routines, playing chess, or acquiring language skills.

7. **Feedback and Self-Assessment:** Regular feedback and self-assessment play crucial roles in skill development. Constructive feedback from teachers, mentors, or peers helps individuals identify areas for improvement and make necessary adjustments.

8. **Motivation and Goal Setting:** Setting clear goals and having the motivation to achieve them can drive skill acquisition. Having a sense of purpose and commitment to mastering a skill can significantly enhance the learning process.
9. **Social Learning and Collaboration:** Learning in a social context, such as group activities, workshops, or collaborative projects, can foster skill development. Interacting with others can provide different perspectives and ideas.
10. **Adaptation and Flexibility:** Adaptability is essential in skill acquisition. Being open to learning and adjusting techniques based on changing circumstances or new information is crucial for continued improvement.

It's important to note that the effectiveness of these methods may vary depending on the nature of the skill being learned, individual learning styles, and the specific context in which the learning takes place. Often, a combination of these methods is employed for successful skill acquisition.

This book may appear repetitive at times, but this is intentional because the building blocks, strategies, and behaviors discussed are crucial to learn. Repetition is a fundamental aspect of learning throughout our lives, not just for academic or professional pursuits but also for honing our skills and becoming more adept at recognizing and countering these tactics in others. By mastering these skills, we empower ourselves to navigate various situations, protecting our boundaries and avoiding unnecessary conflicts and stress.

The clinical approach of this book serves a purpose – it allows you to examine your life patterns and interactions with others objectively. It's like donning a lab coat for your mind, providing insulation against harm. As you gain new insights and information, it's natural to wish you knew these things earlier. However, dwelling on the past won't change it. Instead, focus on learning and preventing future pitfalls.

Our future lies in how we learn from the past, not in carrying its baggage. Let go of regrets and haunting memories. Embrace the knowledge gained from this book to create a brighter today and future. Moving on may be challenging, but it is essential. Remember, "The past luggage has no future for us" (David Alan Binder).

After reading this book, consider how many marks or notes you've taken. These annotations signify your active engagement with the material, reinforcing your commitment to applying these insights to empower yourself moving forward.

The number of times a person must read something to fully understand and comprehend it can vary significantly depending on several factors, including:

Complexity of the Material: The complexity and difficulty of the material being read will impact the number of times needed for comprehension. More complex topics or dense academic texts may require multiple readings.

Prior Knowledge: If the reader already has some background knowledge or familiarity with the subject matter, it can expedite the comprehension process, requiring fewer readings.

Reading Skills: Strong reading skills, such as effective skimming, scanning, and critical reading, can contribute to quicker comprehension.

Motivation and Engagement: A reader who is highly motivated and engaged in the material is more likely to understand it more quickly than someone who lacks interest.

Reading Speed: Some individuals naturally read faster and may grasp the content in fewer readings compared to slower readers.

External Factors: External distractions, fatigue, or stress can affect comprehension, necessitating additional readings.

In general, most people may need to read something at least a few times to gain a good understanding. According to Chewe Kalamata "You need to read a book 6 to 9 times and not less than 3 times in order to memorize it. Our brains recall things in three's because if something happens once we over look it, if it happens twice we call it a coincidence, when it happens three times we recognise it as a pattern and stays with us."

"YOUR FUTURE IS WORTH NO LESS THAN READING THIS BOOK 3 TIMES!" — David Alan Binder

Often, it's helpful to approach the material with different reading strategies. For instance:

a. **Skimming:** An initial quick read-through to get an overview of the content and main ideas.

b. **Scanning:** Searching for specific information or details.

c. **Close Reading:** A more thorough and careful reading to understand the finer nuances and details.

d. **Revisiting:** Returning to specific sections that were challenging or unclear during the initial reads.

Ultimately, there is no fixed number of times that universally guarantees full comprehension. Each person's learning style, cognitive abilities, and prior knowledge will influence the number of readings required. The most important thing is to remain patient, persistent, and engaged with the material until a satisfactory level of comprehension is achieved.

Red Flags:

1. **Overemphasis on Control:** The book advocates for excessive control over others' thoughts, emotions, or actions, promoting manipulation as a powerful tool.
2. **Lack of Ethical Considerations:** The book encourages unethical or morally questionable tactics to achieve personal goals or manipulate others.
3. **Promises of Instant Results:** Claims that the techniques or strategies provided will yield immediate and guaranteed outcomes may raise suspicion of unrealistic promises.
4. **Appeal to Negative Emotions:** The book relies heavily on fear, anger, or guilt to motivate readers, potentially manipulating their emotions for the author's benefit.
5. **Isolation and Alienation:** The book encourages readers to isolate themselves from others, making them vulnerable to manipulation.
6. **Emphasis on Exploiting Weaknesses:** Strategies that focus on exploiting others' vulnerabilities or weaknesses may indicate harmful intent.
7. **No Consideration for Consent:** Encouragement of actions that disregard the consent or autonomy of others is a significant red flag.

Red Flag Behaviors:

1. **Gaslighting:** Techniques that manipulate or distort another person's perception of reality, leading them to doubt their own thoughts or emotions.
2. **Manipulative Language:** The book uses manipulative language or persuasive techniques designed to influence the reader's thoughts or behavior.
3. **Deception and Lying:** Encouraging dishonesty or deception to achieve personal goals or manipulate others.
4. **Guilt-Tripping:** Encouragement of using guilt as a tool to control or manipulate others' actions or decisions.

5. **Narcissistic Behavior:** The book promotes narcissistic attitudes or behaviors, such as self-centeredness and a lack of empathy.
6. **Emotional Exploitation:** Tactics that exploit others' emotions or vulnerabilities for personal gain.
7. **Isolation Techniques:** Strategies that advocate for cutting off social support systems or relationships to control others.
8. **Emotional Blackmail:** Encouraging readers to use emotional manipulation to gain compliance or control over others.

It is important to remember that honesty and truth-telling are essential in many situations. However, there are also times when lies and half-truths can be used as tools. It is important to be aware of these principles and to use them judiciously.

There are a few reasons why lies and half-truths can be used as tools. For example, they can be used to protect someone from harm, to prevent conflict, or to achieve a greater good. However, it is important to use them sparingly and only when absolutely necessary. Lies and half-truths can have negative consequences, such as damaging trust and relationships.

It is also important to remember that there are times when honesty is the best policy. For example, if someone asks you a direct question, you should always tell the truth. Lying in these situations can damage trust and relationships.

Ultimately, the decision of whether or not to tell a lie or half-truth is a personal one. However, it is important to be aware of the potential consequences of your actions and to use these tools wisely.

REFERENCES

Babiak, P., & Hare, R. D. (2006). Snakes in Suits: When Psychopaths Go to Work. HarperBusiness.

Cialdini, R. B. (2006). Influence: The Psychology of Persuasion. Harper Business.

Simon, G. K. (2020). In Sheep's Clothing: Understanding and Dealing with Manipulative People. Parkhurst Brothers Publishers Inc.

Stout, M. (2006). The Sociopath Next Door: The Ruthless Versus the Rest of Us. Harmony.

Zimbardo, P. G. (2008). The Lucifer Effect: Understanding How Good People Turn Evil. Random House.

Vaknin, S. (2005). Malignant Self-Love: Narcissism Revisited. Narcissus Publications.

Forward, S., & Frazier, P. (1997). Emotional Blackmail: When the People in Your Life Use Fear, Obligation, and Guilt to Manipulate You. William Morrow Paperbacks.

Sternberg, R. J. (2014). Dark Psychology and Manipulation: Techniques to Influence and Manipulate People. CreateSpace Independent Publishing Platform.

Cleckley, H. (1988). The Mask of Sanity: An Attempt to Clarify Some Issues about the So-Called Psychopathic Personality. Emily S Cleckley.

Hare, R. D. (1993). Without Conscience: The Disturbing World of the Psychopaths Among Us. The Guilford Press

ACTIVITY

Decode the Manipulator

Objective: Get ready to dive deeper into the intriguing world of manipulation and dark psychology explored in "Mind Games: The Dual Facets of Manipulation and Dark Psychology." This interactive activity is designed to enhance your understanding of the book's themes and encourage critical thinking.

Instructions:

Meet the Characters: In your journey through this activity, you'll encounter select characters from the book who exemplify manipulation and dark psychology traits. Below, you'll find brief descriptions of these characters and the tactics they employ.

Character 1: [Description and tactics]

Character 2: [Description and tactics]

Character 3: [Description and tactics]

Decode the Manipulator: Your task is to decode the manipulative tactics used by these characters. As you read through the book, pay close attention to their actions, words, and behavior. Can you spot manipulation techniques such as gaslighting, guilt-tripping, or emotional coercion? Take notes and jot down your observations.

Join the Discussion: Share your insights and discoveries with fellow readers. You can do this by participating in book club discussions, engaging in online forums, or even starting a conversation with friends who have also read the book. Discuss the characters' motivations and the consequences of their manipulative behavior on the story's outcomes.

Apply It in Real Life: Reflect on your own life experiences. Have you ever encountered manipulation or dark psychology tactics in your personal or professional life? Consider how a deeper understanding of these concepts, gained from reading this book, might have influenced your responses or decisions in those situations.

Unleash Your Creativity: Get creative and put your newfound knowledge to the test. Write short stories or scenarios that explore alternative outcomes for characters who fell victim to manipulation in the book. This exercise allows you to think critically and empathize with the characters.

Author Insights: If you're curious and want to delve deeper into the book's themes, keep an eye out for opportunities to engage with the author. Look for virtual Q&A sessions or author interviews where you can ask questions about character development, psychological insights, or any other aspects of the book.

We hope you enjoy this interactive journey through "Mind Games: The Dual Facets of Manipulation and Dark Psychology." By participating in this activity, you'll not only gain a richer understanding of the book but also apply its concepts to your own life, fostering critical thinking and insightful discussions.

Happy reading and decoding!

ABOUT DAVID ALAN BINDER

David Alan Binder is of mixed racial heritage, a professional, a freelance editor, a proofreader, an assessor and an author of two published books and the recipient of four writing awards. He currently holds 62 Certificates & 3 Degrees from Courses, Colleges and Universities.

Education:

Bachelors from Mount Mercy University (hons-Dean's List)

Masters from San Diego State University 3.4 GPA

Writing Experience:

Award Winning Author, 8 Awards, Ghost Writer
Books Published:
The Manager's Manager: Strategies and Tactics for Effective Leadership
ALL ABOUT ALGAE - Exploring Phycology or Algology: A Comprehensive Guide to Algae and their Significance

Submittals:

Beach Book Festival Award, New England Book Festival Award, Reading Life Award, Astra Writing Contest Award, Awarded the Golden Wizard Book Prize, Won 3rd place in the Children's Stories Anthology Something Or Other Publishing

Other Published Works:

Effects of environmental pollution on properties
A Chapter Book
An Anthology of Children's Stories
8 Children's Picture Books
An Anthology of Poetry 1971 to present

www.ingramcontent.com/pod-product-compliance
Ingram Content Group UK Ltd.
Pitfield, Milton Keynes, MK11 3LW, UK
UKHW041842190726
13854UKWH00002B/681

9 789359 839158